Essays on Writing

OTHER TITLES IN THE LONGMAN TOPICS READER SERIES

A LONGMAN TOPICS READER

Essays on Writing

LIZBETH A. BRYANT
Purdue University Calumet

HEATHER M. CLARK
Ivy Tech Community College

Longman

New York   San Francisco   Boston
London   Toronto   Sydney   Tokyo   Singapore   Madrid
Mexico City   Munich   Paris   Cape Town   Hong Kong   Montreal

Acquisitions Editor: Lauren A. Finn
Senior Marketing Manager: Sandra McGuire
Production Manager: Savoula Amanatidis
Project Coordination and Text Design: Elm Street Publishing Services
Electronic Page Makeup: Integra Software Services Pvt. Ltd.
Cover Design Manager: Nancy Danahy
Cover Photo: Desk in office with laptop and paper work © Hisayoshi
    Osawa/Taxi Japan, Getty Images, Inc.
Senior Manufacturing Buyer: Roy L. Pickering, Jr.
Printer and Binder: LSC Communications
Cover Printer: LSC Communications

For permission to use copyrighted material, grateful acknowledgment is made
to the copyright holders on pp. 211–212, which are hereby made part of this
copyright page.

Library of Congress Cataloging-in-Publication Data
Bryant, Lizbeth A.
Essays on writing / Lizbeth A. Bryant and Heather M. Clark.
    p. cm.—(Longman topics reader)
  ISBN-13: 978-0-205-52144-9 (alk. paper)
  ISBN-10: 0-205-52144-4
    1. English language—Composition and exercises—Study and
teaching (Higher)   2. English language—Rhetoric—Study and teaching
(Higher)   3. Report writing—Study and teaching (Higher)   4. College prose.
I. Clark, Heather, M. 1973   II. Title.

PE1404.B777 2009
808'.042—dc22   2008030614

Copyright © 2009 by Pearson Education, Inc.

Please visit us at www.pearsonhighered.com

ISBN-13: 978-0-205-52144-9
ISBN-10:   0-205-52144-4

Longman
is an imprint of

www.pearsonhighered.com

5 2019

CONTENTS

Writing is everywhere. It surrounds us. As you read this introduction, apply for a job, read the directions to an iPod, or compose the many pieces of work required in college, you encounter writing. The problem often is that many of us hate writing. It's a chore: something to be tolerated at best. As we tackled this book, we were reminded of some of our own experiences with writing. Heather was reminded of her freshman composition class where she was accused of plagiarism after the title of her argument paper "Guns Don't Die—People Do" turned out to be the title of a book by Pete Shields. She went on to earn a "C" in that class. It took quite a while for her to overcome the grudge she held against that teacher and to rewrite her own attitude toward writing.

We have learned that while attitude is an important factor of writing and its process, colleges and businesses don't care what our attitudes toward writing are; they want clear and insightful prose. To that end, we have put together this collection of essays, hoping to support your growth as writers.

The book is broken into five chapters. The first is "Attitudes." While colleges and businesses may not care about our attitudes toward writing, we have seen how writers' attitudes influence their ability to write. Often our experiences shape our attitudes for better or worse. Heather's experience drove her to be a more diligent researcher. Another student wrote to Liz about a teacher who locked him in a closet and told him to write. Six years later, the details were still crystal clear in his memory. Whether writing is used as punishment or our efforts are supported by a wonderful teacher, our writing experiences shape our attitudes. Perhaps many of the experiences in this chapter will seem familiar to you.

The second chapter, "Practice," deals with just that: the practice of writing. There's no magic formula. Trust us; over the past twenty-five years, we've looked! Even armed with the best spell check and five-paragraph formula, writing takes time and practice. Authors in Chapter Two offer tools and pearls of wisdom that will support you in fine-tuning a process that works for you. With practice, you will be able to streamline and refine your process into your own magic formula.

As you hone your own formula, we hope you'll take a look at Chapter Three, "Voice," which deals with how, as writers, we struggle with finding our academic voice while still holding onto our own unique vision of the world. Even a voice as strong and powerful as Dr. Martin Luther King, Jr., struggled to find its way in the academic world, but as the authors in this chapter help us see, the battle to hold onto your voice is worth the outcome.

We couldn't do a book without including a discussion of technology. Technology offers support for writing with online searching tools and simple cut-and-paste to revise text. Because of this ease of use, research tells us that 41% of college students will commit one or more instances of cut-and-paste Internet plagiarism (Granitz and Loewy, 2007). The possibility of copying and pasting information from the Web into essays presents a significant choice. Authors in Chapter Four, "Technology and Integrity," cover the positive and negative impact technology has had on the quality and practice of writing. From bending your voice to sharpening your craft, technology has become an everyday tool in writing.

Armed with a positive attitude, a fine-tuned writing process, and the support of technology, you're ready to tackle Chapter Five, "Impact." This chapter gives some examples (and offers some suggestions) on how writing can impact our world. This is an incredibly volatile time in our country and our world. The tasks ahead may seem daunting, but today, more than ever, the old adage "The pen is mightier than the sword" rings true. Well-written prose can not only help land the perfect job, but it can also affect the outcome of the next election.

The truth is this: Heather and Liz (and most writers) still struggle with the writing process. We've been in your shoes. We're still learning, and we hope you'll take this journey with us. We want to leave you with an understanding of how writing can impact the world, and we want you to study the practice of writing— and yourself as a writer. By doing this, you will understand how to be a successful writer who impacts your world.

If you gain nothing else from this book, we hope that you will be fearless in your writing. There is no other time or place in your life where you will get so much feedback about your ideas. Good, bad, or otherwise, get your ideas on the page, read what you write, listen to what others have to say, and then write what you mean. Gain control over your writing; don't let it control you. After this course, you may not love writing, but we hope you'll be on speaking terms with it.

Wishing you a wonderful semester,

LIZBETH A. BRYANT AND HEATHER M. CLARK

Granitz, Neil and Dana Loewy. "Applying Ethical Theories: Interpreting and Responding to Student Plagiarism." *Journal of Business Ethics* 72 (2007): 293–306.

"What do you think of when you think of writing?" Heather asks her students this question every semester, and every semester she gets responses like, "I hate it!" or "It's boring," or "What's the point?" *Essays on Writing* is a response to these questions: "I hate it!" is about attitudes in Chapter One; "It's boring" relates to the practice of writing in Chapter Two and constructing voices in Chapter Three; and "What's the point?" is answered in Chapter Five on impact. We also included a chapter on technology and integrity to address the proliferation of the Web in our students' lives and the choices they face regarding plagiarism and paper mills.

As we looked for texts about writing that would encourage our students to read and to see the power of writing, we could not find a collection that focused exclusively on writing. So, we created our own. As a collection of previously published pieces, it can be used by itself with only a handbook or as a supplement to a composition textbook.

We selected both pieces that interest students and pieces for the teacher that address the aspects of writing covered in most classes, such as analyzing rhetorical situations and revising. *Essays on Writing* includes magazine articles, book chapters, newspaper articles, academic essays, a poem, and a cartoon. We chose pieces such as "Shitty First Drafts" that have worked with our students (even though some might be offended by the language). Anne Lamott's colloquial voice attracts students to the piece. Her sarcasm and images of the "vinegar-lipped Reader Lady" (72) who is criticizing her prose and the "mouse people clawing" (73) to get out of the glass jar create the persona that draws our students to Lamott's ideas. With pieces that students "like," we are closer to achieving the purpose of *Essays on Writing*: to prompt students to think critically about and write about writing. We have also included academic voices such as Stanley Aronowitz, Maureen Hourigan, and Rebecca Moore Howard.

We envisioned and built *Essays on Writing* on the Outcomes Statement for First-Year Composition developed by the Council of Writing Program Administrators. We directly address the WPA Outcomes concerning rhetorical knowledge; critical thinking, reading, and writing; and processes. In addition, we also address technology, which is currently being considered as an addtion to the Outcomes.

We start the book with a letter to the students in a colloquial voice that invites them to read. We tell stories of our writing and stories of our students that have helped our students know that they are not alone as they struggle to compose and to grow as writers, readers, and thinkers. We make it a point to acknowledge the writing and reading difficulties students face. Naming the struggles allows students to address and move past these struggles to writing experiences that bring them accomplishment and success.

Each chapter introduction sets the rhetorical stage for the issues discussed and the conversations going on about that issue. Chapter introductions include paragraph summaries of each piece that address what that piece is adding to the conversation. We end the chapter introductions with prereading questions that focus the readers' attention on the issues in the following chapter. These prereading questions might be used as short writing activities in which students tap their prior knowledge, generate questions they want answered, and predict what the articles will say.

The headnotes for each article add to the rhetorical context of the piece by focusing on the professional and writing histories of the authors. This background helps students discern the author's angle of vision and reason for writing. The headnotes end with a one-sentence summary of the piece and where it was originally published.

The Thinking and Writing Questions at the end of each piece are designed to get students interacting with the ideas in the piece, talking to their peers, and developing their ideas through writing. Each set of questions follows the same pattern with the first question as a knowledge-based, reading comprehension question. Question Two asks students to analyze some rhetorical aspect of the piece. Question Three is intertextual, bringing one piece into conversation with another piece. Questions Four and Five ask students to examine the content of the essay through analysis and application.

The end-of-chapter Thinking and Writing Questions are writing prompts that ask students to synthesize the ideas in the chapter. Most writing prompts offer some questions and prewriting activities to get students thinking. There are prompts for a literacy narrative, a writing process analysis, a poem, an I-Search paper, exploratory essays, and a multi-genre research paper. These writing prompts bring students back to the major goal of our text: for students to read and write about their reading, writing, and thinking in the hope of getting students to grow as readers, writers, and thinkers.

Chapter One, "Attitudes," focuses on how writers' attitudes influence their writing abilities and how teachers can affect students' attitudes. Authors in this section examine what teachers have done to make us dread writing, how teachers inspire us to write, the struggle to get insightful words into coherent prose, and arguments that writing is an art—not a skill. Chapter Two, "Practice," focuses on how writers get this art done, including invented spelling, rituals, writing to learn, shitty first drafts, revision, and editing. While Chapter Two covers the cognitive aspects of writing, Chapter Three brings in some social and cultural aspects. The pieces in Chapter Three, "Voice," examine the struggle between the voices of home and community that students bring to the classroom and the formal scholarly voices they meet in academics. The pieces address voice both as the power and agency to speak and be heard and the development of a written persona through choices ranging from types of words to the topic. In Chapter Four, "Technology and Integrity," authors examine the impact that technology has had on the quality of our writing and on the personas we develop online. We also chose pieces that address the issue of buying term papers from the perspective of the student who buys the papers, the author who writes these papers, and the instructor who receives these papers. In Chapter Five, "Impact," we end with many examples of how writing influences our lives from the capacity of writing to reduce physical pain, to the cost of having to train writers on the job, to the impact that poor writing can have on a nuclear meltdown.

Encourage students to send their creations to us. We want to know what they think about writing and the pieces in *Essays on Writing*. Let us know how the articles work with your students. Input from you and your students can impact the next version of this book. Isn't this the point of writing: to impact our world? Please email us: *hclark28@ivytech.edu* or *bryant@calumet.purdue.edu*.

We're looking forward to hearing from you.

LIZBETH A. BRYANT AND HEATHER M. CLARK

ACKNOWLEDGMENTS

There are so many people without whose help this book would simply not have been possible. We would especially like to thank Traci Bryan, Toni Donahue, Jeff Honnold, Mary Howe, Christine Hunter, Jadelee Lynch, Lora Mendenhall, Jason Pete, and Suzanne Weber for their hours of editing and proofreading articles. We're grateful to Julie Osborn for her fantastic transcription, and to Sue Speichert, Mike Dobberstein, Dan Punday, and students in English 391 and 590 in spring 2008 for their insight and consideration. Thank you to Bob Clark for his research and patience. We would also like to thank the many reviewers: Harvey Wiener, CUNY/LaGuardia Community College; Deborah C. Teague, Florida State University; Mary Stewart, Shippensburg University; Chitra Duttagupta, Arizona State University; Diana Lurz, Rogers State University; Connie Wasem, Spokane Falls Community College; Anne Stafford, University of Tennessee; Lanette Cadle, Missouri State University; Eileen Seifert, DePaul University; Sarah Allen, University of Mary Washington; and Lynn Lewis, University of Oklahoma, who have carefully examined this book each step of the way and helped us shape it into what it is today. We are truly indebted to the talent and wisdom of Maureen Hourigan, not only for her stellar article, but also for her careful reviews and thoughtful guidance. And finally, we would like to express our sincere gratitude to our students, who push us to be better teachers year after year and give us something to look forward to each and every class.

LIZBETH A. BRYANT AND HEATHER M. CLARK

CHAPTER 1

Attitudes

Many writing specialists believe that one's attitude toward writing influences one's ability to write. If we believe we are successful, we will approach writing with confidence. If we have negative attitudes, thinking that writing takes too much of our time or that we are "bad" writers, our chances of being successful are not too great. This chapter explores various attitudes toward and beliefs about writing: the intricate process whereby we generate our thoughts, move our ideas to words on page or computer screen, and transform the words into texts that our readers will understand.

Sometimes attitudes are formed through experiences with writing. In the eleventh grade, Liz's English teacher was returning essays. As she handed Liz her paper, the teacher declared in front of the entire class, "Liz, if you're going to college, you need to learn how to write." That moment crystallized Liz's perception of herself as a "bad writer." She avoided writing and college for the next nine years until she ventured into a college history class. After two American history classes, the professor encouraged her to take a writing class. With trepidation, she enrolled in the first-semester writing course. Liz found a writing instructor who conferenced with her and taught her how to prewrite, focus, organize her ideas, draft, revise, and edit. From this class, she developed a desire to learn how writers learn to write, which lead to a career of writing, studying writing, and teaching writing. This crystallizing incident with her eleventh grade teacher formed an attitude toward writing that influenced Liz's college and professional careers.

Many of our attitudes toward writing are formed long before we get to college. Most of us, at some point, had to write an "I will not . . ." list à la Bart Simpson. In "I Won't Use Writing As Punishment. I Won't . . . ," Roy Peter Clark examines the impact on students when writing is used as punishment. If writing is associated with punishment early in our school careers, students can develop negative attitudes toward writing. We avoid writing because it is associated with the message that we are troublesome: "Because you are bad, you have to write." Clark contends that in creating this association, students are robbed of academic success.

In "Writing about General Apache," Dick Harrington tells his story of working with his student General Apache. In a college classroom that focused on writers telling their stories—not on error or punishment—General Apache came to write his stories about Vietnam. Harrington creates a writing class that encourages students to trust and to tell their stories. General Apache's attitude toward writing improved as he experienced the need to tell his stories.

From a teacher's perspective in "Making Children Hate Reading," John Holt identifies other experiences that may have created our attitudes toward reading and writing. He reminds us of times in elementary school when we were reading aloud, and the person behind us corrected our pronunciation. When faced with humiliation and failure, a dislike of reading and writing can easily develop. Holt wonders why teachers take "what should be the most flexible, exciting, and creative of all school courses and make it into something that most children can hardly wait to see the last of" (26).

In her literacy narrative, "Inspiration," Melissa Duffy tells us about teachers and friends who encouraged her writing. In ninth grade she struggled to write a story, "Paco the Taco." Her teacher Mr. Wright supported her and asked, "Have you ever thought about being a children's author?" These crystallizing experiences fostered a positive attitude toward writing, leading Duffy to write this literacy narrative in her first-semester writing class in college.

In "writing autobiography," bell hooks continues the chapter with a literacy narrative that recounts her struggle to put her autobiography into words. bell hooks, written without capital letters, is the pen name of Gloria Jean, about whom hooks struggles to write. Thinking it would be simple to tell the story of Gloria Jean, hooks encounters a writing block. Finally getting past her block, hooks finds the beauty and benefit of telling one's story: how writing "enabled [her] to look at [her] past from a different perspective and to use this knowledge as a means of self-growth and change" (35). Like Duffy, hooks talks about an encouraging experience with her writing.

In "Bonehead Writing," Craig Vetter focuses on the struggle to write. Bemoaning its difficulty, Vetter characterizes writing as "a blood sport, a walk in the garden of agony" (37). The difficulty of writing is that it is thinking, much like the thinking that hooks had to do to write her autobiography. Writing is not just a skill of stringing together clauses and semicolons, nor spelling words correctly. Vetter contends that our writing records our thinking. And because it is critical thinking, no one can teach a person to write. In fact, he will tell you that your school is stealing students' money.

In "Writing is Not a Skill," Stanley Aronowitz agrees with Craig Vetter, that writing is more than just mastering "techniques and rules" (39). Aronowitz argues that writing is not just a skill, but also an art and a form of thinking. Because writing entails critical thinking and imagination, it is an art. If an instructor sees writing as simply a set of skills, that instructor limits the art of writing and prevents it from being a meaning-making process. Aronowitz challenges instructors in all disciplines to teach the writing of their disciplines as the art of making meaning.

Aronowitz's argument on skill and art in writing takes us back to the beginning articles that claim how we perceive writing impacts, not only how we succeed at writing, but also how we are taught writing. Your teacher's attitude toward writing influences how he or she teaches, which in turn impacts you as a writer. As you read these pieces, examine your attitude toward writing and your teachers' attitudes. How well do these authors' attitudes and beliefs fit with yours? Look for the arguments laid out by these authors. How are they trying to persuade you? Do you buy it? Why or why not?

I Won't Use Writing as Punishment. I Won't . . .

Roy Peter Clark

Author Roy Peter Clark is the vice president and senior scholar at the Poynter Institute for Media Studies in St. Petersburg, FL. Dr. Clark has taught writing at every level from school children to Pulitzer

Prize-winning authors for more than thirty years, and has spoken about the writer's craft on The Oprah Winfrey Show, *National Public Radio, and* Today. *He writes a regular column, "Writing Tools," for PoynterOnLine. Clark is the author or editor of several books on journalism and writing. His most recent work is* Writing Tools: 50 Essential Strategies for Every Writer. *A version of "I Won't Use Writing as Punishment. I Won't . . ." appeared in the* St. Petersburg Times. *Clark explores the impact on students when writing is used as punishment.*

———————— ◆ ————————

[Author's note: More than 20 years after I wrote this essay, I wish I could say that it was too old-fashioned or obsolete to reprint. Heck, it was even written on a typewriter. Alas, the use of writing as punishment is still with us. One California high school teacher just sent me a message to complain that the math teachers at her school were giving writing assignments to students who misbehaved. In a delicious act of insurgency, the English teachers threatened to punish students with math problems if the math teachers didn't desist.

Another teacher wrote a moving message in which she described how a child, undergoing counseling and rehabilitation, was made to copy monotonous paragraphs for her misdeeds. Imagine the good it might do for such a child to use writing in encouraging ways.

And if such evidence were not enough, we have another icon of literacy testifying to the grotesque consequences of using writing as punishment. I mean none other than the great Harry Potter. In the fifth book and movie in the series by J.K. Rowling, Harry is punished by the world's most horrible teacher, Dolores Umbridge. The toadlike tyrant gives Harry detention for telling a terrible truth, that the evil Voldemort is back. Umbridge gives Harry a special pen and makes him write "lines" over and over, that he must not tell lies. With each stroke of the pen an excruciating bloody line forms on the back of Harry's hand, a wound that never fully heals.

I hope that Harry writes his own memoirs some day. But don't count on it.

ROY PETER CLARK – JULY 24, 2007]

One day Sam Ficarrotta strolled into the library of Sandy Lane Elementary in Clearwater, where he is principal, and found two sweet-faced children doing research for a term paper. One was reading up on chipmunks, the other on hummingbirds.

Ficarrotta rules his school with the tender passion of an Italian nobleman, exchanging lines of poetry with members of his staff and talking effusively about the need to introduce children to a world of truth and beauty.

He pulled a volume from the library shelf and displayed it for the children, two fifth- grade girls named Carri Lantto and Becky Miller. The book contained the plays of Shakespeare, written in language that children could understand. He convinced them that *A Midsummer's Night Dream* and *King Lear* would be more engaging than chipmunks and hummingbirds.

In the days that followed Becky and Carri devoured the plays, wrote reports on the life and works of Shakespeare and introduced the Bard to their classmates.

RECENTLY, Ficarrotta introduced the girls to me. We talked about the universality of Shakespeare's plays, his marvelous plots and intriguing characters and even got down to the nitty gritty, chatting about the humiliation of Bottom and the blinding of Gloucester.

We then walked into Becky and Carri's classroom, where about 75 students waited to show me their work. They had been writing every day since the beginning of the school year for their teacher, Mary Osborne.

She has them explore ideas for stories, carefully plan their work, write rough drafts, rework the story after consultation, make changes and corrections and publish their work in a class booklet. Mark Beery handed me his story on "Teenagers and Drugs." He writes: "It is easier to prevent drug abuse than to stop the practice after it has started. If you know what drugs do to you, then you will have a better chance of not taking them. I wrote this opinion paper because teenagers need to know what drugs can do to them." The final version of his story was stapled to 11 other drafts! Each draft brought the paper closer to publication, and Mark was as proud of his efforts as he was of his final story.

Mrs. Osborne has so thoroughly converted her class to the values of good writing that the class is carrying her standard into Bonnie Lewison's second-grade class. Groups of fifth graders take the younger children to the library, where they write stories together. The older kids consult with the second graders, evaluating the stories and suggesting revisions. The fifth graders have compiled a "yucky list" to help the little ones avoid common second-grade errors and have even created a handy model of the writing process in language that second graders can understand.

THESE LITTLE miracles of collaboration are being worked throughout Pinellas County by teachers turned on to the teaching of writing. From Bay Point in the south to Ozona in the north,

I have seen students and teachers writing their way toward excellence in education.

The Pride Awards now recognize the outstanding student writers in the county; "Alligator Express" has provided space in this newspaper for the work of hundreds of students; and Writer's Camp, a team effort of The Poynter Institute and the school system, will bring together 20 teachers and 60 students for a summer of writing and learning.

An important part of this effort is a modest proposal by Dr. J. Howard Hinesley, executive assistant superintendent for curriculum and instruction, to eliminate writing as a form of punishment.

• • •

In Aldous Huxley's *Brave New World*, his vision of a dehumanized future society, doctors take infants and load them into rooms filled with pretty books and flowers. Attracted to the bright colors, the infants crawl over to these, feel the silky petals and crumple the bright pages. Then something happens. A nurse throws a switch, and: "There was a violent explosion. Shriller and ever shriller, a siren shrieked. Alarm bells maddeningly sounded. The children started, screamed; their faces were distorted with terror."

The mad scientist behind this experiment explains: "They'll grow up with what the psychologists used to call an 'instinctive' hatred of books and flowers . . . They'll be safe from books and botany all their lives."

With Huxley's parable in mind, imagine a scene in which a fifth grader is misbehaving. He's throwing spitballs, or dropping books on the floor, or laughing in the library, or giving the finger.

IMAGINE THE teacher saying, "Johnny, because you've been bad, you have to draw a picture." Or, "You have to do a scientific experiment." Or, " You have to play something on the piano."

These forms of discipline seem absurd. Yet for years teachers have told Johnny, "Because you were bad, you have to write." Perhaps a student will have to write an essay under the title "Why I Must Not Laugh in the Library." Perhaps the teacher will work over the paper with a red pen, marking every flaw in crimson hieroglyphics. The exercise leaves one indelible mark on the psyche of the student: WRITING IS PUNISHMENT.

Most adults I know suffer some form of writing neurosis. I feel it, even as I type these words on my Royal Standard. And how would you feel, oh reader, if you were given a writing assignment today, knowing that your work would be published next

Sunday on this page? When is the last time you wrote anything, even a letter? What force keeps you from writing? I sit on airplanes next to strangers and tell them that I "teach writing." Sometimes they look like they want to hold up a cross to keep me at bay. A sour expression passes over their faces as if they would have me, like Jonah, jettisoned from the plane. "Oh," they keen, "I tried to write—once."

I want to respond, imitating Sigmund Freud, "Tell me, ven did you begin to have zese feelings about your writing?" My guess is that you can trace the writing neurosis to childhood. Something happened—or did not happen—in elementary school. It is there the twig is bent, or broken, by the association of writing and punishment.

IN PURE Skinnerian terms it works this way. Teachers try to modify the behavior of students by creating negative consequences for misbehavior. In one school, for example, students who misbehave badly are given a choice between suspension or writing an essay (the death penalty or life imprisonment). The unintended side affect of this process is to create in the mind of the student a perpetual association between suffering and the act of writing, in the same way that the protagonist of *A Clockwork Orange* was conditioned to hate Beethoven.

A teacher recently described how her colleague in a Miami high school gets students to show up for exams. If they show up, they get to take an objective test, multiple choice, and the like. If they miss the test, the makeup is an essay exam. In other words, writing is the punishment for missing a test. Attendance for his exams is almost perfect. "Do anything, sir, but don't make me write."

My daughter once had a teacher who gave writing as punishment. She would come into the house, slam her books on the table, and proceed to her room to write 50 times: "I must not talk in the library." I noticed that the next time she went to her desk to undertake a real writing assignment, she did so with less enthusiasm. She was coming to associate the act of writing with punishment.

WATCHING HER made me recall my early school days. We often received writing as punishment, and we developed clever defense mechanisms against different types of punishment assignments.

If the teacher told us to write 100 times, "I will not talk in the library," we would write one word at a time.

I
I
I

I

I

I

etc.

If the teacher asked us to write a hundred-word essay, we would inflate each sentence with clutter and redundancy, and count the words after every sentence: "The library should always be a quiet place, a very quiet place, a place where no talking goes on, a place where people come to study because there is always quiet there, at least in my opinion." Two more sentences like that, and the snow job is complete.

Sometimes a teacher would tell us to write an essay that would be "two sides of a piece of paper" in length. Ha, ha. It was always fun to outsmart her by writing in our most immature cursive, puffing out the length and width of each letter so that a few worthless sentences filled up the space.

THE TENDENCY to equate writing with punishment is so deeply ingrained in our educational system that it has been reflected in popular culture. During a recent episode of the television comedy *Diff'rent Strokes*, an otherwise enlightened teacher gives Arnold and his classmates a 100-word essay to write as punishment for misbehaving in the hallway.

In a nostalgic reminiscence of his Indiana childhood, Jean Shepherd remembers a teacher this way:

> Miss Bodkin; after recess, addressed us: "I want all of you to write a theme . . ." A theme! A rotten theme before Christmas! There must be kids somewhere who love writing themes, but to a normal air-breathing human kid, writing themes is a torture that ranks only with the dreaded medieval chin-breaker of Inquisitional fame. A theme!

In a recent film version of Shepherd's story, Miss Bodkin is portrayed in a dream sequence as a cackling witch who marks student papers with an F.

Fred Hechinger of the *New York Times* reported the story of a father, a professional writer, who complained to a teacher after his child was made to write a punitive essay. "Only once have I written an angry letter to one of my children's teachers, and that was when our son was made to write an essay as a penalty for some transgressions in class." The teacher admitted that she never considered the consequences of using writing as punishment.

The issue was addressed by Linda Lewis, principal of LeMay Elementary School in Bellevue, Neb., in an article in *Principal* magazine. During job interviews for three candidates, she asked each teacher how discipline could be maintained in the classroom. "I make them write something for me," said one. "I have offenders copy pages from the dictionary," said the second. A "fresh-faced 1981 college graduate" said, "Oh, I make them memorize poetry."

"Is it any wonder," says Lewis, "that English teachers find it difficult to whip up kids' enthusiasm for writing?"

In the *Times*, Hechinger argues that "the joy of writing is not dead in today's children unless it is killed in the bud by adults."

WHAT THEN is the appeal for some teachers and administrators in using writing as punishment?

> It is easy to control, requiring little supervision. Students can be stuck in a room and required to write till their hands fall off.
>
> It creates the illusion of an educational and counseling purpose. Students who write essays about why they should not smoke are thought to benefit from the exercise.
>
> It seems a humane alternative to suspension or paddling.

None of these justifies the practice. Because there is often little supervision, students are not encouraged to carefully plan these essays. Students may not be required to consult with teachers, to discuss the issues and strategies of the essay, to write several drafts, to polish and correct their own work and to share it with others. When writing becomes punishment, all the positive elements of learning—organization, discovery and communication—disappear.

Moreover, there are dozens of alternatives to beating or suspending kids, many of which are now being explored in the county through an "assertive discipline" program. One of the best ways to create a positive, disciplined atmosphere for learning is to teach writing the way Mary Osborne does at Sandy Lane. Her students always seem too busy to be bad. This goes for her weaker students as well as her Pride Award winners because Mary has discovered, like so many other teachers, that writing is for all students.

THE WEAKEST students, those who most often received writing as punishment and who most fear the act of writing, need most desperately to discover the value of their own words. Fear of writing, argues John Daly of the University of Texas, "is related to low self-concept and low self-confidence" as well as various kinds of academic failure.

Recently I spent two weeks teaching a group of sixth graders who had been grouped together at the "basic skills" level. Students in this group sometimes refer to themselves as "the dumb class."

Students in this class expected little of themselves and each other. They distrusted me at first. They seemed a bit beaten down and demoralized. They did not laugh at my jokes, and I often saw a look of collective hopelessness on their faces.

When I asked them about their writing, many answered in one-word responses and spoke so softly they could not be heard. Some students wrote their names in the tiniest script as if they were trying to hide their identities in the farthest corner of the paper. Their body language was defensive. They were trying to protect themselves from me. Over the years they had developed sophisticated strategies for avoiding teacher scrutiny.

I TRIED to break through these barriers by being unshakably positive in my response to their work. I told them that by the end of two weeks, each student will have written the best story of his or her life, published it in a class booklet, and read it aloud in front of the principal. They looked at me as if I were an oily used car salesman.

But it worked. Some students wrote three or four drafts, and one student wrote four complete stories. They read their work to each other and perhaps for the first time in their lives, began to take charge of their own education by revising and correcting their own work. They wrote about pets, friends, games, and trips. Some students wrote deeply personal narratives, which revealed much about their learning problems. I saw looks of satisfaction and triumph when, on the final day, they read their stories aloud and the principal applauded.

We will experience more and more of these triumphs as the good writing movement sweeps from school to school, from classroom to classroom, and from student to student. We should be teaching the Golden Rule. And we should embrace the Silver Rule as well: "Thou shalt not give writing as punishment." If you disagree, your punishment is to write it out 100 times.

Thinking and Writing Questions

1. Why, according to Clark, do teachers assign writing as a form of punishment? Why don't teachers give us math problems as a form of punishment?

2. Examine the structure of Clark's piece. Even though the title says it's about writing as punishment, why might he start and end the piece with examples of teachers and students working on authentic writing? What purpose does Clark accomplish with this structure?

3. The authors in Chapter Two speak about the practice of writing as a process of making many choices as one decides what and how to compose. What happens to a writer's ability to make decisions and choices when the writer is told to write one hundred times, "I will not talk in class"?

4. Clark argues that when writing is associated with punishment, a neurosis can develop that leads many to avoid writing. Students tell us of their attempts to write big, using bigger fonts and wider margins. To what lengths have you gone to avoid writing?

5. Clark writes that Mrs. Osborn has "thoroughly converted her class to the values of good writing" (5). What are these "values of good writing"? How is this different from the value placed on writing when it is used as punishment?

Writing about General Apache
DICK HARRINGTON

Educator Dick Harrington taught college composition, college-prep writing, American literature, and poetry writing for thirty-one years at Piedmont Virginia Community College. Since retiring, he gives workshops to college and university faculty worldwide on developing teaching practices that result in student success. Dr. Harrington is working on a piece of literary non-fiction about Kevin Crowe, a wood-firing potter in Nelson County, Virginia. As a guitar player for Troublesome Creek String Band on their CD "Fast as Time Can Take Me," Harrington has been invited to play his guitar as far away as Denmark. In "Writing about General Apache" Harrington recounts the stories of two writers: how his student General Apache came to write stories about his experiences in Vietnam and how Harrington struggles to write a story about his student General Apache.

--------------- ✦ ---------------

My poem "General Apache Talks with His Writing Teacher" is a true story though I can hardly portray the degree of pain and triumph of this man, this student, this Vietnam vet who in the war had come to be known as General Apache. He took developmental writing for two quarters, progressed to college composition, and then in midterm dropped his classes because the bullet lodged next to his spine had started to move. If it moved far enough away, the surgeons could take it out. If it moved closer, they might be powerless to stop paralysis. I phoned his home a while later and learned he is doing fine, working at the post office.

What's so special about him, given his history, is his capacity to make peace with the world and his tremendous desire to communicate his experience. Once while visiting Washington, DC, he paid a homeless man $20 for an inside tour of the streets. The next week he came to class with an article on the surprises of that afternoon. He'd thought he'd known just about everything about the streets because he'd lived there himself, but he'd been mistaken.

In the early days of developmental writing he seemed very quiet but industrious. Not more than five foot ten, he reminded me of a wiry NFL cornerback who always shows up where he's supposed to be. His shoulders were unusually broad, his arms muscular, his hands big. He walked with quiet grace.

I always sit down with my developmental students to talk and to listen. I don't want to miss that phrase or that look in the eye revealing an interest they might not yet be able to verbalize, especially to a teacher. After years of trying to think up stimulating assignments for the whole class, I now encourage students to satisfy course requirements with subjects of their own choosing, preferably subjects which, as Ken Macrorie is fond of saying, choose them. I get much more and better writing these days by learning what stimulates them to think and write.

I'd just finished conferring with a woman in her midtwenties who had told me she was interested in writing about alcoholism. Our conversation had revealed her great need to write the story of her husband's drunken rampage with his shotgun, threatening to kill her and the four kids as they huddled screaming behind the bed. She had seemed excited to learn I would guide her in writing that story.

And so in the first days, I sat down with this vet and asked to see the list of subjects he might like to pursue. There weren't many items in his daybook because he felt reluctant. He was not used to a teacher sitting so close. As we talked, I was struck by his gentle directness. His head seemed to buzz with possibilities.

He wanted to write about his experience as a drug counselor for the children of Vietnam veterans; about his trip to *The Wall* after years of alcoholism, drug addiction and brawling; about the jungle itself at night; about misrepresentations of the war; about the chaos of a firefight. He'd been quite something in the war, often decorated.

Afterward he'd been chosen, despite his physical impairment, to train officers how to fight and survive in jungle combat. He wanted to write it all "so people will understand what happened to guys." We talked in class. We talked in my office. At first, of course, he was skeptical about me. I hadn't gone. I was a teacher, a Ph.D. What did I know? But somehow he began to trust that I listened to what he said. More important, I didn't judge him and didn't fear him for having cut so many human throats. Not that he bragged. He talked with humility and grace about things that probably would have broken me. If there were old fashioned heroes in Vietnam, he was surely one. His unit twice took Hamburger Hill.

One day I sat down and asked, "What are you working on?" He said, "Special." I said, "What?" He said, "Special. All my life growing up, my momma and my grandmother and others always said I was special. The coaches said I was special. I was even special in Nam because everybody looked to me for what to do next. But when I come back, people spit on me and called me baby killer. For over 20 years I was lost in alcohol, nightmares, and I don't know what else. And then just the other day a young boy I was counseling told me I was a very special person. I'm writing about that. Special."

I wanted to write down the many things he told me about his life. As I began, the poem took shape. I worked on it for at least a month off and on. When I finally got up the nerve, I told him I'd written something about him that I wanted him to read. I admitted I was very nervous but I wanted him to come to my office. In the office I fidgeted, tried to explain, started to hand it to him, and pulled back again. At last I gave it up. He read it carefully, deliberately, which is his way, and then looked up with a kind of bashful smile. "That's me. That's my whole life right there. I wish I could find words to put things like you can."

I said with practice he would improve his own writing. I told him I appreciated his response and needed to ask him about the accuracy of one part. He'd told me everything else in the poem except the details of the throat cutting. I told him I'd never cut anyone's throat, so I'd had to imagine what it must be like. He said it was exactly as I'd described. Writing about it had made me feel I was forcing myself into one of his nightmares of reality, yet I felt I had to be true to what he'd done and had been. I guess part of me feared the throat-cutting passage might set him off, but it didn't perhaps because I didn't judge or shy from the act of deliberate killing.

Showing him this poem was one of the most liberating experiences of my life, and I want to share my experience with readers of *TETYC*.

GENERAL APACHE TALKS WITH HIS WRITING TEACHER

I was just out of school
playing ball for Cincinnati
when my notice come.
Marines taught me to kill people
every kind of way,
sent me to Nam,
made me a bush rat.

In the monsoon jungle
on night patrol
I'd always take point.
The other guys would
follow after me,
listening for the VC's
gurgle when my knife
cut the jugular
and vocal cords.

First they just
called me Apache.
But I done the job so well
they got to calling me
General Apache.
When our time come
the whole outfit got surrounded.
AK-45 slug paralyzed me,
kept me laying almost a whole day
till the choppers come,
looking at my buddy's face,
his head spewing out brains.

I still dream about it.
That bullet still in me
here next to my spine.
Back in the States people'd ask,
"You really do all them
things they say you did?"

Tried out for the Reds,
but they cut me,
my arm being numb and all.
I got to drinking more

and looking for guys
that could fight me.

Instead of just jailing me again
one judge got me a shrink.
I went to The Wall in DC,
found each name,
thirty-five bush rats.
Didn't find my name.
Just stood there crying.

I do counseling myself now
with kids hooked on drugs and alcohol.
Missed class yesterday,
up all night with a kid
wanting to kill his parents.
My own son, the oldest,
about to graduate from college.
Time to make something of me now.
When I start to remember
I don't sleep.
Some nights I feel
I got to have a drink.

I want you to help me
write it all down
so people will understand
what happened to guys.
Been flying round and round
on a plane since Nam
and now I know
it's about to land.

Thinking and Writing Questions

1. Why does Harrington let his students find their own subjects to explore? What do you think about this?
2. Harrington's goal is to share his experience of writing the poem "General Apache Talks with His Writing Teacher": "the most liberating experience of [his] life" (13). General Apache tells Harrington that he wants to write "'so people will understand what happened to guys'" in Vietnam (13). Both writers are struggling to share their experiences and tell their stories. How does the structure and content of this piece achieve Harrington's purpose?

3. In *Writing to Change the World* Mary Pipher explains how "writing is designed to change the world, at least a small part of the world, or in some small way perhaps a change in a reader's mood or in his appreciation of a certain kind of beauty" (202). How does Harrington's poem work to change the world? How did General Apache work to change the world with his writing?

4. Harrington uses the fact that General Apache's "unit twice took Hamburger Hill" to claim that he is an old-fashioned hero (13). Research the significance of Hamburger Hill to the Vietnam conflict. With this information, explain what makes General Apache a hero.

5. Harrington explains a teaching strategy used by many writing teachers called conferring. The teacher sits down beside the student to confer about the student's writing and progress. Collaboratively, the teacher works with the student to decide what to revise rather than returning the paper with notes that tell the student what to change. Does this conferencing work with Harrington's students? How do you know this? Would this conferencing work with you?

Making Children Hate Reading
JOHN HOLT

Educator John Holt taught elementary math in the 1950's. He studied flaws within the public school system and became a fierce advocate for children and championed education reform. He published on education theory and practice, and lectured at Harvard University and University of California, Berkeley. His first book, How Children Fail *from 1964, and* How Children Learn *from 1967 have sold over a million and a half copies and have been translated into fourteen languages. In the mid 1970's Holt realized that meaningful school reform was not possible and advocated for home schooling. He began his own magazine* Growing Without Schools. *Holt died in 1985. In "Making Children Hate Reading," which originally appeared in* Redbook *magazine in 1967 and was reprinted in 1969 in* The Underachieving School, *Holt examines teaching practices that make students hate reading and writing.*

———————— ✦ ————————

When I was teaching English at the Colorado Rocky Mountain School, I used to ask my students the kinds of questions that English teachers usually ask about reading assignments—questions designed to bring out the points that I had decided they should know. They, on their part, would try to get me to give them hints and clues as to what I wanted. It was a game of wits. I never gave my students an opportunity to say what they really thought about a book.

I gave vocabulary drills and quizzes too. I told my students that every time they came upon a word in their book they did not understand, they were to look it up in the dictionary. I even devised special kinds of vocabulary tests, allowing them to use their books to see how the words were used. But looking back I realize that these tests, along with many of my methods, were foolish.

My sister was the first person who made me question my conventional ideas about teaching English. She had a son in the seventh grade in a fairly good public school. His teacher had asked the class to read Cooper's *The Deerslayer*. The choice was bad enough in itself; whether looking at man or nature, Cooper was superficial, inaccurate and sentimental, and his writing is ponderous and ornate. But to make matters worse, this teacher had decided to give the book the microscope and X-ray treatment. He made the students look up and memorize not only the definition but the derivation of every big word that came along—and there were plenty. Every chapter was followed by close questioning and testing to make sure the students "understood" everything.

Being then, as I said, conventional, I began to defend the teacher, who was a good friend of mine, against my sister's criticisms. The argument soon grew hot. What was wrong with making sure that children understood everything they read? My sister answered that until this class her boy had always loved reading, and had read a lot on his own; now he had stopped. (He was not really to start again for many years.)

Still I persisted. If children didn't look up the words they didn't know how would they ever learn them? My sister said, "Don't be silly! When you were little you had a huge vocabulary, and were always reading very grown-up books. When did you ever look up a word in the dictionary?"

She had me. I never looked at our dictionary. I don't use one today. In my life I doubt that I have looked up as many as fifty words, perhaps not even half that.

Since then I have talked about this with a number of teachers. More than once I have said, "According to tests, educated and literate people like you have a vocabulary of about twenty-five thousand words. How many of these did you learn by looking them up in a dictionary?" They usually are startled.

Few claim to have looked up even as many as a thousand. How did they learn the rest?

They learned them just as they learned to talk: by meeting words over and over again, in different contexts, until they saw how they fitted.

Unfortunately, we English teachers are easily hung up on this matter of understanding. Why should children understand everything they read? Why should anyone? *Does* anyone? I don't, and I never did. I was always reading books that teachers would have said were "too hard" for me, books full of words I didn't know. That's how I got to be a good reader. When about ten, I read all the D'Artagnan stories and loved them. It didn't trouble me in the least that I didn't know why France was at war with England or who was quarreling with whom in the French court or why the Musketeers should always be at odds with Cardinal Richelieu's men. I didn't even know who the Cardinal was, except that he was a dangerous and powerful man that my friends had to watch out for. This was all I needed to know.

Having said this, I will now say that I think a big, unabridged dictionary is a fine thing to have in any home or classroom. No book is more fun to browse around in—if you're not made to. Children, depending on their age, will find many pleasant and interesting things to do with a big dictionary. They can look up funny-sounding words, which they like, or words that nobody else in the class has ever heard of, which they like, or long words, which they like, or forbidden words, which they like best of all. At a certain age, and particularly with a little encouragement from parents or teachers, they may become very interested in where words came from and when they came into the language and how their meanings have changed over the years. But exploring for the fun of it is very different from looking up words out of your reading because you're going to get into trouble with your teacher if you don't.

While teaching fifth grade two years or so after the argument with my sister, I began to think about reading. The children in my class were supposed to fill out a card—just the title and author and a one-sentence summary—for every book they read. I was not running a competition to see which child could read the most books, a competition that almost always leads to cheating. I just wanted to know what the kids were reading. After a while it became clear that many of these very bright kids, from highly literate and even literary backgrounds, read very few books and deeply disliked reading. Why should this be?

At this time I was coming to realize, as I described in my book *How Children Fail*, that for most children school is a place of danger, and their main business in school is staying out of danger as much as possible. I now began to see also that books are among the most dangerous things in school.

From the very beginning of school we make books and reading a constant source of possible failure and public humiliation. When children are little we make them read aloud, before the teacher and other children, so that we can be sure they "know" all the words they are reading. This means that when they don't know a word, they are going to make a mistake, right in front of everyone. Instantly they are made to realize that they have done something wrong. Perhaps some of the other children will begin to wave their hands and say "Ooooh O-o-o-oh!" Perhaps they will just giggle, or nudge each other, or make a face. Perhaps the teacher will say, "Are you sure?" or ask someone else what he thinks. Or perhaps, if the teacher is kindly, she will just smile a sweet, sad smile—often one of the most painful punishments a child can suffer in school. In any case, the child who has made the mistake knows he has made it, and feels foolish, stupid, and ashamed, just as any of us would in his shoes.

Before long many children associate books and reading with mistakes, real or feared, and penalties and humiliation. This may not seem sensible, but it is natural. Mark Twain once said that a cat that sat on a hot stove lid would never sit on one again, but it would never sit on a cold one either. As true of children as of cats. If they, so to speak, sit on a hot book a few times, if books cause them humiliation and pain, they are likely to decide that the safest thing to do is to leave all books alone.

After having taught fifth-grade classes for four years I felt quite sure of this theory. In my next class were many children who had had great trouble with schoolwork, particularly reading. I decided to try at all costs to rid them of their fear and dislike of books, and to get them to read oftener and more adventurously.

One day soon after school had started, I said to them, "Now I'm going to say something about reading that you have probably never heard a teacher say before. I would like you to read a lot of books this year, but I want you to read them only for pleasure. I am not going to ask you questions to find out whether you understand the books or not. If you understand enough of a book to enjoy it and want to go on reading it, that's enough for me. Also I'm not going to ask you what words mean.

"Finally," I said, "I don't want you to feel that just because you start a book you have to finish it. Give an author thirty or forty pages or so to get his story going. Then if you don't like the characters and you don't care what happens to them, close the book, put it away, and get another. I don't care whether the books are easy or hard, short or long, as long as you enjoy them. Furthermore I'm putting all this in a letter to your parents, so they won't feel they have to quiz and heckle you about books at home."

The children sat stunned and silent. Was this a teacher talking? One girl, who had just come to us from a school where she had had a very hard time, and who proved to be one of the most interesting, lively, and intelligent children I have ever known, looked at me steadily for a long time after I had finished. Then, still looking at me, she said slowly and solemnly, "Mr. Holt, do you really mean that?" I said just as solemnly, "I mean every word of it."

Apparently she decided to believe me. The first book she read was Dr. Seuss's *How the Grinch Stole Christmas*, not a hard book even for most third graders. For a while she read a number of books on this level. Perhaps she was clearing up some confusion about reading that her teachers, in their hurry to get her up to "grade level," had never given her enough time to clear up. After she had been in the class six weeks or so and we had become good friends, I very tentatively suggested that, since she was a skillful rider and loved horses, she might like to read *National Velvet*. I made my sell as soft as possible, saying only that it was about a girl who loved and rode horses, and that if she didn't like it she could put it back. She tried it, and, though she must have found it quite a bit harder than what she had been reading, finished it and liked it very much.

During the spring she really astounded me, however. One day, in one of our many free periods, she was reading at her desk. From a glimpse of the illustrations I thought I knew what the book was. I said to myself, "It can't be," and went to take a closer look. Sure enough, she was reading *Moby Dick*, in the edition with the woodcuts by Rockwell Kent. When I came closer to her desk she looked up. I said, "Are you really reading that?" She said she was. I said, "Do you like it?" She said, "Oh, yes, it's neat!" I said, "Don't you find parts of it rather heavy going?" She answered, "Oh, sure, but I just skip over those parts and go on to the next good part."

This is exactly what reading should be and in school so seldom is—an exciting, joyous adventure. Find something, dive into it, take the good parts, skip the bad parts, get what you can out of it; go on to something else. How different is our mean-spirited, picky insistence that every child get every last little scrap of "understanding" that can be dug out of a book.

For teachers who really enjoy doing it, and will do it with gusto, reading aloud is a very good idea. I have found that not just fifth graders but even ninth and eleventh graders enjoy it. Jack London's *To Build a Fire* is a good read-aloud story. So are spooky stories: "August Heat" by W. F. Harvey and "The Monkey's Paw" by Saki (H. H. Munro) are among the best. Shirley Jackson's "The Lottery" is sure-fire, and will raise all kinds of questions for discussion and argument. Because of a TV program they had seen and that had excited them, I once started reading my fifth graders William Golding's *Lord of the Flies*, thinking to read only a few chapters, but they made me read it to the end.

In my early fifth-grade classes the children usually were of high IQ, came from literate backgrounds, and were generally felt to be succeeding in school. Yet it was astonishingly hard for most of those children to express themselves in speech or in writing. I have known a number of five-year-olds who were considerably more articulate than most of the fifth graders I have known in school. Asked to speak, my fifth graders were overcome with embarrassment; many refused altogether. Asked to write, they would sit for minutes on end, staring at the paper. It was hard for most of them to get down a half-page of writing, even on what seemed to be interesting topics or topics they chose themselves.

In desperation I hit on a device that I named the Composition Derby. I divided the class into teams, and told them that when I said, "Go," they were to start writing something. It could be about anything they wanted, but it had to be about something; they couldn't just write "dog dog dog dog" on the paper. It could be true stories, descriptions of people or places or events, wishes, made-up stories, dreams—anything they liked. Spelling didn't count, so they didn't have to worry about it. When I said, "Stop," they were to stop and count up the words they had written. The team that wrote the most words would win the derby.

It was a success in many ways and for many reasons. The first surprise was that the two children who consistently wrote the most words were two of the least successful students in the class. They were bright, but they had always had a very hard time in school. Both were very bad spellers, and worrying about this had slowed down their writing without improving their spelling. When they were free of this worry and could let themselves go, they found hidden and unsuspected talents.

One of the two, a very driven and anxious little boy, used to write long adventures, or misadventures, in which I was the central character: "The Day Mr. Holt Went to Jail," "The Day Mr. Holt Fell into the Hole," "The Day Mr. Holt Got Run Over," and so on. These were very funny, and the class enjoyed hearing me read them aloud. One day, I asked the class to write a derby on a topic I would give them. They groaned; they liked picking their own. "Wait till you hear it," I said. "It's 'The Day the School Burned Down.'"

With a shout of approval and joy they went to work, and wrote furiously for 20 minutes or more, laughing and chuckling as they wrote. The papers were all much alike; in them the children danced around the burning building, throwing in books and driving me and the other teachers back in when we tried to escape.

In our first derby the class wrote an average of about ten words a minute; after a few months their average was over 20. Some of the slower writers tripled their output. Even the slowest, one of whom was the best student in the class, were writing 15 words a minute. More important, almost all the children enjoyed the derbies and wrote interesting things.

Some time later I learned that Professor S. I. Hayakawa, teaching freshman English, had invented a better technique. Every day in class he asked his students to write without stopping for about half an hour. They could write on whatever topic or topics they chose; the important thing was not to stop. If they ran dry, they were to copy their last sentence over and over again until new ideas came. Usually they came before the sentence had been copied once. I use this idea in my own classes, and call this kind of paper a Non-Stop. Sometimes I ask students to write a Non-Stop on an assigned topic, more often on anything they choose. [Now, (Winter 1969) my students at Berkeley do about 10-15 minutes of this private writing in almost every class—and I with them. We all find our thoughts coming much faster than we can write them, and ever more so with practice. Many students have said they enjoy this very much.] Once in a while I ask them to count up how many words they have written, though I rarely ask them to tell me; it is for their own information. Sometimes these papers are to be handed in; often they are what I call private papers, for the students' eyes alone.

The private paper has proved very useful. In the first place, in any English class—certainly any large English class—if the amount students write is limited by what the teacher can find time to correct, or even to read, the students will not write nearly enough. The remedy is to have them write a great deal that the teacher does not read. In the second place, students writing for themselves will write about many things that they would never write on a paper to be handed in, once they have learned (sometimes it takes a while) that the teacher means what he says about the papers' being private. This is important, not just because it enables them to get things off their chest, but also because they are most likely to write well, and to pay attention to how they write, when they are writing about something important to them.

Some English teachers, when they first hear about private papers, object that students do not benefit from writing papers unless the papers are corrected. I disagree for several reasons. First, most students, particularly poor students, do not read the corrections on their papers; it is boring, even painful. Second, even when they do read these corrections, they do not get much help from them, do not build the teacher's suggestions into their writing. This is true even when they really believe the teacher knows what he is talking about.

Third, and most important, we learn to write by writing, not by reading other people's ideas about writing. What most students need above all else is practice in writing, and particularly in writing about things that matter to them, so that they will begin to feel the satisfaction that comes from getting important thoughts down in words and will care about stating these thoughts forcefully and clearly.

Teachers of English—or, as some schools say (ugh!), Language Arts—spend a lot of time and effort on spelling. Most of it is wasted; it does little good, and often more harm than good. We should ask ourselves, "How do good spellers spell? What do they do when they are not sure which spelling of a word is right?" I have asked this of a number of good spellers. Their answer never varies. They do not rush for a dictionary or rack their brains trying to remember rules. They write down the word both ways or several ways, look at them, and pick the one that looks best. Usually they are right.

Good spellers know what words look like and even, in their writing muscles, feel like. They have a good set of word images in their minds and are willing to trust these images. The things we do to "teach" spelling to children do little to develop these skills or talents, and much to destroy them or prevent them from developing.

The first and worst thing we do is to make children anxious about spelling. We treat a misspelled word like a crime and penalize the misspeller severely; many teachers talk of making children develop a "spelling conscience," and fail otherwise excellent papers because of a few spelling mistakes. This approach is self-defeating.

When we are anxious, we don't perceive clearly or remember what we once perceived. Everyone knows how hard it is to recall even simple things when under emotional pressure; the harder we rack our brains, the less easy it is to find what we are looking for. If we are anxious enough, we will not trust the messages that memory sends us. Many children spell badly because although their first hunch about how to spell a word may be correct, they are afraid to trust it. I have often seen on children's papers a word correctly spelled, then crossed out and misspelled.

There are some tricks that might help children get sharper word images. Some teachers may be using them. One is the trick of air writing; that is, of "writing" a word in the air with a finger and "seeing" the image so formed. I did this quite a bit with fifth graders, using either the air or the top of a desk, on which the fingers left no mark. Many of them were tremendously excited by this. I can still hear them saying, "There's nothing there, but I can see it!" It seemed like magic. I remember that when I was little I loved to write in the air. It was effortless, voluptuous, and satisfying, and it was fun to see the word appear in the air. I used to write "Money Money Money," not so much because I didn't have any as because I liked the way it felt, particularly that y at the end, with its swooping tail.

Another thing to help sharpen children's image-making machinery is taking very quick looks at words—or other things. The conventional machine for doing this is the tachistoscope. But these are expensive, so expensive that most children can have few chances to use them, if any at all. With some three-by-five and four-by-eight file cards you can get the same effect. On the little cards you put the words or the pictures that the child is going to look at. You hold the larger card over the card to be read, uncover it for a split second with a quick wrist motion, then cover it up again. Thus you have a tachistoscope that costs one cent and that any child can work by himself.

Once when substituting in a first-grade class I thought that the children, who were just beginning to read and write, might enjoy some of the kind of free, nonstop writing that my fifth graders had. About 50 minutes before lunch, I asked them all to take pencil and paper and start writing about anything they wanted. They seemed to like the idea, but right away one child said anxiously, "Suppose we can't spell a word?"

"Don't worry about it," I said. "Just spell it the best way you can."

A heavy silence settled on the room. All I could see were still pencils and anxious faces. This was clearly not the right approach.

So I said, "All right, I'll tell you what to do. Any time you want to know how to spell a word, tell me and I'll write it on the board." They breathed a sigh of relief and went to work. Soon requests for words were coming fast; as soon as I wrote one, someone asked me another. By lunchtime, when most of the children were still busily writing, the board was full. What was interesting was that most of the words they had asked for were much longer and more complicated than anything in their reading books or workbooks. Freed from worry about spelling, they were willing to use the most difficult and interesting words that they knew.

The words were still on the board when we began school next day. Before I began to erase them, I said to the children, "Listen, everyone, I have to erase these words, but before I do, just out of curiosity I'd like to see if you remember some of them."

The result was surprising. I had expected that the child who had asked for and used a word might remember it, but I did not think that many others would. But many of the children still knew many of the words. How had they learned them? I suppose each time I wrote a word on the board a number of children had looked up, relaxed yet curious, just to see what the word looked like, and these images and the sound of my voice saying the word had stuck in their minds until the next day. This, it seems to me, is how children may best learn to write and spell.

What can a parent do if a school, or a teacher, is spoiling the language for a child by teaching it in some tired old way? First, try to get them to change, or at least let them know that you are eager for change. Talk to other parents; push some of the ideas in the PTA; talk to the English department at the school; talk to the child's own teacher. Many teachers and schools want to know what the parents want.

If the school or teacher cannot be persuaded, then what? Perhaps all you can do is try not to let your child become too bored or discouraged or worried by what is happening in school. Help him meet the school's demands, foolish though they may seem, and try to provide more interesting alternatives at home—plenty of books and conversation, and a serious and respectful audience when a child wants to talk. Nothing that ever happened to me in English classes at school was as helpful to me as the long conversations I used to have every summer with my uncle, who made me feel that the difference in our ages was not important and that he was really interested in what I had to say.

At the end of her freshman year in college a girl I knew wrote home to her mother, "Hooray! Hooray! Just think—I never have to take English anymore!" But this girl had always been an excellent English student, had always loved books, writing, ideas. It seems unnecessary and foolish and wrong that English teachers should so often take what should be the most flexible, exciting, and creative of all school courses and make it into something that most children can hardly wait to see the last of. Let's hope that we can and soon will begin to do much better.

Thinking and Writing Questions

1. How, according to Holt, do books and reading become "a constant source of possible failure and public humiliation" (19)?
2. John Holt wrote this essay in 1967 for *Redbook*, a magazine focusing on homemaking, beauty, and parenting that you find at the grocery store checkout. Describe the audience he writes this piece for. What content does Holt include to achieve his purpose with the intended audience?
3. Review the pieces in this chapter and list the factors that authors identify as influencing our attitudes toward writing. Which of these factors have influenced your attitude toward writing? How have you dealt with these factors?
4. Select a scene or incident from Holt's essay that you connect with. Write a few paragraphs describing your experience and explain how this experience has influenced your attitudes toward reading and writing.
5. What major indictment does Holt make about the teaching of reading and writing? What alternatives does he propose? Make a list of the things that you can do, your classmates can do, and your teacher can do to avoid the pitfalls that Holt describes.

Inspiration

MELISSA DUFFY

Melissa Duffy wrote this piece for her literacy narrative assignment in a first-year writing class at Purdue University Calumet in Northwest Indiana. She loves to write short stories and poems but has been consumed with writing school papers since she started college. She is working toward a degree in Occupational Therapy and plans to focus on early intervention to work with infants 0–3 years of age. In "Inspiration," Duffy recounts experiences of how two teachers inspired her to write.

---   ◆   ---

Along with all of the stress of becoming a teenager and entering high school came peace of mind as well. Here in high school was where I learned to love reading and writing; they became avenues where I sought solace and respite from everyday life. It was my English teacher, Mr. Wright, who really gave me my first "push" to write. But it was the support from my best friend and another English teacher that kept me going.

Jumping back to my first year in high school, I was a "normal kid." I had a group of friends with whom I hung out, and I was very comfortable joking around with them. We were a good group of kids, always finding ways to have fun that did not involve drugs. Our belief was always: "We don't need things like drugs to have fun." Which was very true; we had a little game which occupied our attention the majority of the time; the purpose of the game was to see who could tell the craziest story. We would take turns telling impromptu stories. They usually did not make sense and had no purpose, but they made everyone laugh, and it was a good way to pass the time.

That year I had a wonderful English teacher; he was young and very active, and he liked to encourage students to be the best they could. One day in English, my teacher, Mr. Wright, assigned us a paper. The paper needed to be a fictional story with a moral behind it. Prior to this, the stories I had been telling were all oral, I had never written one down, or even thought about it for that matter. Now was my chance to show my teacher what wild story I could tell. I struggled at first because I had a hard time coming up with a moral, or at least one that I liked. I was very unsure, but I started writing. Despite my uncertainty, I wrote several stories, all of which I was not pleased with and I did not think seemed "fit" to submit. Finally, after a few days, I came up with "Paco the Taco." It was a simple story about a taco and his band that wanted to "make it big." This short story told of how they gained their "big break" and what happened when they did.

Mr. Wright read and graded my story with the rest of the students. When I received it back, I was surprised to see on the top, "Wonderful paper, have you ever thought about being a children's author?" next to a big green 'A'. Before that moment I had never thought of being an author, let alone a children's author. Actually, I had never thought about what I wanted to be. Those few words made me think a lot and inspired me to write more.

From then on I wrote down every story I told. I wrote every random thought that popped in my head, from stories about snowflakes to a poem about a worm. I was running out of ideas, though. "Drying up." I had spent so much time writing and not enough learning about different cultures and ways of life. So that summer I went camping with my best friend. We would go every weekend with ten new books between the two of us and every weekend we would both finish all of them. We made a contest out of it. How many books could we read in one day? After we had read them, we would compare and contrast what we each thought about the book and how we interpreted it. We often viewed the books in different ways; that opened my eyes to a new perspective. I learned more in that summer than I had ever learned in one school year.

When school started, I then, applied my new-found knowledge to my stories. I took everything I learned and mixed it together, and what transpired was a plethora of good ideas. It was not until the following year, though, that I was fortunate to have another English teacher who would help expand my writing, Mr. Bean. Mr. Bean loved to tell "scary" stories. He was big into description and determined to teach us how to describe and what we saw in our own mind. He wanted to know everything, down to the single curly red thread that lies upon the carpet. He taught us how to add detail to everything we could see, anything at all that would put you into the character's place. He wanted us to explain every feeling, from the churning and aching of an upset stomach to the sharp shooting pain of a hangnail on their little finger. It took a while before I was able to do this. Before then I was so focused on just telling the story, I never thought about details. I guess the picture was already in my head, I just assumed it was in everyone else's as well.

He had us write a fictional story about anything we wanted, but the first sentence had to be one of three options. We were allowed to alter the sentence a little and add the names of our characters, but they generally had to be the same. I started right away. The sentence I chose to use was "The pain shot through like a steam train." I altered the sentence to fit my story: "The pain shot through Carrie's arm like a steam train." The story develops as follows:

A beautiful teenager named Carrie has an unusual addiction of ejecting blood from her body. She gains a rush from the feeling of blood being pulled out of her veins; it becomes a natural high for her. But Carrie is not doing so well; she has lost too much blood and she is thinking it is time to take her addiction to the next level, hoping she will feel better. Carrie decides to go see her "good friend" Devon. Devon is a handsome metro-sexual, but his good looks and smooth talking can be very deceiving. The story tells about the consequences of her actions and what happens to her because of the choices she has made.

This was the first story I truly took pride in. For the first time I felt like the audience received my view clearly, and I made my readers actually feel what Carrie was feeling. That story was the start of my "good" writings. I have become more "in tune" with my writing since then. I have learned to describe details. Each time I write, I become better.

I now look back at the stories I have written like "Paco the Taco" and think to myself, "It really is not that great of a paper." What my English teacher ever saw in me, I will never know. But I am extremely thankful that he saw something. If Mr. Wright had not made that one comment and Mr. Bean did not encourage me, I would have never continued writing, and I might even hate writing today. But because I had support and encouragement, I love writing. I owe thanks to many people because of that.

Thinking and Writing Questions

1. Duffy's literacy narrative presents a positive attitude toward writing. Describe her attitude. What do you think she would say her positive attitude is based upon?

2. In this narrative about her growth as a writer, Duffy explains how Mr. Bean taught her to add more details to her writing. She writes, "I never thought about details. I guess the picture was already in my head. I just assumed it was in everyone else's as well" (28). What did Duffy discover about looking at her work from the audience's perspective? Why is this important?

3. Whereas John Holt and Roy Peter Clark write about the things that make us avoid writing, Duffy writes about an experience that encouraged her to write. Make some notes about an experience that encouraged you to write. Tell your writing partner about this incident and explain what it is that kept you going. How did this incident and your willingness to keep going impact your success as a writer and as a student?

4. Duffy claims that "each time [she] write[s], [she] become[s] better" (29). What do you think about this statement? Is this so for you?

writing autobiography

BELL HOOKS

Feminist bell hooks is a noted author, teacher, and scholar. She is a Distinguished Professor of English at City College in New York where she teaches creative writing, African-American literature, and composition. She earned her Ph.D. in 1983 from the University of California, Santa Cruz. Her writings cover gender, race, teaching, and how media impacts our culture. She has published over fourteen book-length works, including Ain't I a Woman: Black Women and Feminism, *1981;* Feminist Theory: From Margin to Center, *1984; and* Teaching to Transgress: Education as the Practice of Freedom, *1994. Her use of the pseudonym "bell hooks" honors her female ancestors as well as her great-grandmother from whom the name is taken. hooks prefers the lower-case spelling of her name so as to lessen the prominence of the author and to highlight the message of the texts. The following chapter "writing autobiography" from* remembered rapture: the writer at work *describes hooks' struggle to write her autobiography.*

—————————— ✦ ——————————

To me, telling the story of my growing-up years was intimately connected with the longing to kill the self I was without really having to die. I wanted to kill that self in writing. Once that self was gone—out of my life forever—I could more easily become the me of me. It was clearly the Gloria Jean of my tormented and anguished childhood that I wanted to be rid of, the girl who was always wrong, always punished, always subjected to some humiliation or other, always crying, the girl who was to end up in a mental institution because she could not be anything but crazy, or so they told her. She was the girl who sat a hot iron on her arm pleading with them to leave her alone, the girl who wore her scar as a brand marking her madness. Even now I can hear the voices of my sisters saying, "mama make Gloria stop crying." By writing the autobiography, it was not just this Gloria I would be rid of, but the past that had a hold on me, that kept me from the present. I wanted not to forget the past but to break its hold. This death in writing was to be liberatory.

Until I began to try and write an autobiography, I thought that it would be a simple task, this telling of one's story. And yet I tried year after year, never writing more than a few pages. My inability to write out the story I interpreted as an indication that I was not ready to let go of the past, that I was not ready to be fully in the present. Psychologically, I considered the possibility that I had become attached to the wounds and sorrows of my childhood, that I held to them in a manner that blocked my efforts to be self-realized, whole, to be healed. A key message in Toni Cade Bambara's novel *The Salt Eaters*, which tells the story of Velma's suicide attempt, her breakdown, is expressed when the healer asks her, "Are you sure sweetheart, that you want to be well?"

There was very clearly something blocking my ability to tell my story. Perhaps it was remembered scoldings and punishments when mama heard me saying something to a friend or stranger that she did not think should be said. Secrecy and silence—these were central issues. Secrecy about family, about what went on in the domestic household was a bond between us—was part of what made us family. There was a dread one felt about breaking that bond. And yet I could not grow inside the atmosphere of secrecy that had pervaded our lives and the lives of other families about us. Strange that I had always challenged the secrecy, always let something slip that should not be known growing up, yet as a writer staring into the solitary space of paper, I was bound, trapped in the fear that a bond is lost or broken in the telling. I did not want to be the traitor, the teller of family secrets—and yet I wanted to be a writer. Surely, I told myself, I could write a purely imaginative work—a work that would not hint at personal private realities. And so I tried. But always there were the intruding traces, those elements of real life however disguised. Claiming the freedom to grow as an imaginative writer was connected for me with having the courage to be open, to be able to tell the truth of one's life as I had experienced it in writing. To talk about one's life—that I could do. To write about it, to leave a trace—that was frightening.

The longer it took me to begin the process of writing autobiography, the further removed from those memories I was becoming. Each year, a memory seemed less and less clear. I wanted not to lose the vividness, the recall and felt an urgent need to begin the work and complete it. Yet I could not begin even though I had begun to confront some of the reasons I was blocked, as I am blocked just now in writing this piece because I am afraid to express in writing the experience that served as a catalyst for that block to move.

I had met a young black man. We were having an affair. It is important that he was black. He was in some mysterious way a link to this past that I had been struggling to grapple with, to name in writing. With him I remembered incidents, moments of the past that I had completely suppressed. It was as though there was something about the passion of contact that was hypnotic, that enabled me to drop barriers and thus enter fully, rather reenter those past experiences. A key aspect seemed to be the way he smelled, the combined odors of cigarettes, occasionally alcohol, and his body smells. I thought often of the phrase "scent of memory," for it was those smells that carried me back. And there were specific occasions when it was very evident that the experience of being in his company was the catalyst for this remembering.

Two specific incidents come to mind. One day in the middle of the afternoon we met at his place. We were drinking cognac and dancing to music from the radio. He was smoking cigarettes (not only do I not smoke, but I usually make an effort to avoid smoke). As we held each other dancing those mingled odors of alcohol, sweat, and cigarettes led me to say, quite without thinking about it, "Uncle Pete." It was not that I had forgotten Uncle Pete. It was more that I had forgotten the childhood experience of meeting him. He drank often, smoked cigarettes, and always on the few occasions that we met him, he held us children in tight embraces. It was the memory of those embraces—of the way I hated and longed to resist them—that I recalled.

Another day we went to a favorite park to feed ducks and parked the car in front of tall bushes. As we were sitting there, we suddenly heard the sound of an oncoming train—a sound that startled me so that it evoked another long-suppressed memory: that of crossing the train tracks in my father's car. I recalled an incident where the car stopped on the tracks and my father left us sitting there while he raised the hood of the car and worked to repair it. This is an incident that I am not certain actually happened. As a child, I had been terrified of just such an incident occurring, perhaps so terrified that it played itself out in my mind as though it had happened. These are just two ways this encounter acted as a catalyst, breaking down barriers, enabling me to finally write this long-desired autobiography of my childhood.

Each day I sat at the typewriter and different memories were written about in short vignettes. They came in a rush, as though they were a sudden thunderstorm. They came in a surreal, dream-like style that made me cease to think of them as strictly autobiographical because it seemed that myth, dream, and reality had merged. There were many incidents that I would talk about with my siblings to see if they recalled them. Often we remembered together a general outline of an incident but the details were different for us. This fact was a constant reminder of the limitations of autobiography, of the extent to which autobiography is a very personal storytelling—a unique recounting of events not so much as they have happened but as we remember and invent them. One memory that I would have sworn was "the truth and nothing but the truth" concerned a wagon that my brother and I shared as children. I remembered that we played with this toy only at my grandfather's house, that we shared it, that I would ride it and my brother would push me. Yet one facet of the memory was puzzling—I remembered always returning home with bruises or scratches from this toy. When I called my mother, she said there had never been any wagon, that we had shared a red wheelbarrow, that it had always been at my grandfather's house because there were sidewalks on that part of town. We lived in the hills where there were no sidewalks. Again I was compelled to face the fiction that is a part of all retelling, remembering. I began to think of the work I was doing as both fiction and autobiography. It seemed to fall in the category of writing that Audre Lorde, in her autobiographically based work *Zami*, calls bio-mythography. As I wrote, I felt that I was not as concerned with accuracy of detail as I was with evoking in writing the state of mind, the spirit of a particular moment.

The longing to tell one's story and the process of telling is symbolically a gesture of longing to recover the past in such a way that one experiences both a sense of reunion and a sense of release. It was the longing for release that compelled the writing but concurrently it was the joy of reunion that enabled me to see that the act of writing one's autobiography is a way to find again that aspect of self and experience that may no longer be an actual part of one's life but is a living memory shaping and informing the present. Autobiographical writing was a way for me to evoke the particular experience of growing up southern and black in segregated communities. It was a way to recapture the richness of southern black culture. The need to remember and hold to the legacy of that experience and what it taught me has been all the more important since I have since lived in predominately white communities and taught at predominately white colleges. Black southern folk experience was the foundation of the life around me when I was a child; that experience no longer exists in many places where it was once all of life that we knew. Capitalism, upward mobility, assimilation of other values have all led to rapid disintegration of black folk experience or in some cases the gradual wearing away of that experience.

Within the world of my childhood, we held on to the legacy of a distinct black culture by listening to the elders tell their stories. Autobiography was experienced most actively in the art of telling one's story. I can recall sitting at Baba's (my grandmother on my mother's side) at 1200 Broad Street—listening to people come and recount their life experience. In those days, whenever I brought a playmate to my grandmother's house, Baba would want a brief outline of their autobiography before we would begin playing. She wanted not only to know who their people were but what their values were. It was sometimes an awesome and terrifying experience to stand answering these questions or witness another playmate being subjected to the process and yet this was the way we would come to know our own and one another's family histories. It is the absence of such a tradition in my adult life that makes the written narrative of my girlhood all the more important. As the years pass and these glorious memories grow much more vague, there will remain the clarity contained within the written words.

Conceptually, the autobiography was framed in the manner of a hope chest. I remembered my mother's hope chest, with its wonderful odor of cedar, and thought about her taking the most precious items and placing them there for safekeeping. Certain memories were for me a similar treasure. I wanted to place them somewhere for safekeeping. An autobiographical narrative seemed an appropriate place. Each particular incident, encounter, experience had its own story, sometimes told from the first person, sometimes told from the third person. Often I felt as though I was in a trance at my typewriter, that the shape of a particular memory was decided not by my conscious mind but by all that is dark and deep within me, unconscious but present. It was the act of making it present, bringing it into the open, so to speak, that was liberating.

From the perspective of trying to understand my psyche, it was also interesting to read the narrative in its entirety after I had completed the work. It had not occurred to me that bringing one's past, one's memories together in a complete narrative would allow one to view them from a different perspective, not as singular isolated events but as part of a continuum. Reading the completed manuscript, I felt as though I had an overview not so much of my childhood but of those experiences that were deeply imprinted in my consciousness. Significantly, that which was absent, left out, not included also was important. I was shocked to find at the end of my narrative that there were few incidents I recalled that involved my five sisters. Most of the incidents with siblings were with me and my brother. There was a sense of alienation from my sisters present in childhood, a sense of estrangement. This was reflected in the narrative. Another aspect of the completed manuscript that is interesting to me is the way in which the incidents describing adult men suggest that I feared them intensely, with the exception of my grandfather and a few old men. Writing the autobiographical narrative enabled me to look at my past from a different perspective and to use this knowledge as a means of self-growth and change in a practical way. In the end I did not feel as though I had killed the Gloria of my childhood. Instead I had rescued her. She was no longer the enemy within, the little girl who had to be annihilated for the woman to come into being. In writing about her, I reclaimed that part of myself I had long ago rejected, left uncared for, just as she had often felt alone and uncared for as a child. Remembering was part of a cycle of reunion, a joining of fragments, "the bits and pieces of my heart" that the narrative made whole again.

Thinking and Writing Questions

1. Explain what bell hooks means when she writes that she wanted to "kill"—in writing—the Gloria Jean of her childhood so that she could become the "me of me" (30).
2. How is hooks' autobiography similar to and different from journal writing, blogging, or writing in a diary? What do you think she might suggest is the purpose of her writing? How does hooks' purpose compare to the purpose of the majority of your writings?
3. The pieces in this chapter are about attitudes toward and beliefs about writing. Vetter characterizes writing as a "blood sport" (37). Holt declares that writing "should be the most flexible, exciting, and creative of all school courses" (26). Aronowitz writes that, "writing is an art—since it entails thought, the adroit use of language . . . imagination, genuine knowledge" (40). What do you think hooks would say about her attitude toward writing? From what do you infer her attitudes?
4. What actually happened to Gloria Jean and bell hooks as a result of writing her autobiography? What does hooks' narrative add to your understanding of her decision to publish under the name of bell hooks rather than her given name, Gloria Jean?

Bonehead Writing
CRAIG VETTER

Author Craig Vetter has taught magazine writing in the Medill School of Journalism at Northwestern University in Evanston, IL. He has worked on staff for Playboy, Outside, *and* Sunset *magazines, and has been freelancing for the past twenty-five years for a wide range of national magazines. He graduated from the University of San Francisco with a BA in English Literature. In "Bonehead Writing," which first appeared in* Playboy, *Vetter shares a lecture he would give to a first-year writing class about the struggles of writing.*

───────────── ✦ ─────────────

There's a sort of low moan that goes up periodically from the English departments at colleges and universities across the country over the fact that most students, even the good ones, can't write a lick—not a love letter or a suicide note, much less an essay or a term paper. It's nothing new, but according to the teachers who have to read this crap for a living, the further we get into the computer era the worse it's becoming. So at places like Harvard and Yale and Brown, they're holding faculty conferences to hash the problem through; they're designing bonehead writing courses and setting up special peer-group tutoring programs in an all-out, last-ditch effort to ensure that their graduates will at least be able to fill out applications for day labor without embarrassing themselves.

They haven't gone so far as to suggest that a student be required to write, say, one short coherent paragraph in order to graduate, but there are signs that they're getting a little desperate. For one thing, they're hiring more and more writers, and I don't mean just the cocktail-party lions of big fiction, either. They're actually cleaning out the mop closets to make office space for journalists and other freelance grubs who have spent most of their careers below decks, sweating and wiping the greasy pipes in the engine room of the profession.

Somehow, I haven't been asked. I am qualified, though: at it almost 20 years with nothing to show except a world-class alcohol/tobacco habit, debt that follows me like a huge pet rat and a small, used Olivetti with a leatherette case. Credentials, in other words. And I know some things about writing that others are not likely to tell you; ugly things. I think I could cram most of them into the first lecture, which, given the size of the problem, would probably have to be held in a fairly large room. If I did it right, though—if I were honest with my students—I think we could most likely hold the second class in a Datsun and get everybody in comfortably.

So picture me now, walking across the quad in my uniform— torn bathrobe, bolo tie, blown-out L.L. Bean boating mocs—smelling like a ripe field of Cannabis, making little Italian hand signals to the Jordache and Calvin coeds, then gripping the lectern and looking out into the small bay of faces that are waiting for me to teach them about writing.

"Good morning, children, and brace yourselves. This is Writing One-A. I wanted to subtitle it 'Writing for those who still sign their name with an X,' but the administration said, 'No, these kids aren't stupid or uneducated, just writing-impaired.' I love that. Makes you sound like Helen Keller at the pump, waiting for a miracle. It's not entirely your fault, though; I know that. There isn't one in a thousand teachers who knows the first damn thing about writing. All your lives, they've been reducing it to widgets and screws, clauses and semicolons for you, till what you think you're working with is a dainty sort of parlor art, something like embroidery.

"The truth is that writing is a blood sport, a walk in the garden of agony every time out, which is why those who are any good at it look older than their contemporaries, snap at children on the street, live alone. Like me.

"So you can pretty much forget the polite approach to writing in here. What I'm going to show you this semester is that you don't have what it takes to write well. You never did and you never will. In fact, you probably ought to think of this class as one of those wilderness-survival courses that are popular these days. Except that instead of taking you out in a happy little group and encouraging you to face trouble and danger as a team, I want you to imagine that you are going to be hustled into deep woods at midnight, trussed up, beaten senseless and left to die. If you do make it back to camp, we'll give you a nice T-shirt that says, I SURVIVED THE DOWNWARD BOUND SCHOOL OF WRITING, you'll be rebeaten, then dragged to a less benign part of the forest.

"And if you think that metaphor exaggerates what's ahead of you, take a look at this. Don't turn away, you wormy little cowards. This is your enemy: a perfectly empty sheet of paper. *Nothing* will ever happen here except what you make happen. If you are stupid, what happens will be like a signed confession of that fact. If you are unfunny, a humorless patch of words will grow here. If you lack imagination, your reader will know you immediately and forever as the slug you are. Or let me put it to you this way—and you may want to tattoo this somewhere on your bodies—BLANK PAPER IS GOD'S WAY OF TELLING US THAT IT'S NOT SO EASY TO BE GOD.

"But I'm not here to give you just the good news this morning, so let's get right to the ugliest of today's ironies. I'm stealing your money. I couldn't teach you how to write if I wanted to, if *you* wanted me to. Everybody who ever learned this wretched craft taught himself, and he did it despite the lettered fools who got into the process here and there, because writing is not, first, the gathering up and stringing together of words. Writing is *thinking*, which means that every time you sit down to it, you get another chance to find out just how perceptive you *aren't*. To come up with one simple, interesting or funny thought on anything is the hardest, dirtiest shoveling any of us ever has to do, and no one can teach you how to do it.

"There is one trick I can give you, however; a way for you to seem smarter and more clever than you really are. All you have to do is spend 40 or 50 hours working up an idea, a sentence, that looks when you've written it as if it took 90 seconds to make. You don't have to tell anyone how long you were alone in your own weak mind, floundering and whining—that it took you eight full days to write a dopey little 900-word column.

"But—and this is what I'd like you to ask yourselves before our next meeting—why in hell would anybody want to learn to do that?"

Thinking and Writing Questions

1. According to Vetter, writing is not widgets and screws—it is thinking. He states "BLANK PAPER IS GOD'S WAY OF TELLING US THAT IT'S NOT SO EASY TO BE GOD" (37). What is Vetter saying about writing and thinking in this statement?

2. Describe Vetter's voice in this essay. Think of voice as simply the presence or personality behind the writing. What type of personality does his choice of words, images, and ideas project? What does Vetter accomplish by using this voice?

3. In his special way, Vetter says that students "can't write a lick—not a love letter or a suicide note, much less an essay or a term paper" (36). The authors of "The Neglected 'R'" report that by "grade 12, most students are producing relatively immature and unsophisticated writing" (National Commission). Sam Dillon reports in "What Corporate America Can't Build: A Sentence" that "a third of employees in the nation's blue-chip companies wrote poorly and that businesses were spending as much as $3.1 billion on remedial training" (177). What conclusions can you draw from these three quotes?

4. Vetter claims that because teachers don't know anything about writing, they reduce it to "widgets and screws, clauses and semicolons" (37). What types of widgets-and-screws teaching strategies have your teachers used? How have these teaching strategies helped you?
5. Can your teacher or a writing class teach you how to write? How do we learn to write? What can you, your classmates, and the instructor do to help you learn to write and think?

Writing Is Not a Skill
STANLEY ARONOWITZ

Social activist Stanley Aronowitz has authored and edited over twenty-three books and published more than two hundred articles and reviews in publications such as Harvard Educational Review, Social Policy, The Nation, *and* The American Journal of Sociology. *He has taught at the Graduate Center of the City University of New York since 1983, where he is a Distinguished Professor of Sociology. He studies labor, social movements, science and technology, education, social theory and cultural studies and is director of the Center for the Study of Culture, Technology and Work at the Graduate Center. He is founding editor of the journal* Social Text. *Aronowitz writes that he has always been a public intellectual and social activist. In 1952, he dropped out of college and went to work at a steel mill in New Jersey. He took on leadership positions in the various unions and became active in the Civil Rights Movement. In 1967 he returned to college. In "Writing is Not a Skill," taken from his book* The Knowledge Factory, *Aronowitz argues that writing is an art because it involves critical thinking and imagination.*

--- ◆ ---

Is "writing" a skill, an art, or a kind of critical literacy? Are its various forms—fiction, poetry, discourse, and argument, embodied in memos, papers, essays, and treatises—mastered by learning techniques and rules? If writing is a skill, then it can be compared to the instrumental activity of tying a shoelace, replacing a light bulb, operating a computer, a lathe, or a photocopying machine. We seldom think about what is involved in these activities because, after repetitive use, they become habitual. But learning a skill takes time, particularly for the neophyte. One must find out how to turn on the machine before discovering how to retrieve the work from a hard disk and use the various commands and the screen properly. The lathe operator must learn how to put the metal or the wood part into a chuck, the machine part that holds the work, before he gets started; the photocopier operator must know how [sic] place the paper correctly on the surface of the photocopier in order to get the job done.

Writing, too, would be a skill if its mastery were confined to habituating the student to such mechanical features. To be sure, writing incorporates skills: the practitioner must learn how to use pen or pencil or master the mechanics of typing. And in the case of computer-driven word processing, there are a fair number of technical features of some complexity to be assimilated, compared to the relatively simple operation of a typewriter. Further, the formulation of a simple sentence, which embodies spelling, grammar, and syntax, has certain skill components.

But since semantic issues always intrude in writing, making meaning is not a skill but both an art and a form of critical learning. If writing is an art—since it entails thought, the adroit use of language, and rules of expression, none of which is mechanical in nature—the process of learning involves imagination, genuine knowledge, and more or less self-conscious familiarity with logical sequences. Even the most mundane memorandum that goes beyond mere conveyance of information—"The office will be closed at 12:00 P.M. on Thursday, 31 December, for New Year's Eve"—and instead makes a proposal for a course of action, or contests a course of action proposed by another, entails complexity and narrative coherence. Learning the formal apparatus of a memo is a necessary step, but only a first step. Almost everything else must be artfully as well as skillfully wrought, both with respect to its order and its rhetoric, for the object of the exercise is to persuade others of the rightness of one's perspective. In this sense, rhetoric must not be understood pejoratively but in the sense used by the Greeks: like logic, it is inextricably intertwined with argument. It involves careful choices of words, a sense of dramatic presentation, an awareness of the questions that might arise from some of the author's statements, the mood of the audience, and many other considerations.

Every good writing teacher is aware of these and many other issues. She knows that, however much the visual has become a cultural force, words retain their power, and those who are able to use them effectively—to tell stories, invent slogans, construct arguments, and to paint word pictures that have visceral appeal—tend to acquire influence. In short, many writing teachers understand that the skills are subordinate to the art of writing. And they understand that writing is not only a form of communication and expression but signifies a content itself, modifying and infusing all other forms of knowledge. The notion of "writing across the curriculum" demonstrates at all levels of schooling that some teachers have become convinced that the idea that knowledge acquisition is independent of its expression is untenable. Yet few framers of the undergraduate core seem to have taken these insights into account; they persist in using the term "skill" to describe the nature of writing. This term reflects the persistence of the rest of the curriculum to transmit a fixed, specialized body of knowledge acquired by the instructor in graduate school and to which he has become habituated. That a sociologist or economist should consider himself a writing teacher and a guide to close textual reading would embarrass most professors in these fields, except some who understand that the reading and writing are properly learned at all levels of the academic system.

Thinking and Writing Questions

1. Stanley Aronowitz argues that writing is not a skill; it is an art. Lay out his rationale for this statement.

2. Writers compose pieces for a reason: to achieve a purpose, to create an effect. What purpose does Aronowitz have for this piece? What choices does he make to achieve this purpose?

3. Where Vetter uses words such as "bonehead" and "crap," Aronowitz uses "habituating" and "semantic." The words a writer chooses contribute to the personality or voice that the writer has decided to create in the text. Compare and contrast the vocabulary and voices of Vetter and Aronowitz.

4. Presenting writing as a skill, Aronowitz compares it to operating a photocopier which has a clear set of directions to follow: how to insert the original, how to select back-to-front copies, and what buttons to press to make twenty-five copies. Presenting writing as an art, what might we compare it to? Generate a metaphor for writing as an art of making meaning and critical thinking.

5. Aronowitz claims that "reading and writing are properly learned at all levels of the academic system" (41). What does a student continue to learn about writing at various academic levels? Has this been so for you? What might you continue to learn through your college career?

Chapter 1: Thinking and Writing

1. In "writing autobiography," bell hooks tells her story of working through a writing block. In "Inspiration," Melissa Duffy tells her story of becoming a writer. In "Shitty First Drafts," Anne Lamott tells her story of writing to a deadline each month. Compose an autobiographical essay in which you tell your story of a literacy event. There are two basic components of a literacy narrative: the narrative and the analysis of the narrative. To begin, you might draw a literacy timeline, starting with the first time you read a book such as *Hop on Pop* or the first time you wrote—maybe on the wall with crayons—and ending with an argument paper you wrote in high school in which you learned how to revise your first draft and build a solid argument.

   After selecting a literacy event, reread the hooks, Duffy, and Lamott pieces, noting how they tell their narratives and how they develop the significance of the literacy event. Use dialogue and description to let your readers experience the events. Explain the significance of these incidents by illustrating how they have influenced your life and your growth as a reader, writer, and thinker.

2. In "Bonehead Writing," Vetter claims that neither teachers nor a writing class can teach you to write. And yet, you're sitting in a classroom, planning on becoming a better writer. And, teachers and writers in Chapter Two tell you what to do to become a better writer. Write a narrative that records your exploration of Vetter's claim that neither a teacher nor a writing class can teach you to write. You might begin your exploratory essay with the question, "Can a teacher and a writing class teach me how to write?" To get yourself thinking, try to remember how you have learned what you know about writing. How have you been learning to write?

   Cover at least two authors from *Essays on Writing* in your explorations. Record your thinking as you explore this question. Your goal is to examine various sides of this issue. You might not come to a definitive answer to your question; however, you will know what to say to Craig Vetter when you meet him.

3. General Apache was on his way to being a good writer. Melissa Duffy, in "Inspiration," is on her way to becoming a good writer. bell hooks, Anne Lamott, and other authors in this book explore how they have developed into good, experienced writers. These success stories contradict the stories of incompetent writers in other essays. Vetter says that you "can't write a lick" (36). The authors of "The Neglected 'R'" report that by "grade 12, most students are producing relatively immature and unsophisticated writing" (National Commission). Sam Dillon reports in "What Corporate America Can't Build: A Sentence" that "a third of employees in the nation's blue-chip companies wrote poorly and that businesses were spending as much as $3.1 billion on remedial training" (177). How can this discrepancy be explained? How can we explain both the poor quality

of writing that has been reported in recent studies and the stories of experienced accomplished writers? Write an essay in which you present what appears to be the discrepancy between studies of "poor" writing and experiences of "good" writers. Then offer a few reasons for this discrepancy. Are hooks, Lamott, and Duffy exceptions? Will you be an exception when you become an experienced writer?

4. Vetter states in capital letters that "BLANK PAPER IS GOD'S WAY OF TELLING US THAT IT'S NOT SO EASY TO BE GOD" (37). The words and sentences that writers put on blank paper and on blank computer screens create ideas and vivid images. Aronowitz calls this God-like act of creation "art."

So, what happens when a teacher plays God and takes over your writing? Maybe telling you what to add to a draft or what to remove? Maybe telling you to copy a page from the dictionary or write one hundred times, "I will not talk in the library"?

Write an essay in which you explore whether students are able to employ the craft and art of writing to tell their own stories. Draw on your experiences and the pieces in Chapter Two to craft your answer to this question: can you write your own story? What kind of support do you think teachers should provide? When Harrington shows his poem to General Apache, he responds, "'That's my whole life right there. I wish I could find words to put things like you can'" (13). Vetter would say that General Apache can't write a lick much less tell his own story. What do you think? Can novice writers tell their own stories?

Works Cited

National Commission on Writing in America's Schools and Colleges. "The Neglected 'R': The Need for a Writing Revolution" College Board, 2003. http://www.writingcommission.org/prod_downloads/writingcom/neglectedr.pdf, 13 October 2007.

CHAPTER 2

Practice

Okay, so how do we do it? How do we write? Is there a magic formula? The authors in this next chapter address just this topic. And the answer is a resounding, "No!" There is no "Ancient Chinese Secret" that will keep the blank-page-blues at bay. All right, before you bang your head into a wall, take a look at the next few essays. While there may be no magic formula, there are some things you can do to develop a process of thinking and writing that will work for you.

Sandra Boynton's cartoon, "The Five Paragraph Theme" vividly illustrates the organizational pattern we've all been taught (whether we were listening or not) at some point in our academic careers. Teachers have often given students the idea that this structure might just be the Holy Grail we've all been looking for: the magic formula. Boynton's whimsical "monster" gives way to some sarcastic undertones; perhaps pointing out the childishness in thinking there is some magic structure in which to fit our ideas.

While reading "Dyr Mom: Wy R You So Laveabl?" you might stumble over the words of a five-year old who uses invented spelling. Gayle Brandeis shares the early writing of her daughter Hannah who struggles to get her ideas down on paper and to be heard by her parents. Brandeis claims that as Hannah enters the world of literacy "she seems to know that writing is a safe place to explore the taboo" and to tell her mother "DED IS ALWYS MEYN" (50). Hannah struggles to put her feelings of anger toward her father into words, creating the words she doesn't know how to spell. Without a magic formula, Hannah is left to her own devices to create and express her meaning.

Whereas Hannah's situation pushed her to write, many writers have to create environments that foster thinking and writing.

In "Time, Tools, and Talismans," Susan Wyche focuses on writing rituals: behaviors and patterns that both support and prevent successful writing. While many of the following authors will discuss the importance of drafting and revision, Wyche stresses location, location, location: the physical and mental spaces in which writers place themselves to foster the art of writing and thinking. To acknowledge these rituals, Liz has added another category to the writing process called pre prewriting. Heather's pre prewriting rituals are extraordinary. She claims that the following list is "pretty accurate" yet "not exhaustive."

1. Clean house.
2. Do laundry.
3. Be sure desk area is clean.
4. Send daughter to babysitter.
5. Get diet Pepsi.
6. Call Debbie.
7. Discuss project/thesis/idea/weather.
8. Hang up and start writing.
9. Get through one paragraph.
10. Call Debbie while getting another diet Pepsi.
11. Discuss what has just been written.

In "A Way of Writing," William Stafford explains what can happen when the rituals get writers' ideas moving from head to hand to page. Writers learn to engage in composing activities that produce "a whole succession of unforeseen stories, poems, essays, plays, laws, philosophies, religion" rather than "draw on a reservoir" of already formed ideas (66). Stafford compares this process of constructing ideas to that of fishing where one waits for a nibble. Stafford claims that writing is a journey. It is the process that is important. As the author goes through the process, the product will come.

Anne Lamott's chapter, "Shitty First Drafts," builds on Stafford's ideas that we should not judge our first drafts and should even expect shitty first drafts. "You need to start somewhere," Lamott declares, and she explains how she gets through her pre prewriting strategies to her shitty first draft (72). Lamott pulls no punches here. Writing is hard. Anyone who tells you otherwise is lying to you, but as Lamott points out, if you don't write it down, you can't fix it, so get drafting.

Donald Murray builds on Stafford's and Lamott's ideas of drafting, claiming that one hidden truth of writing is that many authors "don't know what they are going to write or even possibly what they have written" (77), which brings Murray to explore the topic of revision. To move beyond our first ideas and first drafts, Murray directs us to use revision as a creative activity rather than just a stage in the writing process. Murray further delineates revision into two types, separating content revision which he calls internal from structural revision which he calls external.

In "Simplicity," William Zinsser argues for editing as a crucial component in writing. Rather than building up, Zinsser suggests that we pare back. He argues that "clutter is the disease of American writing" (85). While he may agree with the likes of Murray, Lamott, and Stafford that writers must build ideas with much writing, he claims, "the secret of good writing is to strip every sentence to its cleanest components" (85). This might be easier said than done, of course, but Zinsser's examples may inspire even the most verbose among us. He charges us to make life easier for our reader by making our prose easier to read.

From Susan Wyche's acceptance of quirky habits to Anne Lamott's embrace of shitty first drafts to William Zinsser's advice to simplify, writing is presented as something authors do from silencing the negative voices in their heads to reading prose backwards. While these authors don't give you the magic formula, they share the things that experienced writers do to get their ideas into words and onto the page. Your job is to figure out what strategies work for you. As you read, think about what you do when you write. How do you pose and solve problems? Do you have any writing quirks? Do you have a favorite place to write? Or time? What about a special pen or computer? What is the hardest aspect of writing for you? How do you overcome that? Don't forget that while there is no magic in any writing formula, there is a magic in writing. It's the journey, not the destination.

The Five-Paragraph Theme
SANDRA BOYNTON

Humorist Sandra Boynton was born in New Jersey in 1953. She began her career with a BA in English from Yale in 1974 and pursued directing until a summer job in the world of greeting cards transformed her path in the mid-1970's. Boynton's cards have sold

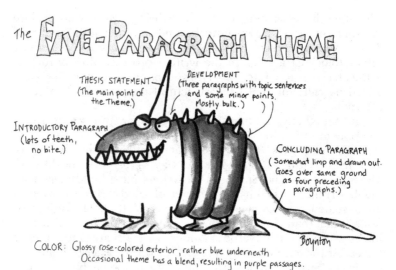

The *Five-Paragraph Theme*

THESIS STATEMENT (The main point of the Theme.)

DEVELOPMENT (Three paragraphs with topic sentences and some minor points. Mostly bulk.)

INTRODUCTORY PARAGRAPH (lots of teeth, no bite.)

CONCLUDING PARAGRAPH (Somewhat limp and drawn out. Goes over same ground as four preceding paragraphs.)

COLOR: Glossy rose-colored exterior, rather blue underneath. Occasional theme has a blend, resulting in purple passages.

Boynton

more than 200 million copies to date; the best known of these is perhaps her 1975 birthday greeting "Hippo Birdie Two Ewes." Boynton is perhaps best known by the mommy-set as the author/illustrator of dozens of "books for discerning children, and some other books for peculiar adults." She has been a best selling author for more than twenty-five years and has received the 1983 Irma Simonton Black Award for her book Chloe & Maude; *the National Cartoonists Society Award in 1993; the National Parenting Publications Awards Gold Medal in 1994 for her book* Barnyard Dance! *In "The Five–Paragraph Theme," which was published in a catalogue for Boynton/Cook Publishers, Boynton gives a visual representation of the five-paragraph theme as a monster.*

———————— ✦ ————————

Thinking and Writing Questions

1. Compose your description of the five-paragraph theme. What rules were you given to follow when creating this genre?
2. Boynton chose to draw the five-paragraph theme as a monster with sharp teeth. What impact does this rhetorical choice have on you?
3. Boynton describes the concluding paragraph as "Somewhat limp and drawn out. Goes over the same ground as four preceding paragraphs." Liz was told,

"In the introduction, tell them what you're going to tell them. In the body, tell them what you want them to know, and in the conclusion tell them what you just told them." What does your writing handbook or textbook say about conclusions? Compare and contrast these descriptions of conclusions. What is the "best" way for teachers to characterize and teach effective conclusions?

4. Why do so many teachers teach and require this rigid structure of a five-paragraph theme?

Dyr Mom: Wy R You So Laveabl?

GAYLE BRANDEIS

Gayle Brandeis is the writer-in-residence for the Mission Inn Foundation's Family Voices Project in Riverside, CA. As a community activist, Brandeis has written about peace and the war in the Middle East. Her novel, The Book of Dead Birds, *won Barbara Kingsolver's Bellwether Prize for Fiction in Support of a Literature of Social Change. Her work has appeared in* Salon.com, The Nation, *and* The Mississippi Review. *In "Dyr Mom: Wy R You So Laveabl?" which first appeared in* Salon.com, *Brandeis tells how her daughter learned to write by experimenting with invented spelling in order to get her feelings on the page.*

---------------- ✦ ----------------

A few months ago, I bought some sugar cookies shaped like the letters of the alphabet. When Jewish children begin to study Torah, rabbis often give them a spoonful of honey so they will always associate learning with sweetness. I figured the cookies would provide a most delicious reading lesson for my 5-year-old daughter. I could picture us at the table together, spelling CAT and LOVE and APPLE on paper plates, our mouths full of shortbread and sugar and the lingering sweetness of words.

When I got home, though, I discovered my daughter had already created her own movable feast. Hannah had been sent to her room for some minor infraction while I was out, and she was not happy about it. Did she whine? Maybe. Did she cry? Most likely. I wasn't there to hear her protests. She did leave some evidence behind, though. She wrote.

Hannah had never written anything all on her own before, other than her own name and the names of our family members. She had never constructed a sentence, never sat down with the intention of getting her thoughts on paper. In the hour that I was gone, though, she essentially figured out the whole writing process.

As I walked through her door, Hannah handed me a piece of paper.

"DYR MOM," it said. "DED IS ALWYS MEYN."

Rough drafts of the letter were scattered around her room: "DRY MOM," one began. "DYR MAM" read another.

I was blown away. Not only had Hannah written a sentence for the first time, she had edited her own work! After years as a writer, I have only recently made friends with the revision process. Hannah shook hands with it her first time out. My heart filled to bursting—my little girl, a writer!

My husband was amazed, too, although he was not completely thrilled to be the villain of her first literary undertaking. This gave us a little peek into what it must feel like to read a daughter's tell-all memoir. Wait, the author's parents must want to say, that's not the whole story! We're not bad people! We bought her a Sno-Cone from the ice cream truck just minutes before the alleged incident! And, you know, she never would have been sent to her room if she hadn't thrown a stick at her brother's head!

Before we could get too worked up about her initial angry outpouring of words, though, Hannah began another series of letters, sweet as any sugar cookie.

"DYR PYPIL," she wrote. "I LAV AVRYWON."

"DYR IDAHO," another said. "I WD LIK TO GO THAR."

It didn't take long for her to return to her writergrrl roots, though. In a little heart-covered, pastel-papered notebook, she wrote more scathing critiques of her dad, and even more of her brother. So far, I've managed to escape her writerly wrath. " MOM," she wrote in her journal. "WY R YOU SO LAVEABL?" I know I won't be immune to her poison pen forever, but for now, I enjoy being the subject of her little tributes. Who needs good reviews when your own daughter writes "THAT DANS WS GROOVY" and "MI MOM IS A POET. YOU CN TEL BCS OF HR BUKS"?

Hannah often sits on the couch, one leg crossed over the other like a stenographer from a '40s movie, pencil and notebook in hand. She loves to write lists—"LOBSDR, FISH, SHRIMP, SHRK"; "CHIKIN, TRKY, DAK, ROOSDR"—little inventories of the world she knows. She has her own "dictionary of bad words," which right now reads "ASS ASS ASS HL." She seems to know that writing is a safe place to explore the taboo, to delve into rage and joy and the enchantment of the ordinary.

"I have my own way of spelling," Hannah says excitedly, like she's created her own civilization. When she asks me how to spell something correctly, I tell her, but I love the playful, fluid way she chooses to spell words. I want to give her some more time to swim around in her own language before she has to worry about spelling tests and red pencil marks and grammar and precision. That will come soon enough.

I think of Margaret Atwood's poem "Spelling," which opens:

My daughter plays on the floor
with plastic letters,
red, blue & hard yellow,
learning how to spell,
spelling,
how to make spells

Hannah is learning how to make spells. Her own spells. Her own magic.

Hannah and I never did have our sugar-cookie spelling lesson. Our family polished off the container of treats like speed readers, spilling spelling crumbs everywhere, before we had a chance to act out my plan. Hannah taught herself more than those cookies ever could, though.

The very last page of Hannah's heart notebook reads, in large letters, "I AM JIST FYN." Isn't that, ultimately, what we all try to say when we write? Aren't we all trying to convince our readers and, even more so, ourselves, that we are just fine? That our words are valid? That we deserve to be heard?

Atwood writes later in the same poem, "A word after a word/after a word is power." It is very cool for me, as a writer and a woman, to watch my daughter discover that power inside her. She helps me remember my own power as well: words sweet and biting, pungent and nourishing, in all of our fingers, on both of our tongues.

Thinking and Writing Questions

1. Why did Hannah begin to write? What social interaction pushed her to put her ideas into written words?

2. Brandeis begins her piece with a narrative about buying letter-shaped cookies. Compare her introduction to other introductions in this chapter. For

example, in "A Way of Writing," Stafford starts with his definition of a writer. Experienced writers carefully choose the first thing their readers read, gauging what will hook them. Explain why Brandeis starts her essay with a story. Consider her topic, purpose for writing, and audience.

3. In "Writing to Connect," Mary Pipher says that, "All writing is designed to change the world, at least a small part of the world, or in some small way perhaps a change in a reader's mood or in his appreciation of a certain kind of beauty" (202). How do Hannah's few new words change her mother? How does Brandeis' story influence your perception of invented spelling?

4. At the beginning of Hannah's writing career, she used invented spelling to write her ideas. Do you ever use invented spelling when you are drafting and don't know how to spell a word? Why? Why not? How do you invent when your brain won't bring up the word or the ideas that you need?

Time, Tools, and Talismans
SUSAN WYCHE

Writing teacher Susan Wyche-Smith formerly served as Director of Composition at Washington State University and more recently as the founding director of the University Writing Program at CSU Monterey Bay. Currently, she has struck out on a new path of learning: studying Landscape Architecture at the University of California Berkeley Extension Program, working part-time as a landscape designer, and taking long walks with her border collie, Shadow. In "Time, Tools, and Talismans," which first appeared as an essay in The Subject Is Writing, *Wyche explores the rituals writers have developed that both support and hinder their writing processes.*

---- ✦ ----

Famous writers have been known to do a lot of crazy things to help them write: Dame Edith Sitwell sought inspiration by lying in a coffin. George Sand wrote after making love. Friedrich Schiller sniffed rotten apples stashed under the lid of his desk. A hotel room furnished with a dictionary, a Bible, a deck of cards, and a bottle of sherry suits Maya Angelou. Fugitive writer Salman Rushdie carries a silver map of an unpartitioned India and Pakistan. Charles Dickens traveled with ceramic frogs.

Writers also mention less bizarre practices. They describe eating, drinking, pacing, rocking, sailing, driving a car or riding in a bus or train, taking a hot bath or shower, burning incense, listening to music, staring out windows, cleaning house, or wearing lucky clothes. What do these rituals do for writers? The explanations are as varied as the rituals themselves. Tolstoy believed that "the best thoughts most often come in the morning after waking, while still in bed, or during a walk." Sonia Sanchez says that she works at night because "at that time the house is quiet. The children are asleep. I've prepared for my classes . . . graded papers . . . answered letters. . . . [A]t a quarter to twelve all that stops . . . then my writing starts." Although interpretations differ, one need not read extensively in the journals, letters, essays, and interviews of writers to know that they consider rituals an essential component of their work.

Do these behaviors serve a purpose in the composing process? Are some practices more common than others? Do rituals make for better writers? Until recently, the answer was usually "No," but anthropologists and others who study the subject of consciousness now say that private rituals are used by individuals to selectively and temporarily shut out the daily world. Researchers in psychophysiology have observed that rhythmic activities that can be performed "mindlessly" alter brainwaves into a more relaxed, creative state. Walking, pacing, and some kinds of exercise have this effect. So does staring out windows, which some researchers now believe may actively trigger daydreaming rather than being a symptom of it. Although coffins and frogs are probably effective only in the personal psychology of a Sitwell or a Dickens, scientists at Yale have discovered that rotting apples produce a gas that suppresses panic—a reminder that we should be careful not to scoff too soon at writers' rituals.

I became interested in the subject of rituals after suffering through my master's thesis with a bad case of writer's block. When a counselor asked me to describe my work habits, I became aware of the condition under which I had chosen to work: at school in the afternoon (my worst time of day) in an office where I was constantly interrupted or at home (also in the afternoon) while my husband's band practiced in the living room. I answered the phone, made coffee, and tried to shut out mentally what the walls could not. As Tillie Olsen points out, writing under such conditions produces a "craziness of endurance" that silences the writer. After awhile, even when I wasn't interrupted, I'd create my own distractions by calling friends, scrounging food in the kitchen, or escaping the house to run errands.

At the counselor's prompting, I began looking for a protected place to work—at first in the library and later at coffeeshops, where the conversational buzz and clatter of dishes provided consistent background noise. Somehow the interruptions in these places were less disruptive than those at home. I also began to pay attention to those moments when ideas bubbled up effortlessly, like on my walks to and from the university or while soaking in a hot bath late at night. I realized that ideas had always come in offbeat moments, but I had rarely been able to recapture them at "official" writing times. In the next three years, I gradually revamped my work habits and was able to face writing my doctoral dissertation, not with fear-producing blank pages, but pocketfuls of short passages scribbled in the heat of inspiration.

As a teacher of writing who works with unprepared students who are "at risk" in the university, I began to wonder what they did when they wrote. I knew there were times when they, too, became frustrated, blocked, and turned in work that did not represent their actual abilities. In spring 1990, I conducted a project with two writing classes in the Academic Skills Department at San Diego State University. I wanted to know

> What rituals did students practice when they wrote for school?
>
> What explanations would they offer for their practices?
>
> Where did they get their best ideas?
>
> What did they do when they blocked?
>
> Were they aware of habits that sabotaged their composing processes?

Students filled out several pages of a questionnaire on their schedules, their rituals, and the amount of time they allocated for writing school assignments. Afterward, several met with me for follow-up interviews. In the following section, I present edited transcripts of three students who represented the range of responses I received.

INTERVIEWS

The first student, Adriana, provides a profile of work habits typical of other students in her class. She takes five classes, works twenty hours each week, and spends six to ten hours per week on homework:

> I create a schedule for a day but if there's one particular thing I'm supposed to do, and I fall behind, I just throw it out. Sometimes I

call my friends on the phone and tell them what I'm writing about in the essay, and they give me ideas.

Everything has to be clean and neat because if I see my clothes hanging everywhere, I can't study; I can't concentrate. So I have to straighten it up—everything—before I start. I do most of my writing at night. Last night I stayed up till three o'clock. Before, I used to go to the public library, but it got too loud because of all these high school students jumping around. Now I work primarily at home. Pacing gives me time to relax and jot down what I'm doing. I can't stay in one place, like for five hours and write a paper. I have to stand up, walk around, watch a little bit of TV and then start again. If my favorite program comes on I just have to watch it. Sometimes its hard to do both—writing and TV.

To relax, I breathe deeply, stuff like that. I lay in my bed, looking at the ceiling. Nothing special. I work sitting down or lying down. I stare out a window. That's how I get my thoughts all together. I guess it helps, I find myself doing it a lot. I also have this one cassette with all piano solos by George Winston.

At times I put off working on an assignment until it's too late to do my best work, because I work better under pressure. If I start maybe a month before, I won't really concentrate. If I start three days before, then I'll get on it. If I have a month to do a project, and I sit down the week before, I'm not even thinking about it the other three weeks. Sometimes I work when I'm too exhausted, because I have a deadline to make. I've got to do it or fail the class.

I get my ideas sometimes right away, but most of the time it takes an hour to sit and think about it. I also get ideas from reading essays or from the person next to me. I'd ask what they're writing about, and sometimes I get some ideas. When I do go blank, I get frustrated—don't even know what I do. I think I just sit there and keep staring at my paper.

Adriana has difficulty creating and following through on self-made schedules. Her problems are further compounded by being unable to concentrate for extended periods of time; instead, she takes numerous breaks, including watching television. By her own account she begins drafts cold, using only the hour prior to drafting to give the paper serious thought.

Given all this, it is surprising to note how many beneficial rituals she practices. She cleans her workspace, paces, and breathes deeply to relax. She stares out windows to gather her thoughts and focuses her attention by listening to instrumental music. However, she mitigates the effect of these practices by placing herself under the pressure of imminent deadlines. It's no wonder that she becomes frustrated when she blocks. She has little time left for delays, and her coping strategy—to sit staring at the blank page—is more likely to create stress than to relieve it. The conditions she chooses would torpedo even a stronger writer's chance for success.

The second student, Marcia, also has five classes, averages eighteen hours each week at a job, and spends sixteen to twenty hours each week (twice as much as Adriana) on homework.

> Usually I study in the evening. I start at seven or eight, and lately I've been finishing about one or two. I talk my paper over with my friends. I ask if it's OK to write on this, or I ask them to read it when I'm finished, to see if it's OK. I usually work in my room, sometimes on my bed or in the living room on the floor. For some reason, I can't do my homework on my desk. When I'm in the family room, I just lie down on the couch, and do my homework with my legs up on the table. I play the radio, sometimes I'll watch TV. If it's an interesting show, I'll continue working during the commercials.
>
> I guess I'm just a procrastinator. I always tend to do my writing assignments at the last minute. Like when they give it to you, and they say, this is due a month later, I'll start on it a week before it's due. Sometimes when I'm thinking about a paper, I think, oh, I could write that in my paper, but when I come to writing it, I forget. I get distracted when I watch TV, or when there's people there and I say, OK, I won't do this now, I'll do it later when I'm by myself. Sometimes I'm on the phone or I go out. Then I end up not doing it, or starting late. When I was doing one assignment, I wrote it in about an hour.
>
> If I block, I put it down for a while, or I ask somebody to read it, or do something else. Then I'll go back to it. When I block, I feel mad, yeah, frustrated. I don't cry. I just think, I hate writing, I hate writing. Why do I have to do this? That kind of stuff. Writing is not my subject.

Marcia writes in the evening, after a full day of work and school. Like Adriana, she describes herself as a procrastinator. She has no designated workspace and often seeks distraction in friends or television. Although Adriana describes using an hour to generate and organize her ideas, Marcia mentions no such practice. She doesn't write down ideas and often doesn't remember them when she is ready to draft the assignment. There are other clues to serious problems. Although help from peers can be useful, she seems overly reliant on her friends for ideas and approval. She looks to them to tell her whether her choice of subject is a good one, to help her when she blocks, and to tell her whether her draft is adequate. She spends very little time on the work and may not even finish if interrupted. Her frustration with writing is obvious; her rituals—what few she practices—sabotage her efforts.

The third student, Sam, represents a highly ritualistic writer. He is enrolled in four classes, works twenty-five hours, and spends six to ten hours on homework.

> I'm really into driving. When I drive I notice everything. Things like, Oh, that billboard wasn't like that yesterday. I notice if my car feels different. I'm constantly looking and thinking. What's going on? And so, when I have time to prepare for my paper, all the thought goes into that, from there.
>
> In high school, my thoughts used to go down on microrecording. But I haven't used it since college. My batteries went dead. I do a little bit of performing stand-up comedy, so now I carry a little book for when I see something funny or some kind of story I want to keep. I've probably been through three of those books. I lose a lot of creative energy when I don't write things down.
>
> My roommates and I lift weights every day. A lot of thoughts come from that. I don't like to sit. When I'm thinking, I pace. I do a lot of what you could call role playing. I think, if I come from here, then I gotta hit the next paragraph this way. I actually look this way, then turn the other way. I really get into my papers, I guess. I'm Italian, I talk with my hands. It's a way to release energy both physically and mentally.
>
> Ideas come at different times. I've been known to write paragraphs on napkins at work. At home, I don't have a desk. I have my computer, which just sits on top of my dresser. I usually sit on my bed. A lot of times I lie down; a lot of times I'll stand up, just depends. I write in the afternoon, I feel a lot better than I do when I write at night. I look out a window and just write. But, when it comes to the mid hours, six o'clock, seven o'clock, there's too many things going on. I'm too jumpy, too hyper to concentrate then.
>
> I'm a very procrastination kind of guy. If I had a paper due in two weeks, there would be a lot of afternoon writing, a lot of jotting down. I'd probably end up pulling it all together late one

evening. You never know, that last week, I might come up with something more. But at all times, I'm actively thinking about it. I never keep working on a problem once I've blocked. I feel this is useless. So, I'll stop, and a half hour later, it'll hit me. If I block at night, I'll stop for the rest of the night. If it's in the day, I'll try to get it again at night. I prefer a sleep period in between. Everybody believes in a fresh new day. A new outlook.

Like Adriana and Marcia, Sam considers himself a procrastinator. But unlike either of them, he actively makes use of the interim between assignment [sic], noting down ideas, even writing entire sections if they take shape in his mind. Because he works better in the afternoon than late at night after he's put in a full day, he tries to schedule his work periods early. He seems to be a kinetic thinker—getting ideas in motion—and he takes advantage of that by allowing himself to pace and act out ideas rather than work at a desk. His interest in stand-up comedy has taught him to pay attention to the world around him, and this has become a source of material for his school assignments. In a way, Sam is always preparing to write. The result? He spends less time on his homework than Marcia and rarely experiences, as Adriana does, the frustration of being blocked.

I appreciated the candor of these and other students in responding to my questions but, as a teacher of writing, I was disheartened by many of the things I learned. Over half of the students surveyed spent fewer than ten hours per week on homework for a full schedule of classes, and three-quarters averaged twice as many hours on the job. The picture that emerged of their composing processes, from both statistics and interviews, was even bleaker. Few practiced rituals to help them write, most wrote under conditions hostile to concentration, and more than two-thirds admitted that procrastination regularly affected the quality of their work.

HOW RITUALS HELP

Rituals cannot create meaning where there is none—as anyone knows who has mumbled through prayers thinking of something else. But a knowledge of rituals can make a difference for students who want to make better use of the time they spend on writing. For one thing, rituals help writers pay attention to the conditions under which they choose to work. Some people think, for example, that fifteen minutes spent writing during TV commercial breaks is the equivalent of fifteen minutes of continuous, uninterrupted time. If they knew more about the nature of concentration—such as the destructive effect of interruptions on one's ability to retain and process information—they would recognize the difference. If they knew that language heard externally interferes with tasks requiring the production of inner speech, they would know that instrumental music or white noise (like the hum heard inside a car) might enhance their ability to write but that television or music with lyrics is likely to make work more difficult.

A knowledge of rituals can also encourage more effective use of the time spent on assignments. While many teachers consider two hours of homework a reasonable expectation for each hour in class, the students I talk to spent half that time and projects were typically written in one stressful sitting. Writing teacher Peter Elbow calls this "The Dangerous Method" and warns that it not only increases the pressure but depends for its success on a lack of any mishaps or mental blocks.

The problem with waiting until the last minute to write is that ideas rarely appear on demand. Instead, they come when listening to others, while reading or dreaming, or in the middle of other activities. Certain conditions stimulate their production, such as when a writer is relaxed and the mind is not strongly preoccupied with other matters. These moments may occur at particular periods of the day, for example, during "hypnagogic" states, the stage between waking and dreaming. Automatic, repetitious activity has a similar effect, which may be why writers often mention the benefits of walking, pacing, or exercising of some kind. They learn to make use of those times by noting down ideas or combining naturally productive times with their scheduled writing time.

Having some ideas to start with is an advantage to the writer, but not enough in itself. Ideas seldom occur as full-blown concepts, complete with all of the details, order, and connections that are required for formal writing. More often, they begin as an image, sensation, key word or phrase, or a sketchy sense of shape and structure. Transforming these bits into a full-fledged piece— whether poem, essay, or short story—usually requires one or more periods of concentration. The term concentration means "to bring together, to converge, to meet in one point" and in reference to thinking, it refers to keeping one's attention and activity fixed on a single problem, however complex. For the kind of writing required at the college level, concentration is crucial.

Most of us know that it is hard to concentrate when we are tired, when interrupted or preoccupied, ill or under stress—thus we recognize, experientially, that writing requires the concerted effort of mind and body. Some people can concentrate under adverse conditions—they could work unfazed in the middle of a hurricane if they wanted to—but most of us aren't like that. Concentration comes naturally to a few things that we like to do or are vitally interested in—music, perhaps, or sports. The rest of the time, we juggle several things at once, like jotting down a shopping list while we watch TV or organizing the day ahead while we take a shower. Switching from this kind of divided or scattered mental activity to a state of concentration often generates resistance, especially when the task is unpleasant or formidable.

Mihaly Csikszentmihalyi (1975), a psychologist at the University of Chicago, refers to this state of intense concentration as "flow," and from interviews with athletes, artists, and various professionals, theorizes that flow can only be achieved when a person is neither bored nor worried, but in control, possessing skills adequate to meet the challenge at hand. The key to achieving and maintaining flow is to balance one's skills against the challenge. "What counts," he says, "is the person's ability to restructure the environment so that it will allow flow to occur" (53).

Although rituals can take a bewildering number of forms, they help writers restructure their environment in one or more ways: clear the deck of competing preoccupations, protect from interruptions, encourage relaxation, reduces anxiety, and provide a structure (through established limitations of time) for dividing projects into manageable increments. This last use is especially important as writing assignments increase in length and complexity. The transition from the shorter assignment that can be completed in the space of two or three hours to an assignment that requires weeks of reading, research, and multiple drafts can be devastating to those who have conditioned themselves to write in only one, high-pressured session. In such cases, the writer needs strategies to help him or her overcome mental resistance and make good use of scheduled work-time.

USING RITUALS

Because no two writers are alike, no formula for effective rituals exists. Even the same writer may use different rituals for different projects, or for different stages of a project. One writer may need several rituals involving workspace, time, and repetitive activities; another may need only a favorite pen. Every writer must learn to pay attention to his or her own needs, the demands that must be juggled, the mental and biological rhythms of the day, and the spontaneous moments of inspiration. Here are some suggestions for establishing productive rituals:

1. Consider the times of the day in which you are most and least alert. Most people have two or three cycles each day. Note the times that are your best.

2. Identify those times and activities in which ideas naturally occur. These may include certain times of day (when waking up, for example), during physical activities, or when engaged in repetitive or automatic behaviors (driving a car or washing dishes). Carry a tape recorder, small notebook, or some means of recording your ideas as they occur.

3. Draw up a schedule of a typical week. Mark those hours that are already scheduled. Note those times that are left open that correspond with the times identified in items 1 and 2. These are the most effective times to schedule writing. If possible, plan to do your writing during these times instead of "at the last minute." Each semester, once I know when my classes meet, I draw up such a schedule and post it on my refrigerator. Although I can't always use my writing time to work on writing, the schedule serves as a constant reminder of my priorities.

4. Consider the amount of time that you are normally able to maintain concentration. Even experienced writers tend to work for no more than three or four hours a day. They may spend additional time reading, making notes, or editing a text, but these activities can tolerate more interruptions and can be performed at less-than-peak times. Remember, too, it sometimes takes time to achieve a full state of concentration—an hour may provide only fifteen to twenty minutes of productive time. Writing frequently for short periods of time may be best. Many writers advocate working a little bit every day because the frequency helps lessen the initial resistance to concentration.

5. Consider the conditions under which you work best. Do you need absolute silence or background noise? Does music help you to focus or does it distract you? Do you prefer to work alone or with other people around? Do you prefer certain kinds of pens, inks, or paper, or do you need access to a typewriter or computer? Do you work best when sitting, standing, or lying down? Does it help you to

pace or rock in a rocking chair or prepare a pot of coffee? Do you prefer natural, incandescent, or fluorescent light? Is the temperature comfortable? Is this a place you can work without being interrupted? Identify these needs and assemble an environment in which you are most comfortable.

6. Cultivate rituals that help you focus. Many writers use meditational exercises, write personal letters, or read recreationally to relax and prime the inner voice with prose rhythms. Some writers eat and drink so as not to be bothered with physical distractions; others eat or drink while they work because the repetitive activity helps them stay focused. Some writers feel they are more mentally alert if they write when they are slightly hungry. Experiment with different rituals and choose what works best for you.

Once concentration is achieved, writers tend to lose awareness of their rituals, but when concentration lapses or writers become blocked, they may consciously use rituals to avoid frustration and regain concentration as quickly as possible. The rituals vary according to the writer, the situation, the task, and the cause of the interruption or block, but common practices suggest several options:

1. Take a short break from the work and return later. If pushed for time, a short break may be most efficient. The trick is to stay away long enough to let strong feelings that may sabotage the writing subside, without letting one's focus shift too far away from the project overall. This is time to get something to drink, stretch out, or put the clothes in the dryer—activities that don't require one's full attention.

2. Shift attention to a different part of the same task and work on that. If you don't need to take a break, work on a section of the project with which you are not blocked. If you know, for example, that you plan to describe a personal experience later in the draft and you know what you want to say about it (even though you are not yet sure how that experience fits within the overall organization of the piece), go ahead and write it and set it aside for later.

3. Shift attention to a different task and return later. Other tasks can provide a break from the writing and, simultaneously,

maintain the feeling of productivity; some professional writers juggle more than one writing project at a time for this very reason.

4. Switch to reading—notes or other texts—to stimulate new ideas and to help regain focus. If you are working from notes or research materials, sometimes browsing through them will remind you of things you wanted to say. If that doesn't work, try reading materials that are not related to your task. One student told me that he used articles in *Rolling Stone* to help him get into a "voice" that helped him write. If you are working on a computer and have lost your sense of direction ("What should I say next?"), printing out your work and reading that may also help you regain your flow of thoughts.

5. Talk to someone about the problem or, if no one is around, write about it. Writers frequently use a friend or family member to talk through their ideas aloud (notice how often family members are thanked in the acknowledgments of books); reading or talking to someone not only offers a respite, but may result in the needed breakthrough.

6. Take a longer break, one which involves physical activity, a full escape from the task, or a period of sleep. If the block seems impenetrable or if you are so angry and frustrated that a short break won't make any difference, then spend enough time away from the task that you can begin afresh. Get out of your workspace, go for a hike, see a movie, or spend an evening shooting pool. Intense physical workouts can burn off tension created by writing blocks. If you're tired, take a nap. Some people can work well when tired, and pulling an all-nighter is possible for them, but others are far better off sleeping first and working later, even if that means waking up at 3:00 A.M. to write.

CODA

Writing this article has reminded me that knowing about rituals and making use of them are not always the same thing. Parts of this developed easily; others had to be teased out line by line. Ideas came while walking the dog, stoking the woodstove, taking hot baths, and discussing my work with others. After reading the last draft, my husband asked me how I intended to conclude.

By discussing X, Y, and Z, I answered. I knew exactly what I wanted to say.

That was several nights ago, and today, I can't for the life of me remember what I said. If only I had thought to write it down.

ANNOTATED BIBLIOGRAPHY

The writers' rituals described here were gathered from a variety of sources—interviews, published diaries and letters, biographical and autobiographical materials—but anecdotes about rituals appear almost anytime writers discuss their writing processes. For further reading, see the *Paris Review Interviews with Writers* series, Tillie Olsen's *Silence*, or *Working It Out: 23 Women Writers, Artists, Scientists, and Scholars Talk About Their Lives and Work*, edited by Sara Ruddick and Pamela Daniels.

For further reading on writing and altered states of consciousness, see Csikszentmihalyi's *Beyond Boredom and Anxiety*, Richard Restak's *The Brain* (based on the PBS television series *The Brain*), and Diane Ackerman's *A Natural History of the Senses*. For an older but excellent introduction to the subject of psychophysiology see *Altered States of Consciousness*, edited by Charles T. Tart.

Although the subject of rituals is not a common one for most teachers of composition, a few have discussed the personal and idiosyncratic needs of writers. See especially several of the self-reflective articles in *Learning by Teaching* by Donald M. Murray, Peter Elbow's *Writing with Power*, and James Moffett's essay, "Writing Inner Speech, and Meditation," in *Coming On Center*.

Work Cited

Csikszentmihalyi, Mihaly (1975). *Beyond Boredom and Anxiety.* New York: Jossey-Bass.

Thinking and Writing Questions

1. Wyche's study of her students' work habits revealed that their procrastination, which they thought was pushing them to write, was actually preventing them from writing. Explain how this happens.
2. All writers must eventually give their piece a title. Based on the content of her essay, why did Wyche use the word "talisman"? The Merriam Webster 11th Collegiate Dictionary defines "talisman" as "an object held to act as a charm to avert evil and bring good fortune."

3. While Wyche focuses on practical ways to move our writing brains to a space of thinking, focus, and creativity, Brandeis in "Dyr Mom" focuses on the emotional desire of Hannah to be heard. bell hooks in "writing autobiography" focuses on her emotional need to understand her childhood. Karen Cangialosi in "Healing through the Written Word" focuses on how writing enables patients to lessen physical pain and heal their bodies. Is it worth the effort, time, and energy to develop and use the practical aspects of writing to achieve one's desired emotional result? Why? Why not?

4. Write a piece like Adrian's, Marcia's, and Sam's that describes your work habits and rituals. Add a paragraph that explains why you work this way. Then, read your piece to a friend and discuss how your habits and rituals support and sabotage your thinking and writing processes. What might you need to change? What do you sacrifice when you sabotage yourself?

5. Wyche quotes psychologist Mihaly Csikszentmihalyi who writes that what one needs to achieve a state of intense concentration is the "ability to restructure the environment so that it will allow flow to occur" (60). What things can you restructure in your environment to make writing time productive?

A Way of Writing
WILLIAM STAFFORD

Poet and pacifist William Stafford kept a daily journal for fifty years, composed nearly 22,000 poems, of which roughly 3,000 were published in fifty-seven volumes of poetry. When drafted into the military in 1941, he registered as a conscientious objector and worked in the Civilian Public Service from 1942–1946. He earned bachelor's and master's degrees from the University of Kansas and a doctorate from the University of Iowa. In 1970 he served as poetry consultant to the Library of Congress, a post now designated "American Poet Laureate." He was a professor of English at Lewis and Clark College in Portland, Oregon, until his retirement in 1990. He died in August 1993. In "A Way of Writing," which first appeared as a chapter in Writing the Australian Crawl, *Stafford describes his writing process to explain how he uses the act of composing to discover.*

✦

A writer is not so much someone who has something to say as he is someone who has found a process that will bring about new things he would not have thought of if he had not started to say them. That is, he does not draw on a reservoir; instead, he engages in an activity that brings to him a whole succession of unforeseen stories, poems, essays, plays, laws, philosophies, religions, or—but wait!

Back in school, from the first when I began to try to write things, I felt this richness. One thing would lead to another; the world would give and give. Now, after twenty years or so of trying, I live by that certain richness, an idea hard to pin, difficult to say, and perhaps offensive to some. For there are strange implications in it.

One implication is the importance of just plain receptivity. When I write, I like to have an interval before me when I am not likely to be interrupted. For me, this means usually the early morning, before others are awake. I get pen and paper, take a glance out of the window (often it is dark out there), and wait. It is like fishing. But I do not wait very long, for there is always a nibble—and this is where receptivity comes in. To get started I will accept anything that occurs to me. Something always occurs, of course, to any of us. We can't keep from thinking. Maybe I have to settle for an immediate impression: it's cold, or hot, or dark, or bright, or in between! Or—well, the possibilities are endless. If I put down something, that thing will help the next thing come, and I'm off. If I let the process go on, things will occur to me that were not at all in my mind when I started. These things, odd or trivial as they may be, are somehow connected. And if I let them string out, surprising things will happen.

If I let them string out. . . . Along with initial receptivity, then, there is another readiness: I must be willing to fail. If I am to keep on writing, I cannot bother to insist on high standards. I must get into action and not let anything stop me, or even slow me much. By "standards" I do not mean "correctness"—spelling, punctuation, and so on. These details become mechanical for anyone who writes for a while. I am thinking about such matters as social significance, positive values, consistency, etc. I resolutely disregard these. Something better, greater is happening! I am following a process that leads so wildly and originally into new territory that no judgment can at the moment be made about values, significance, and so on. I am making something new, something that has not been judged before. Later others—and maybe I myself—will make judgments. Now, I am headlong to discover. Any distraction may harm the creating.

So, receptive, careless of failure, I spin out things on the page. And a wonderful freedom comes. If something occurs to me, it is all right to accept it. It has one justification: it occurs to me. No one else can guide me. I must follow my own weak, wandering, diffident impulses.

A strange bonus happens. At times, without my insisting on it, my writings become coherent; the successive elements that occur to me are clearly related. They lead by themselves to new connections. Sometimes the language, even the syllables that happen along, may start a trend. Sometimes the materials alert me to something waiting in my mind, ready for sustained attention. At such times, I allow myself to be eloquent, or intentional, or for great swoops (Treacherous! Not to be trusted!) reasonable. But I do not insist on any of that; for I know that back of my activity there will be the coherence of my self, and that indulgence of my impulses will bring recurrent patterns and meanings again.

This attitude toward the process of writing creatively suggests a problem for me, in terms of what others say. They talk about "skills" in writing. Without denying that I do have experience, wide reading, automatic orthodoxies and maneuvers of various kinds, I still must insist that I am often baffled about what "skill" has to do with the precious little area of confusion when I do not know what I am going to say and then I find out what I am going to say. That precious interval I am unable to bridge by skill. What can I witness about it? It remains mysterious, just as all of us must feel puzzled about how we are so inventive as to be able to talk along through complexities with our friends, not needing to plan what we are going to say, but never stalled for long in our confident forward progress. Skill? If so, it is the skill we all have, something we must have learned before the age of three or four.

A writer is one who has become accustomed to trusting that grace, or luck, or—skill.

Yet another attitude I find necessary: most of what I write, like most of what I say in casual conversation, will not amount to much. Even I will realize, and even at the time, that it is not negotiable. It will be like practice. In conversation I allow myself random remarks—in fact, as I recall, that is the way I learned to talk—so in writing I launch many expendable efforts. A result of this free way of writing is that I am not writing for others, mostly; they will not see the product at all unless the activity eventuates in something that later appears to be worthy. My guide is the self, and its adventuring in the language brings about communication.

This process-rather-than-substance view of writing invites a final, dual reflection:

1. Writers may not be special—sensitive or talented in any usual sense. They are simply engaged in sustained use of a language skill we all have. Their "creations" come about through confident reliance on stray impulses that will, with trust, find occasional patterns that are satisfying.

2. But writing itself is one of the great, free human activities. There is scope for individuality, and elation, and discovery, in writing. For the person who follows with trust and forgiveness what occurs to him, the world remains always ready and deep, an inexhaustible environment, with the combined vividness of an actuality and flexibility of a dream. Working back and forth between experience and thought, writers have more than space and time can offer. They have the whole unexplored realm of human vision.

Thinking and Writing Questions

1. Many new writers believe that good writers are born with a talent that affords them a deep reservoir of ideas and creativity. In the opening paragraph, Stafford says, loudly, NOT SO! What does Stafford attribute good writing and writers to?

2. Compare and contrast the voices of Stafford and Anne Lamott in "Shitty First Drafts."

3. Do you think that Stafford would agree with Aronowitz's argument that writing is not a skill but an art? Why? Why not?

4. How does Stafford's concept of writing as a discovery process of finding and creating ideas fit into the phenomenon of Writing that we are addressing in this book?

5. Here is a focused freewrite by Liz to develop questions for the Stafford essay:

   Maybe I can write a question about the difficulty I am having with writing all of these questions. My brain just won't push forward into any new ideas to ask you to focus on in this article.

   Reminder #1: Trust the process. The "something" I want will come. So review what I have written. Question on Stafford's voice, how to apply Stafford to the classroom, the secret and myth about writers having ideas that he debunks, a connection to Aronowitz's ideas about writing as art.

Okay—next tactic. How does this article fit in the chapter and into the entire book? Broaden my view. Stafford's idea of writing to learn fits in this chapter on the phenomenon of Writing with a capital "W." He explains how writers develop their ideas that they share with their readers. This is important for students to realize that they too can be writers if they work the process. It is not some inborn trait that only special people get. Maybe this idea will be good for the students who read this book to think about. Bingo—another question. This is working.

Twelve minutes of focused freewriting led Liz to pull another idea from her brain. We want you to try this. Pick a topic or issue to explore. Write freely about the issue. Let your hand and your thoughts move across the page. Don't stop. If you lose focus, pull yourself back by writing "now, getting back to my topic." Give your brain a chance to discover a new focus or perspective on the issue. If your brain is not accustomed to this type of thinking, it might take some practice.

Shitty First Drafts
ANNE LAMOTT

Born in San Francisco in 1954, humorist and writer Anne Lamott is a graduate of Goucher College in Baltimore. She has taught at the University of California Davis and conducted many writing workshops across the country. She received a Guggenheim Fellowship, and is the author of six novels and four best-selling books of non-fiction. Her nonfiction books include Operating Instructions: A Journal of My Son's First Year *(1993), in which she describes her adventures as a single parent, and* Tender Mercies: Some Thoughts on Faith *(1999), in which she charts her journey toward faith in God. She has also been the food reviewer for* California *magazine, a book reviewer for* Mademoiselle, *and a regular contributor to* Salon's *"Mothers Who Think." In the following selection, taken from Lamott's popular book about writing,* Bird by Bird, *she argues for the need to let go and write those "shitty first drafts" that lead to clarity and sometimes brilliance in second and third drafts.*

◆

Now, practically even better news than that of short assign-ments is the idea of shitty first drafts. All good writers write them. This is how they end up with good second drafts and terrif-ic third drafts. People tend to look at successful writers, writers who are getting their books published and maybe even doing well financially, and think that they sit down at their desks every morn-ing feeling like a million dollars, feeling great about who they are and how much talent they have and what a great story they have to tell; that they take in a few deep breaths, push back their sleeves, roll their necks a few times to get all the cricks out, and dive in, typing fully formed passages as fast as a court reporter. But this is just the fantasy of the uninitiated. I know some very great writers, writers you love who write beautifully and have made a great deal of money, and not *one* of them sits down routinely feeling wildly enthusiastic and confident. Not one of them writes elegant first drafts. All right, one of them does, but we do not like her very much. We do not think that she has a rich inner life or that God likes her or can even stand her. (Although when I mentioned this to my priest friend Tom, he said you can safely assume you've cre-ated God in your own image when it turns out that God hates all the same people you do.)

Very few writers really know what they are doing until they've done it. Nor do they go about their business feeling dewy and thrilled. They do not type a few stiff warm-up sentences and then find themselves bounding along like huskies across the snow. One writer I know tells me that he sits down every morning and says to himself nicely, "It's not like you don't have a choice, because you do—you can either type, or kill yourself." We all often feel like we are pulling teeth, even those writers whose prose ends up being the most natural and fluid. The right words and sentences just do not come pouring out like ticker tape most of the time. Now, Muriel Spark is said to have felt that she was taking dicta-tion from God every morning—sitting there, one supposes, plugged into a Dictaphone, typing away, humming. But this is a very hostile and aggressive position. One might hope for bad things to rain down on a person like this.

For me and most of the other writers I know, writing is not rapturous. In fact, the only way I can get anything written at all is to write really, really shitty first drafts.

The first draft is the child's draft, where you let it all pour out and then let it romp all over the place, knowing that no one is going to see it and that you can shape it later. You just let this childlike part of you channel whatever voices and visions come through and onto the page. If one of the characters wants to say, "Well, so what, Mr. Poopy Pants?," you let her. No one is going to see it. If the kid wants to get into really sentimental, weepy, emotional territory, you let him. Just get it all down on paper because there may be something great in those six crazy pages that you would never have gotten to by more rational, grown-up means. There may be something in the very last line of the very last paragraph on page six that you just love, that is so beautiful or wild that you now know what you're supposed to be writing about, more or less, or in what direction you might go—but there was no way to get to this without first getting through the first five and a half pages.

I used to write food reviews for *California* magazine before it folded. (My writing food reviews had nothing to do with the magazine folding, although every single review did cause a couple of canceled subscriptions. Some readers took umbrage at my comparing mounds of vegetable puree with various ex-presidents' brains.) These reviews always took two days to write. First I'd go to a restaurant several times with a few opinionated, articulate friends in tow. I'd sit there writing down everything anyone said that was at all interesting or funny. Then on the following Monday I'd sit down at my desk with my notes and try to write the review. Even after I'd been doing this for years, panic would set in. I'd try to write a lead, but instead I'd write a couple of dreadful sentences, xx them out, try again, xx everything out, and then feel despair and worry settle on my chest like an x-ray apron. It's over, I'd think, calmly. I'm not going to be able to get the magic to work this time. I'm ruined. I'm through. I'm toast. Maybe, I'd think, I can get my old job back as a clerk-typist. But probably not. I'd get up and study my teeth in the mirror for a while. Then I'd stop, remember to breathe, make a few phone calls, hit the kitchen and chow down. Eventually I'd go back and sit down at my desk, and sigh for the next ten minutes. Finally I would pick up my one-inch picture frame, stare into it as if for the answer, and every time the answer would come: all I had to do was to write a really shitty first draft of, say, the opening paragraph. And no one was going to see it.

So I'd start writing without reining myself in. It was almost just typing, just making my fingers move. And the writing would be *terrible*. I'd write a lead paragraph that was a whole page, even though the entire review could only be three pages long, and then I'd start writing up descriptions of the food, one dish at a time, bird by bird, and the critics would be sitting on my shoulders, commenting like cartoon characters. They'd be pretending to snore, or rolling their eyes at my overwrought descriptions, no matter how hard I tried to tone those descriptions down, no matter how conscious I was of what a friend said to me gently in my early days of restaurant reviewing. "Annie," she said, "it is just a piece of *chicken*. It is just a bit of *cake.*"

But because by then I had been writing for so long, I would eventually let myself trust the process—sort of, more or less. I'd write a first draft that was maybe twice as long as it should be, with a self-indulgent and boring beginning, stupefying descriptions of the meal, lots of quotes from my black-humored friends that made them sound more like the Manson girls than food lovers, and no ending to speak of. The whole thing would be so long and incoherent and hideous that for the rest of the day I'd obsess about getting creamed by a car before I could write a decent second draft. I'd worry that people would read what I'd written and believe that the accident had really been a suicide, that I had panicked because my talent was waning and my mind was shot.

The next day, though, I'd sit down, go through it all with a colored pen, take out everything I possibly could, find a new lead somewhere on the second page, figure out a kicky place to end it, and then write a second draft. It always turned out fine, sometimes even funny and weird and helpful. I'd go over it one more time and mail it in.

Then, a month later, when it was time for another review, the whole process would start again, complete with the fears that people would find my first draft before I could rewrite it.

Almost all good writing begins with terrible first efforts. You need to start somewhere. Start by getting something—anything—down on paper. A friend of mine says that the first draft is the down draft—you just get it down. The second draft is the up draft—you fix it up. You try to say what you have to say more accurately. And the third draft is the dental draft, where you check every tooth, to see if it's loose or cramped or decayed, or even, God help us, healthy.

What I've learned to do when I sit down to work on a shitty first draft is to quiet the voices in my head. First there's the vinegar-lipped Reader Lady, who says primly, "Well, *that's* not very interesting, is it?" And there's the emaciated German male who writes these Orwellian memos detailing your thought crimes. And there are your parents, agonizing over your lack of loyalty and discretion; and there's William Burroughs, dozing off or shooting up because he finds you as bold and articulate as a houseplant; and so on. And there are also the dogs: let's not forget the dogs, the dogs in their pen who will surely hurtle and snarl their way out if you ever *stop* writing, because writing is, for some of us, the latch that keeps the door of the pen closed, keeps those crazy ravenous dogs contained.

Quieting these voices is at least half the battle I fight daily. But this is better than it used to be. It used to be 87 percent. Left to its own devices, my mind spends much of its time having conversations with people who aren't there. I walk along defending myself to people, or exchanging repartee with them, or rationalizing my behavior, or seducing them with gossip, or pretending I'm on their TV talk show or whatever. I speed or run an aging yellow light or don't come to a full stop, and one nanosecond later am explaining to imaginary cops exactly why I had to do what I did, or insisting that I did not in fact do it.

I happened to mention this to a hypnotist I saw many years ago, and he looked at me very nicely. At first I thought he was feeling around on the floor for the silent alarm button, but then he gave me the following exercise, which I still use to this day.

Close your eyes and get quiet for a minute, until the chatter starts up. Then isolate one of the voices and imagine the person speaking as a mouse. Pick it up by the tail and drop it into a mason jar. Then isolate another voice, pick it up by the tail, drop it in the jar. And so on. Drop in any high-maintenance parental units, drop in any contractors, lawyers, colleagues, children, anyone who is whining in your head. Then put the lid on, and watch all these mouse people clawing at the glass, jabbering away, trying to make you feel like shit because you won't do what they want—won't give them more money, won't be more successful, won't see them more often. Then imagine that there is a volume-control button on the bottle. Turn it all the way up for a minute, and listen to the stream of angry, neglected, guilt-mongering voices. Then turn it all the way down and watch the frantic mice lunge at the glass, trying to get to you. Leave it down, and get back to your shitty first draft.

A writer friend of mine suggests opening the jar and shooting them all in the head. But I think he's a little angry, and I'm sure nothing like this would ever occur to you.

Thinking and Writing Questions

1. What is the essence of a "shitty first draft"? Why is this concept so significant to Lamott that she gives a whole chapter to it?

2. Lamott uses many images as metaphors to describe and develop her concepts. For example, "The first draft is the child's draft, where you let it all pour out and then let it romp all over the place" (70). Make a list of these images. Why does she use these images? How does she use them to create her sarcastic, playful voice?

3. Drawing on Susan Wyche's explanation of writing rituals, list the rituals that Lamott employs to write a restaurant review.

4. One of our favorite images is of snarling dogs that represent the voices in a writer's head. Many of us have messages in our head that we have internalized about writing: messages from teachers, parents, and textbooks that have shaped our view of writing. Every time Heather sits down to write, one of Heather's voices says, "Who are you kidding? You can't even string two sentences together to make sense." Record the voices and messages that you give yourself about writing. Identify messages that subvert your writing process. Develop some tactics to shut down these voices. Compose and repeat to yourself some positive messages that support your writing.

5. Try a little of your own image making. What is your writing process like? An Easter egg hunt in which you run frantically from tree to bush to porch, pushing all of the other children out of the way, looking for eggs and ideas? You fill up your basket and find a secluded corner to evaluate your discoveries. After pouring all of your candies on the floor, you sort them. You put the rich butter creams back into your basket where the ideas will grow and develop. You take the jelly beans and Peeps to your friends, hoping to trade for some more butter creams. This is a shitty first draft, but do you get the idea?

Internal Revision

DONALD MURRAY

Writer Donald Murray won the Pulitzer Prize in 1954 for editorials he wrote on National Defense for the Boston Herald. *He taught writing at the University of New Hampshire and championed the process of teacher-to-student conferencing to teach writing. He authored books on the craft of writing and teaching writing, including* Learning by Teaching; Expecting the Unexpected; *and* Crafting a Life in Essay, Story, Poem. *He wrote a column for the* Boston Globe *on aging until his death in December 2006. Part of Murray's article, "Internal Revision," is reprinted here. It was originally published in* Research on Composing—Points of Departure *and reprinted in* Learning by Teaching. *Murray explores revision as a process of first making meaning and second making meaning clear to the reader.*

◆

Writing is rewriting. Most writers accept rewriting as a condition of their craft; it comes with the territory. It is not, however, seen as a burden but as an opportunity by many writers.

Neil Simon points out, "Rewriting is when playwriting really gets to be fun. . . . In baseball you only get three swings and you're out. In rewriting, you get almost as many swings as you want and you know, sooner or later, you'll hit the ball." Rewriting is the difference between the dilettante and the artist, the amateur and the professional, the unpublished and the published. William Gass testifies, "I work not by writing but rewriting." Dylan Thomas states, "Almost any poem is fifty to a hundred revisions—and that's after it's well along." Archibald MacLeish talks of "the endless discipline of writing and rewriting and rerewriting." Novelist Theodore Weesner tells his students at the University of New Hampshire his course title is not "Fiction Writing" but "Fiction Rewriting."

And yet rewriting is one of the writing skills least researched, least examined, least understood, and—usually—least taught. The vast majority of students, even those who take writing courses, get away with first-draft copy. They are never introduced to the opportunities of serious revision.

A search of the literature reveals relatively few articles or books on the rewriting process. I have a commonplace book which has grown from one thin journal to 24 3-inch-thick notebooks with more than 8,000 entries divided into prewriting, writing, and rewriting. Yet even with my interest in the process of rewriting—some of my colleagues would say my obsession—only four of those notebooks are labeled rewriting.

I suspect the term rewriting has, even for many writers, an aura of failure about it. Rewriting is too often taught as punishment, not as an opportunity for discovery or even as an inevitable part of the writing process. Most texts, in fact, confuse rewriting with editing, proofreading, or manuscript preparation. Yet rewriting almost always is the most exciting, satisfying part of the writing process.

THE WRITING PROCESS

The most accurate definition of writing, I believe, is that it is the process of using language to discover meaning in experience and to communicate it. I believe this process can be described, understood and therefore learned. Prewriting, writing, and rewriting have been generally accepted as the three principal divisions of the writing process during the past decade. I would like to propose new terms for consideration, terms which may emphasize the essential process of discovery through writing: *prevision, vision,* and *revision.*

Of course, writing will, at times, seem to skip over one part of the writing process and linger on another, and the stages of the process also overlap. The writing process is too experimental and exploratory to be contained in a rigid definition; writers move back and forth through all stages of the writing process as they search for meaning and then attempt to clarify it. It is also true that most writers do not define, describe, or possibly even understand the writing process. There's no reason for them to know what they are doing if they do it well, any more than we need to know grammatical terms if we speak and write clearly. I am convinced, however, that most writers most of the time pass through the following distinct stages.

Prevision. This term encompasses everything that precedes the first draft—receptive experience, such as awareness (conscious and unconscious), observation, remembering; and exploratory experience, such as research, reading, interviewing, and note-taking. Writers practice the prevision skills of selecting, connecting, and evaluating significant bits of information provided by receptive and exploratory experience. Prevision includes, in my opinion, the underestimated skills of title and lead writing, which help the student identify a subject, limit it, develop a point of view towards it, and begin to find the voice to explore the subject.

Vision. In the second stage of the writing process, the first draft—what I call a discovery draft—is completed. This stage takes the shortest time for the writer—in many cases it is written at one sitting—but it is the fulcrum of the writing process. Before this first draft, which Peter Drucker calls "the zero draft," everything seems possible. By completing this vision of what may be said, the writer stakes out a territory to explore.

Revision. This is what the writer does after a draft is completed to understand and communicate what has begun to appear on the page. The writer reads to see what has been suggested, then confirms, alters, or develops it, usually through many drafts. Eventually a meaning is developed which can be communicated to a reader.

THE IMPORTANCE OF DISCOVERY

My main concern in this chapter is revision. But to be able to understand what I consider the most important task in the revision process, we have to appreciate the fact that writers much of the time don't know what they are going to write or even possibly what they have written. Writers use language as a tool of exploration to see beyond what they know. Most texts and most of our research literature have not accepted this concept or dealt with its implications.

Elie Wiesel say's, "I write in order to understand as much as to be understood." The poet Tony Connor gives a recipe for writing a poem: "Invent a jungle and then explore it." William Stafford states, "You don't know what's going to happen. Nobody does." I have included at the end of this chapter forty-seven other quotations from my commonplace book which testify to the essential ignorance writers feel many times about what they are writing.

In teaching writing I often feel that the most significant step is made when a student enters into the writing process and experiences the discovery of meaning through writing. Yet this process of discovery has not been generally explored or understood for a number of reasons. First of all, it has not been experienced by nonwriters or admitted when it is experienced by writers in the less imaginative forms of writing. One professor of philosophy, after reading a text of mine, confessed he had been ashamed of the way he wrote, that he didn't know what to say or how to say it when he sat down to write. He had to write and write and write to find out what he had to say. He was embarrassed and didn't want his colleagues to know how dumb he was. When he read my book he found his activities were legitimate. I suspect such unjustified shame is more prevalent than we like to admit. Another professor told me recently that he makes assignments he could not complete by his own deadline. He explained, "My students are smarter than I am. I have to rewrite and rewrite many drafts." Yet he neither "confesses" this to his students nor allows them the opportunity to perform the writing task essential for them to achieve publication.

Most professors who are aware of the process of rewriting to discover meaning are uncomfortable thinking about it, to say nothing of discussing it in class. Discovery seems the province of the "creative writer," the writer who deals in poetry, fiction, or drama. Such activities are not quite respectable in the academic community, where we too often have a sex manual attitude: it's okay to read about it as long as you don't do it. But I am an academic schizophrenic, a "creative" writer and a "noncreative" writer. As the chairperson of a rather large department, I spend a good deal of my time writing memos to deans and vice provosts. (That's really creative writing.) I also moonlight occasionally as a corporate ghostwriter. I publish texts, novels, poems, and "papers." And in all of these roles I find the process of discovery through language taking place. I do not agree with the educational segregation of functional and imaginative writing, creative and noncreative writing. I know the process of discovery takes place when I write fiction and nonfiction, poetry and memos. To produce letters, reports, novels, essays, reviews, poems, and academic papers that say something, you have to allow language to lead you to meaning.

In drafting this paper I found myself writing, as I attempted to define the writing process, that the writer, after the first draft, is "not dealing with the vision but a fact." The word vision surprised me. It appeared on the page without premeditation. In reading it over I cut the sentence but decided the word was a better term than *writing* to describe the second stage of the writing process and, working from that point, saw the virtue of using the term *revision* for rewriting and then tried on the term *prevision* for size and found it fit, although I can't find it in my dictionary. I'm not sure that this is a discovery of enormous value, but it was fun; and I think this accident of language, this business of using words I didn't know I was going to use, has helped me understand the writing process a little bit better.

I suspect most of us have experienced many similar discoveries, but we feel it a failure: if we had a bit more IQ, we would have known the right word. I find few English teachers are comfortable with the concept of uncalculated discovery. They simply do not believe the testimony of writers when they say they write what they don't know, and this may indeed be an uncomfortable concept if you spend your classroom hours analyzing literature and telling your students exactly why the writer did what he or she did, as if literature resulted from the following of a detailed blueprint. Writing, fortunately for writers, is much more exciting than that. The writer does plan but keeps adapting those plans to what is discovered on the page.

The writer, however, who lives in the academic community— and today most of us do—is surrounded by people who seem to know precisely what happens in a piece of literature. The other night my colleague, the poet Charles Simic, said his favorite poems were the ones he didn't understand, an unsettling confession in a department of English. It is hard to admit that you don't know what you're doing when you write. It seems a bit undignified, perhaps even cause for the removal of tenure. Surely my governor would think I ought to know what I'm doing when I sit down to write—I'm a full professor, for goodness sake—and yet I don't. And hope I never will.

Listening to a lecture the other day, I found myself doodling with language. (The better the lecture the more likely a piece of writing will start to happen on my notebook page.) From where I sat in the lecture hall, I could see an office door, and I watched a person in that office get up and shut the door against the lecture. It was an ordinary act, yet, for no reason I can recall, I found myself writing this on the page:

> I had an office at a university, an inside office, without window or air. The classrooms up and down the corridor would fill up with words until they spilled over and reached the edge of my half-opened door, a confident, almost arrogant mumble I could no longer bother to try to understand. Was I to be like the makers of those words, was I already like the students in my own Freshman sections? Perhaps the only good thing about this position was that Mother was dumbly proud and Father puzzled and angry, "Is this where they put you, an educated man? The union would kill me."
>
> If I hadn't killed a man, my life would have seemed trite. . . .

I have followed this short story for only a couple of pages in the past few days. I am ashamed to reveal the lines above—I don't know if they will lead me to a story—but I'm having fun and think I should share this experience, for it is revealing of the writing process. I did not intend to write a short story. I am working on a novel, a book of poems, and articles such as this one. Short fiction is not on the menu. I did not intend to write an academic short story. I do not like the genre. I do not particularly like the character who is appearing on my page, but I am interested in being within his head. I have not yet killed a man, to my knowledge, and I have never been a teaching assistant, although I have known many.

I want to repeat that there was absolutely no intent in what I was doing. The fact that the character had killed a person came as a total surprise to me. It seems too melodramatic, and I don't like this confessional voice, and I do not like the tense, and I have trouble dictating these words from my notebook to my wife, because they keep changing and leading me forward. I do not know if the killing was accidental or premeditated. I don't know the victim. I don't know the method. I don't know if it was imaginary. I do know the phrase "killed a man" appeared on the page.

It may have come there because of what the father said; or, since in the next paragraph I discovered that the young man feels this one act gives him a certain distance from life, a sort of scenic overlook from which to view life, perhaps that idea came from the word "position" in the first paragraph. In my lower middle-class background, even a teaching assistant had a position, not a job. A little more of this kind of thing, however, and the story will never be written.

Writers must remain, to some degree, not only ignorant of what they are going to do but what they are doing. Mary Peterson just wrote me about her novel, "I need to write it before I can think about it, write it too fast for thought." Writers have to protect their ignorance, and it is not easy to remain ignorant, particularly in an English department. That may be one reason we have deemphasized the experience of discovery in writing.

Discovery, however, can be a frightening process. The terror of the empty page is real, because you simply do not know what you are going to say before you say it or if indeed you will have anything to say. I observe this process most dramatically at those times when I dictate early drafts of nonfiction to my wife, who types it on the typewriter. We have done this for years, and yet rather regularly she asks me to repeat what I have said or tell her what I am going to say so that she can punctuate. I don't think, after many books and many years, that she really believes me when I claim I can't remember what I've just said or that I don't know what I'm going to say next.

This process is even more frightening when you engage in the forms of writing that take you inside yourself. "There's not any more dangerous occupation in the world," says James Dickey of poetry. "The mortality rate is very, very high. Paul Valéry once said, 'one should never go into the self except armed to the teeth.' That's true. The kind of poets we're talking about—Berryman, Crane, Dylan Thomas—have created something against which they have no immunity and which they can not control."

Finally, many expert readers who teach English, and therefore writing, are ignorant of the process of discovery because it is not, and should not be, apparent in a finished work. After a building is finished, the flimsy scaffolding is taken away. Our profession's normal obsession with product rather than process leads us towards dangerous misconceptions about the writing process. I believe increasingly that the process of discovery, of using language to find out what you are going to say, is a key part of the writing process. In light of this I would like to reexamine the revision process.

THE TWO PRINCIPAL FORMS OF REVISION

The more I explore the revision process as a researcher and the more I experience it as a writer, the more convinced I am that there are two principal and quite separate editorial acts involved in revision.

Internal revision. Under this term, I include everything writers do to discover and develop what they have to say, beginning with the reading of a completed first draft. They read to discover where their content, form, language, and voice have led them. They use language, structure, and information to find out what they have to say or hope to say. The audience is one person: the writer.

External revision. This is what writers do to communicate what they have found they have written to another audience. It is editing and proofreading and much more. Writers now pay attention to the conventions of form and language, mechanics, and style. They eye their audience and may choose to appeal to it. They read as an outsider, and it is significant that such terms as polish are used by professionals: they dramatize the fact that the writer at this stage in the process may, appropriately, be concerned with exterior appearance.

Most writers spend more time, much more time, on internal revision than external revision. Yet most texts emphasize the least part of the process, the mechanical changes involved in the etiquette of writing, the superficial aspects of preparing a manuscript to be read, and pass over the process of internal revision. It's worth noting that it is unlikely intelligent choices in the editing process can be made unless writers thoroughly understand what they have said through internal revision.

Although I believe external revision has not been explored adequately or imaginatively, it has been explored. I shall concentrate on attempting to describe internal revision, suggesting opportunities for research, and indicating some implications for the teaching of writing.

The Process of Internal Revision

After the writer has completed the first draft, the writer moves toward the center of the writing process. E. M. Forster says, "The act of writing inspires me," and Valéry talks of "the inspiration of the writing desk." The writer may be closer to the scientist than to the critic at this point. Each piece of writing is an experiment.

Robert Penn Warren says, "All writing that is any good *is* experimental: that is, it's a way of seeing what is possible."

Some pieces of writing come easily, without a great deal of internal revision. The experience is rare for most writers, however, and it usually comes after a lifetime of discipline, or sometimes after a long night of work, as it did when Robert Frost wrote "Stopping by Woods on a Snowy Evening." The important thing to understand is that the work that reads the most easily is often the product of what appears to be drudgery. Theodore Roethke wisely points out that "you will come to know how, by working slowly, to be spontaneous."

I have a relatively short 7-part poem of which there are 185 or more versions written over the past 2 years. I am no Roethke, but I have found it important to share with my students in my seminar on the teaching of writing a bit of the work which will never appear in public. I think they are impressed with how badly I write, with how many false starts and illiterate accidents it took for me to move forward towards some understanding of the climate in a tenement in which I lived as an only child, surrounded by a paralyzed grandmother and two rather childlike parents. The important thing for my students to see is that each word changed, each line crossed out, each space left on the page is an attempt to understand, to remember what I did not know I remembered.

During the process of internal revision, writers are not concerned with correctness in any exterior sense. They read what they have written so that they can deal with the questions of subject, of adequate information, of structure, of form, of language. They move from a revision of the entire piece down to the page, the paragraph, the sentence, the line, the phrase, the word. And then, because each word may give off an explosion of meaning, they move out from the word to the phrase, the line, the sentence, the paragraph, the page, the piece. Writers move in close and then move to visualize the entire piece. Again and again and again. As Donald Hall says, "The attitude to cultivate from the start is that revision is a way of life."

Discovery and Internal Revision

The concept of internal revision is new to me. This essay has given me the impetus to explore this area of the writing process. The further I explore the more tentative my conclusions. This chapter is, indeed, as I believe it was meant to be, a call for research, not a report of research. There are many things I do not understand as I experience and examine the process of internal revision. But in addition to my normal researches, I am part of a faculty which includes seven publishing writers, as well as many publishing scholars and critics. We share our work in process, and I have the advantage of seeing them discover what they have to say. I also see the work of graduate students in our writing program, many of whom are already publishing. And I watch the writing of students who are undergraduates at the university, in high school, in middle school, and in elementary school. And I think I can perceive four important aspects of discovery in the process of internal revision.

The first involves *content*. I think we forget that writers in all forms, even poetry, especially poetry, write with information. As English professors and linguistic researchers, we may concentrate on stylistic differences, forgetting that the writer engaged in the process of internal revision is looking through the word—or beyond the word or behind the word—for the information the word will symbolize. Sitting at a desk, pausing, staring out the window, the writer does not see some great thesaurus in the sky; the writer sees a character walking or hears a character speaking, sees a pattern of statistics which may lead toward a conclusion. Writers can't write nothing; they must have an abundance of information. During the process of internal revision, they gather new information or return to their inventory of information and draw on it. They discover what they have to say by relating pieces of specific information to other bits of information and use words to symbolize and connect that information.

This naturally leads to the discoveries related to *form and structure*. We all know Archibald MacLeish said that a poem should not mean but be, but what we do not always understand is that the being may be the meaning. Form is meaning, or a kind of meaning. The story that has a beginning, a middle, and an end implies that life has a beginning, a middle, and an end; exposition implies that things can be explained; argument implies the possibility of rational persuasion. As writers bring order to chaos, the order brings the writers toward meaning.

Third, *language* itself leads writer to meaning. During the process of internal revision (what some writers might call eternal revision), they reject words, choose new words, bring words together, switch their order around to discover what they are saying. "I work with language," says Bernard Malamud, "I love the flowers of afterthought."

Finally, I believe there is a fourth area, quite separate from content, form, or language, which is harder to define but may be as important as the other sources of discovery. That is what we call *voice*. I think voice, the way in which writers hear what they have to say, hear their point of view towards the subject, their authority, their distance from the subject, is an extremely significant form of internal revision.

We should realize that there may be fewer discoveries in form and voice as a writer repeats a subject or continues work in a genre which he or she has explored earlier and become proficient with. This lack of discovery—this excessive professionalism or slickness, the absence of discovery—is the greatest fear of mature, successful writers. They may know too much too early in the writing process.

Thinking and Writing Questions

1. Compare and contrast internal and external revision. Why does Murray make this distinction?
2. Examine Murray's introduction. Where the introductions in "Dyr Mom: Wy R You So Laveabl?" and "Time, Tools, and Talismans" are stories, the introduction to "Internal Revision" is typical of the introductions of academic pieces. Label the parts of Murray's introduction and explain what makes it an introduction for an academic essay.
3. Murray describes writing anxiety as a terror, "The terror of the empty page is real, because you simply do not know what you are going to say" (80). Anne Lamott describes writing anxiety as ravenous dogs, "the dogs in their pen who will surely hurtle and snarl their way out if you ever *stop* writing, because writing is, for some of us, the latch that keeps the door of the pen closed, keeps those crazy ravenous dogs contained" (72). Craig Vetter calls writing anxiety an agony, "writing is a blood sport, a walk in the garden of agony" (37). Talk to your peers about the writing anxieties that you face. To which parts of the act of writing is your anxiety attached? How can you support each other to work through your anxieties?
4. How have you understood revision? As punishment? Fixing your errors? A waste of time? Just more work? An exploration? An opportunity? Discuss with your peers your attitude toward revision. How did you develop this attitude? Has Murray convinced you to see revision as an opportunity for discovery?
5. What part does reading play in revision? Describe the types of reading writers do when they review their own work.

Simplicity

WILLIAM ZINSSER

Writer William Zinsser began his career with the New York Herald
Tribune *and has been a longtime contributor to leading maga-
zines. His seventeen books include* Writing to Learn, Mitchell &
Ruff, Spring Training, American Places, Easy to Remember: The
Great American Songwriters and Their Songs, *and most recently*
Writing About Your Life. *During the 1970s he taught writing at
Yale, where he was master of Yale's Branford College. He now
teaches at the New School, in New York, and at the Columbia
University Graduate School of Journalism. Based on a course
Zinsser taught at Yale,* On Writing Well *has just been published in
its* 7th *edition.* On Writing Well *covers Zinsser's four principles of
writing: clarity, simplicity, brevity, and humanity. "Simplicity," the
chapter from* On Writing Well *reprinted here, covers the problem
with clutter in writing and how to "strip every sentence to its
cleanest components."*

———————— ✦ ————————

Clutter is the disease of American writing. We are a society
strangling in unnecessary words, circular constructions,
pompous frills and meaningless jargon.

Who can understand the clotted language of everyday
American commerce: the memo, the corporation report, the business letter, the notice from the bank explaining its latest "simpli-
fied" statement? What member of an insurance or medical plan
can decipher the brochure explaining his costs and benefits?
What father or mother can put together a child's toy from the
instructions on the box? Our national tendency is to inflate and
thereby sound important. The airline pilot who announces that he
is presently anticipating experiencing considerable precipitation
wouldn't think of saying it may rain. The sentence is too simple—
there must be something wrong with it.

But the secret of good writing is to strip every sentence to its
cleanest components. Every word that serves no function, every
long word that could be a short word, every adverb that carries
the same meaning that's already in the verb, every passive
construction that leaves the reader unsure of who is doing

what—these are the thousand and one adulterants that weaken the strength of a sentence. And they usually occur in proportion to education and rank.

During the 1960s the president of my university wrote a letter to mollify the alumni after a spell of campus unrest. "You are probably aware," he began, "that we have been experiencing very considerable potentially explosive expressions of dissatisfaction on issues only partially related." He meant that the students had been hassling them about different things. I was far more upset by the president's English than by the students' potentially explosive expressions of dissatisfaction. I would have preferred the presidential approach taken by Franklin D. Roosevelt when he tried to convert into English his own government's memos, such as this blackout order of 1942:

> Such preparations shall be made as will completely obscure all Federal buildings and non-Federal buildings occupied by the Federal government during an air raid for any period of time from visibility by reason of internal or external illumination.

"Tell them," Roosevelt said, "that in buildings where they have to keep the work going to put something across the windows."

Simplify, simplify. Thoreau said it, as we are so often reminded, and no American writer more consistently practiced what he preached. Open *Walden* to any page and you will find a man saying in a plain and orderly way what is on his mind:

> I went to the woods because I wished to live deliberately, to front only the essential facts of life, and see if I could not learn what it had to teach, and not, when I came to die, discover that I had not lived.

How can the rest of us achieve such enviable freedom from clutter? The answer is to clear our heads of clutter. Clear thinking becomes clear writing; one can't exist without the other. It's impossible for a muddy thinker to write good English. He may get away with it for a paragraph or two, but soon the reader will be lost, and there's no sin so grave, for the reader will not easily be lured back.

Who is this elusive creature, the reader? The reader is someone with an attention span of about 30 seconds—a person assailed by many forces competing for attention. At one time those forces were relatively few: newspapers, magazines, radio, spouse, children, pets. Today they also include a galaxy of electronic devices for receiving entertainment and information— television, VCRs, DVDs, CDs, video games, the Internet, e-mail, cell phones, BlackBerries, iPods—as well as a fitness program, a pool, a lawn and that most potent of competitors, sleep. The man or woman snoozing in a chair with a magazine or a book is a person who was being given too much unnecessary trouble by the writer.

It won't do to say that the reader is too dumb or too lazy to keep pace with the train of thought. If the reader is lost, it's usually because the writer hasn't been careful enough. That carelessness can take any number of forms. Perhaps a sentence is so excessively cluttered that the reader, hacking through the verbiage, simply doesn't know what it means. Perhaps a sentence has been so shoddily constructed that the reader could read it in several ways. Perhaps the writer has switched pronouns in midsentence, or has switched tenses, so the reader loses track of who is talking or when the action took place. Perhaps Sentence B is not a logical sequel to Sentence A; the writer, in whose head the connection is clear, hasn't bothered to provide the missing link. Perhaps the writer has used a word incorrectly by not taking the trouble to look it up.

Faced with such obstacles, readers are at first tenacious. They blame themselves—they obviously missed something, and they go back over the mystifying sentence, or over the whole paragraph, piecing it out like an ancient rune, making guesses and moving on. But they won't do that for long. The writer is making them work too hard, and they will look for one who is better at the craft.

Writers must therefore constantly ask: what am I trying to say? Surprisingly often they don't know. Then they must look at what they have written and ask: have I said it? Is it clear to someone encountering the subject for the first time? If it's not, some fuzz has worked its way into the machinery. The clear writer is someone clearheaded enough to see this stuff for what it is: fuzz.

I don't mean that some people are born clearheaded and are therefore natural writers, whereas others are naturally fuzzy and will never write well. Thinking clearly is a conscious act that writers must force on themselves, as if they were working on any other project that requires logic: making a shopping list or doing an algebra problem. Good writing doesn't come naturally, though most people seem to think it does. Professional writers are constantly bearded by people who say they'd like to "try a little writing sometime"—meaning when they retire from their real profession, like insurance or real estate, which is hard. Or they say, "I could write a book about that." I doubt it.

Writing is hard work. A clear sentence is no accident. Very few sentences come out right the first time, or even the third time. Remember this in moments of despair. If you find that writing is hard, it's because it *is* hard.

Thinking and Writing Questions

1. Heather and Liz have students who spend time looking for a "better" word, studying the thesaurus to find an intelligent word. What would Zinsser say to these students?

2. Compare and contrast the prose and style of Zinsser to that of Donald Murray. Both are well published authors addressing the topic of writing using different voices and styles. As you analyze the prose of these two authors, discuss with your peers which of these prose styles you see as more effective and why.

3. Zinsser focuses on cutting the words and getting rid of the clutter. Conversely, the other authors in the chapter demand that you grow your ideas and words. How do both the activities of adding and cutting work together to create effective pieces of writing?

4. Experiment with one of Zinsser's sentences. Inflate a sentence using the constructions that he tells us to get rid of. Try this sentence: "If you find that writing is hard, it's because it *is* hard."

Chapter 2: Thinking and Writing

1. Many of the writers in Chapter Two describe how they write: the process they go through. Try your hand at this. You might recount how you wrote a piece. Record all that you did to complete that piece of writing, for example, what writing utensil you used, when you composed, what content problems you proposed for yourself, how you revised, what you did to edit your prose. Get all that you can remember down on the page. After this first draft, revise by adding information based on the ideas presented in each of the essays in Chapter Two. Drawing on Wyche, add more about the rituals you use and how they affect your writing process. Drawing on Murray, add more about the internal and external revision that you do and don't do. Add an evaluation section. Comment on the success of your writing process. What aspects of your writing process do you want to improve?

2. Sandra Boynton's rendition of the five-paragraph theme represents a tradition with a strong hold on students and their writing. This genre has been

part of our school experience. Boynton pokes fun at the assumption that writers can pour their ideas, three at a time, into this structure. The remaining pieces in this chapter could be seen as attempts to break the hold that the five-paragraph theme has on writing. Write an essay—hopefully not in a five-paragraph form—in which you explain the arguments that the authors in Chapter Two would make against the use of the five-paragraph theme.

3. Review the pieces in Chapter Two and make a list of the elements of writing that are covered, such as prewriting, shitty first drafts, revision, and editing. Write a report in which you compare and contrast what we cover in this chapter to what is covered in your handbook and your writing textbook. What other aspects of the practice of writing should we address? Why add these? Send us an email reporting your conclusions and recommending the topics we should add to this chapter. *bryant@calumet.purdue.edu* and *hclark28@ivytech.edu*

4. In "Time, Tools, and Talismans" Susan Wyche draws on the work of Mihaly Csikszentmihaly (pronounced "CHICK-sent-me-high-ee"), a psychologist who developed his concept of flow at the University of Chicago. Compose an essay or an "I Search" piece in which you apply the work of Csikszentmihaly and Wyche to the writing narratives of Stafford, Lamott, and hooks. How does flow operate in their writing?

As you prepare to write, reread "Time, Tools, and Talismans" and mark those passages where Wyche addresses flow. Next, visit the library or the bookstore and look at Csikszentmihalyi's research on flow. Try his book *Flow: The Psychology of Optimal Experience* (Harper & Row, 1990) in which he collected his research that had been published in scholarly journals from 1970–1990. Or look at a scholarly journal article by Csikszentmihaly or about his concept of flow.

Works Cited

Csikszentmihaly, Mihaly. *Flow: The Psychology of Optimal Experience*. New York: Harper & Row, 1990.

CHAPTER 3

Voice

As you piece together your writing processes, sifting through the pages of advice from previous authors and the lines of notes from previous teachers, you might notice that it's still not easy. You may think to yourself, "Okay fine, so I have this lovely process, but how in the world can I write a paper about linguistic aptitude? Or an argument about the pitfalls of early marriage, or a report about the life cycle of the iguana? Who am I to write this stuff? I can barely write my own story with confidence."

It's this problem—this "X" factor—that this chapter on constructing voice directly addresses. It's you having that knowledge and confidence, that agency, giving yourself permission to say something about an issue. You might have heard voice referred to as perspective in a statement such as, "The voice of the Mexican-American is not heard in the story of the Alamo." Having a voice that is acknowledged and acted upon is having power. Do you remember those verbal arguments in which the person with the last word is the winner?

Voice is also defined as the personality projected by your prose. The words you choose, the sentences you construct, and the topics you choose to write about create a writing persona that readers interpret. After reading Anne Lamott's piece on "Shitty First Drafts" and hearing her describe shitty drafts and the vinegar lipped lady, we might describe her voice as sarcastic and funny. She chooses to create this presence in her writing.

We also create a certain voice for the pages you are reading here. In an early draft of the student letter at the beginning of *Essays on Writing* we wrote, "We hope that you find the voice we've chosen sounds more like a voice you know rather than some distant textbook writer passing down wisdom through the ages."

We made a decision to construct a voice that would sound both authoritative on the subject of writing and also informal—not stodgy—so you would read it. We set out to negotiate the combination of our voices. Lizbeth Bryant came to this writing project with the typical academic voice after a dissertation and two scholarly book projects. Heather Clark came to this project after completing her thesis with her colloquial voice—or "trite" as one of her teachers described it—still intact. Heather tells the story of a high school English teacher who often left the comment "trite" on her papers and negatively judged Heather's colloquial voice. In spite of this teacher's negative judgment, Heather's voice has come in quite handy in this project with her short explicatives and vivid images of the information highway.

We combined our voices to create a voice for *Essays on Writing*. We did not "find" it in some magical writing garden as a brilliant yellow daisy in full bloom; we constructed it. It was indeed a conscious effort. This process of constructing and reconstructing voices is so essential to our writing lives that we based an entire chapter on it.

Liz is an expert on voice, and we've included one of her book chapters. "Disruptive 'Sexual' Voices in English 101" examines voices vying for power in the classroom. Liz analyzes how teachers can misjudge students' attempts to speak their voices of home and community in the classroom. In this classroom story, the voices are struggling with each other. The teacher's authoritative voice attemps to lead a classroom discussion full of insight and analysis. The students "seem" to be disrupting the discussion by speaking their colloquial voices through sexual innuendos. Liz realizes that these "students in their first college semester were establishing a place for themselves in a new social situation by speaking their voices in the best way they knew. How can they establish their presence in a classroom focused on language? Through their own use of language" (98). Liz examines the consequences of a teacher's attempts to silence students' voices

In "Teaching Standard English: Whose Standard?," Linda M. Christensen describes other consequences to students, their voices, and their desire to write when their voices and grammars of home are discounted and diminished in the classroom. Because one's voice and grammar has become an "indication of class and cultural background" (103), people who don't speak Standard Written English (SWE) are considered "substandard." Teachers have been charged with preserving SWE in the classroom to assure students' success in the larger, professional and economic worlds. As teachers respond to students' voices with such messages as "The way you said this is wrong" (103), student writers begin to operate out of shame and fear, resulting in a lack of writing or stilted prose that avoids errors and takes no risks to develop ideas. Christensen offers classroom strategies that support students' voices of home so that students will be able and willing to learn and employ SWE.

In "Flipping the Script: Exploring the Relationship between Form and Content in Teen Writing," Nora McCarthy recounts her experience working with teen writers outside of the classroom to bring their voices of home and community into their writing. Working with teens' writing at the content, sentence, and word level, McCarthy encourages the teens to reconstruct voices that give them the agency to speak about their foster care experiences. She identifies and tutors teens to revise the "signature grammatical pattern[s]" (112) that signify their flat, passive voices. These "beaten-down voice[s]" (111) evolve through revision into voices in which teen writers claim their power to "take charge of their lives" (111).

In "A Plagiarism Pentimento," Rebecca Moore Howard builds a case for supporting the emerging voices of students. As students come to college and begin reading and writing about worldly issues, they struggle to develop voices that will allow them to be heard in the academic community: a voice that follows the rules of the written conversations in each academic discipline. Howard argues that in students' attempts to join these written conversations, students can practice a kind of plagiarism called patchwriting. Students pull the voices, words, and sentence patterns of the writers they are studying into their prose because students haven't acquired the discourse patterns, the language, or the content to enter the academic conversations that college professors have directed them to enter. Rather than "persecut[ing] students for crimes" (115), teachers should show students how this is a step they are taking to "manipulate new academic language" as they work to join written conversations of the academy (116).

It is precisely this patchwriting which Keith D. Miller explores in Dr. Martin Luther King's speeches and sermons. In "Redefining Plagiarism: Martin Luther King's Use of an Oral Tradition," Miller examines the oral traditions that Dr. King learned in the church. He grew up in a "highly oral religious culture that treated songs and sermons as shared wealth, not private property" (Miller "Redefining" 130). Dr. King drew on the words and voices of preachers who had written before him to convey his message. When he got to college, he failed first-year English twice (Miller "Composing" 77). He made it through college into graduate school where he wrote a dissertation to earn the title of Dr. King. Keith Miller and other scholars have documented Dr. King's plagiarism of passages in his dissertation. King took the church's oral traditions and applied them to the written discourse of the academic community. Miller examines the ethical issues that Dr. King's plagiarism poses for the academic community: do we justify or condemn the work and words of a man who "electrified millions of people and helped transform American race relations" ("Redefining" 128)? What exactly is King's voice? If he "patched" together the voices of others in his prose, where is his writing presence?

Clearly, this voice stuff ain't easy. Voice is a complicated aspect, one which, like all components of writing, takes time and practice to refine. Are the voices we use a compilation of the voices of others? In a world that grows smaller by the minute, how can we tell what we've been influenced by and what is really our own? How do we construct these voices as we grow as writers, readers, and thinkers? As you read the pieces in Chapter Three, note the energy of these writers to make their voices heard and to fashion a voice by constructing and reconstructing. What is the result of their energy and struggles? How have you struggled with your voice?

Disruptive "Sexual" Voices in English 101

LIZBETH BRYANT

Teacher and writer Lizbeth Bryant has been studying and teaching composition for twenty-two years. She founded the Mid Ohio Writing Project at Ohio State University—Mansfield, a site of the National Writing Project which teaches teachers how to teach writing. She has written and edited numerous pieces including, Grading in the Post Process Classroom *and* Voice as Process, *from which this chapter is taken. Bryant is currently a professor of English at Purdue University Calumet and a fierce advocate for student success in the first-year writing program. In "Disruptive 'Sexual' Voices in English 101," Bryant examines an experience of dealing with a struggle in the classroom between the voices that students bring and the voices that the academy expects.*

——————————   ✦   ——————————

On the inside cover of a final portfolio I read these words: "If you smoke after sex, you did it too fast." The writer appreciated the play on *smoke* and the indefinite pronoun, *it*. I was not surprised by this seemingly inappropriate quote because it followed the discourse pattern of this first-year, first-semester writing class. Sexual words, images, and innuendoes snuck their way into my class—or what I thought was "my class."

Earlier in the semester, in an exercise on sentence combining and commas, I asked, "Where would we stick the comma as we combine these sentences?" Muffled, from the back right corner in a deep voice I heard, "I wouldn't *stick* mine in there. Don't know what I would catch." Snickers erupted. I smiled and chose not to respond to this seemingly inappropriate response. I repeated my question. At that point, I did not know how to react; my smile only accepted this sexual comment and welcomed their voices to the classroom.

Next week, another student voiced a joke with a sexual innuendo. I asked the class, "Which parts will you be including in your analysis essay?" From the back I heard, "Which body *parts* will you include, Mike?" The snickering began, and I heard, "Not this *part*."

TEACHER DESCRIBES, LABELS, ANALYZES, AND JUDGES

Attempting to understand these persistent sexual innuendoes, I analyzed the rhetorical situation, making assumptions about the students' audiences, decisions, and choices. This rhetorical context was a classroom, a public forum in which personal and intimate topics such as sex are not appropriate. A college classroom calls for academic voices full of insight and analysis—not silly voices full of sexual puns. I characterized these voices as humorous and sarcastic, labeled them as sexual based on the subject of discussion, categorized them as private, and judged them as inappropriate for the classroom. As a result, I composed a response to quell them.

In an exercise to practice analysis, I created a scenario for the class: "Pretend that we went to a great party last night, What made it fun?" They responded with, "The music was loud." "The food was great." "Lots of beer." Giggling, from the back of the room I heard, "Yea, it was great. We had a wild orgy." The class began to snicker, and another student responded, "Yea, man. Great sex." I was ready: "You must stop this expression of your teenage sexual fantasies. They are not acceptable in this public classroom. I would like to hear some intelligent conversation. Knock it off! Now, let's continue with our discussion." The laughing stopped, and the class stared at me in an awkward silence with each of us wondering, "What will happen next?" After a moment of silence, I repeated my question. No one answered, and I called on a student. For the remainder of that class period there were no more jokes.

But my attempts to silence their sexual comments did not work; they continued to resurface, and I wanted to know why. In an interview with two class members, Tammy and Tracy, I asked about the sexual comments. Tammy responded, "We are more laid-back and free in your class, so it's okay to talk about sex. We [the students in the class] are real close. We know each other. We sit at meals together and talk about sex. It's a conversation starter. Everyone's interested in it. I can say to anyone, 'I did *this* on the Empire State Building.' And they can respond with 'You did! Well, I did *this*.'" Listening to her classmate, her face red with embarrassment, Tracy said, "Tammy, I can't believe you said that." Tracy was uncomfortable with these sexual conversations that included me. Tammy was willing to talk about sex in the public arena of our conversation or the classroom.

NEW PERSPECTIVES

Labeling and categorizing these voices was not helping me to understand the discourse patterns in "our" class. First, my labeling was incorrect; a label of sexual and judgment of inappropriate was from my perspective. From the students' perspective their voices were attempting to join the teacher's discourse, combining their sexual words with the academic words. And second, I was seeing the voice struggle from my perspective of getting students to speak in an academic voice. Their agenda was different. I needed a new way to conceptualize voice, an understanding of voice that represented what student writers actually do when the voices of home meet the voices of the academy—not what the academicians and composition theorists say that students should be doing with their voices.

Kay Halasek supports this shift from focusing on what the teacher does in the classroom to what students are doing. Rather than assuming this 101 class was "mine," over which I had control, I had to re-envision the dynamics of "our" class. Halasek asks teachers to examine the preformative nature of our pedagogy as an act that "entails *answer-ability*," answerable to an audience of students as coauthors of our pedagogy (1999, 179). Rather than focusing on inappropriate comments, I could focus on how students react to my demands to quit their "bar-room humor." Rather than relying on what composition scholars say students *should* be doing with their voices, I began to listen to what students were doing as they dealt with the power of academic voices. Students have an essential part in constructing a pedagogy—a part I was not acknowledging. Halasek's vision of pedagogy shifts the focus from what teachers *do* to how "teaching is received, which, in turn, allows us to examine the *ethics* of teaching" (180). And when I understand how student writers approach voice, what is my ethical responsibility?

Mary Louise Pratt labels what students do as "pupiling." She examines what pupils do in light of hierarchical classroom structures, helping me to understand my part in using the power of the academy to impede a student's process of voice development. When a teacher asks Pratt's son Manuel to imagine a helpful invention and write about how this invention would help other people and what it would look like, Manuel replied with some "grate" invented spelling:

> Some inventchins are GRATE!!!!!!!!!!!! My inventchin would be a shot that would put every thing you learn at school in your brain. It would help me by letting me graduate right now!! I would need it because it would let me play with my friends, go on vacachin and, do fun a lot more. (Pratt 1991, 38)

The teacher neither acknowledged nor responded to Manuel's attempt to be humorous and critical, unlike my direct attempts to silence the sexual comments. Manuel wrote a paragraph that "sought ways to resist or subvert" the assignment (38). Pratt asks, "What is the place of unsolicited oppositional discourse, parody, resistance, critique in the imagined classroom community?"

(39), much like my question: What do I do with these sexual voices that are oppositional—not appropriate in the academic discourse community?

Pratt likens Manuel's resistance to that of Guaman Poma who in 1613 wrote to King Philip III of Spain a text in which the conquered one from Peru attempts a dialogue with the conqueror. In his critique of the Spanish occupation of Peru, Poma attempts "to construct a new picture of the world, a picture of a Christian world with Andean rather than European peoples at the center of it" (34). The voice of the conquered enters the tension-filled zone with the authoritative discourse of Spain. Poma positions his text in the contact zone, representing the movement of the marginalized perspective of the conquered group into print culture. Pratt uses the metaphor of a contact zone to characterize "social spaces where cultures meet, clash, and grapple with each other, often in contexts of highly asymmetrical relations of power, such as colonialism, slavery, or their aftermaths as they are lived out in many parts of the world today" (34).

Manuel and my 101 students come from a long line of resisters. Like Manuel in kindergarten and Poma in conquered Peru, my 101 students in their first college semester were establishing a place for themselves in a new social situation by speaking their voices in the best way they knew. How can they establish their presence in a classroom focused on language? Through their own use of the language. They subverted my control of their language by taking selected words—*stick* and *parts*—and using them in the way they found appropriate. They did not directly confront the authoritative discourse of the academy that I yielded as leader and grade-giver; they exercised a subtle resistance through mimicry and parody, accompanied by snickering. This is less about sex and inappropriate voices, and more about disruption and students' attempts to enter the discourse being controlled by the instructor. Pratt describes this type of oppositional discourse as "the attempt to be critical or contestatory, to parody the structures of authority" (39). The authoritative, academic voice of the teacher meets the humorous, disruptive voices of students in the construction zone of the classroom.

INSIGHTS FROM THIS NEW PERSPECTIVE

Rather than delineating the defining features of a voice, I began to look at interactions between voices: how students were navigating, negotiating, rejecting, and combining voices of home, community, and the academy; how I was resisting their voices;

and what forces controlled these interactions. Each student brings a conglomeration of voices to class—a web of voices not easily differentiated. The demarcation between voices is not clear, simple, or fixed. It is very difficult—I would say almost impossible—to hold these voices and their creation process still long enough to qualify and quantify them. Voices merge in and out of one another, daring us to label and categorize them. Remember my mistake of labeling the sexual voices as private. I am not omniscient enough to have a clear picture of this web. Therefore, rather than simply labeling and categorizing voices, I examined the relationships of voices in these webs of words. How do these voices function in the construction zones of our classrooms? What happens in the process of combining and constructing voices?

Events in this 101 class show how students navigated the discourse waters of the academy and decided to bring aspects of their voices of community into the construction zone of the classroom. They asserted their presence and agency by speaking a voice that was part of their discourse system. They positioned their words of sex next to my words of the authoritative discourse to create a hybrid. This contact zone became a construction zone where they took my words *stick* and *parts* and juxtaposed them against the words of their sexual innuendos.

Even after I asked them to stop, they continued to move their voices into the construction zone by mimicking me. Meeting the authoritative discourse of the academy in the construction zone, they began to combine their voices with the academic voice. They constructed new voices that combined the voices they brought to class with the voices I asked them to develop. I envision them trying on these new academic voices, seeing if they fit and adjusting for the correct style. A process was beginning. These interactions in the construction zone can best be studied as a series of events—a combination of mergers and intersections—that create a new voice. As a result, I reconceived voice as a process.

My direction to silence their voices stunted this process of voice development. A process of true interaction and construction is not achieved when elements in the process are silenced— not allowed to enter the zone of contact, a zone I reconceive as a construction area in which new voices are made. The voices that students bring to the classroom are as essential to this process as the authoritative voices already in place. How can any kind of construction happen if students don't bring their own voices into the construction zone to build upon? I realized my attempts to silence the sexual voices and insert an academic voice were actually holding back their process of voice development —stunting their ability to construct voices they could employ in academic discourse. My silencing was not supportive of hybrid voices. My concept of voice as a product was not helping my students to grow. I was not, as Carl Rogers reminds me, supporting my students' "urge to expand, extend, develop, mature" (1961, 351).

WHAT I COULD HAVE DONE

After interviewing the students, reading Pratt, and analyzing the discourse patterns from the students' perspectives, I realized how I could have transformed these conflicts into teaching moments. By examining with the students how voices operate in social contexts, we could have explored:

1. How they analyzed the rhetorical situation of the lunch room and employed a one-upmanship to talk about sex;
2. How they analyzed the rhetorical situation of our 101 class and decided to use their sexual comments;
3. How asymmetrical power relations operate in the academy;
4. Why some voices are deemed more appropriate than others;
5. Who makes these determinations of appropriateness: the educational, governmental, and political factions that enter the argument about students' rights to their own language;
6. How they and others who have been silenced attempt to subvert control by the hegemonic structures;
7. How they combined the voices they brought to the classroom with the voices they encountered: a process of voice construction.

In short—I could have created a metadiscourse about their resistance by bringing to the forefront the conflict between the authoritative voices of the academy that I represented and their disruptive voices.

As usual, my hindsight is a perfect 20/20. But this is one of the joys of teaching: another teaching moment will come around. My encounter with these disruptive voices in English 101 began my journey to develop the pedagogies and theoretical underpinnings that support students' processes of voice development.

Thinking and Writing Questions

1. Bryant discusses contact and construction zones. What is a voice construction zone? How does it work? Point out examples of voice construction zones in Bryant's piece. Identify examples of construction zones operating in your prose. What and how are you constructing? Do you see this construction operating in the work of your peers? How?

2. Bryant describes a problem in her classroom that she struggles to solve: outbursts of "sexual" voices. Describe the voice Bryant constructs to tell this story. How would you describe her ethos: her "credibility and trustworthiness" (Ramage, Bean, and Johnson 79)? When authors pose problems that they don't resolve, is their ethos diminished? Do you trust what they are saying? Why or why not?

3. Read and interpret the story of students in Bryant's class through the lens of Margaret Atwood's poem "Spelling" in Chapter Five. Atwood writes, "A word after a word/after a word is power" (199) How are Bryant's students striving for a bit of power in the dominant structures of the authoritative discourse? How are Bryant's students, "learning how to spell,/ spelling,/ how to make spells" (199)?

4. What voices do you hear in your writing classroom environment? The disruptive voices that Bryant examines? Resistant voices that challenge the teacher? The "know-it-all" student? The bossy student? The voice of the class clown? How do these voices "navigate" the conversations of the classroom? Do these voices change from course to course, say from writing class to math class? Or are they relatively stagnant? What makes you think so? How does your voice change from class to class?

5. Bryant lists a series of things she could have changed to work with the "sexual" voices. How effective do you think these changes would be? Why?

Teaching Standard English: Whose Standard?

LINDA CHRISTENSEN

Teacher and social activist Linda Christensen has taught high school Language Arts and worked as a Language Arts Curriculum Specialist in Portland, Oregon, for the last thirty years. Currently, she directs the Oregon Writing Project at Lewis & Clark College, a site of the National Writing Project network which teaches teachers how to teach writing. Christensen *is the author of* Reading, Writing, and Rising Up: Teaching about Social Justice and the Power of the Written Word *and co-editor of* Rethinking School Reform: Views from the Classroom. *She has given keynote addresses at local, national, and international conferences about her work on literacy and social justice. She received the Fred Heschinger Award from the National Writing Project in 1998 for use of her research in teaching and writing. In "Teaching Standard English: Whose Standard?," which was originally published in* English Journal *and reprinted in* Reading, Writing, and Rising Up, *Christensen laments how students' voices of home can be silenced and altered when teachers discount the voices that students bring to the classroom.*

---------------- ✦ ----------------

When I was in the ninth grade, Mrs. Delaney, my English teacher, wanted to demonstrate the correct and incorrect ways to pronounce the English language. She asked Helen Draper, whose father owned several clothing stores in town, to stand and say "lawyer." Then she asked me, whose father owned a bar, to stand and say "lawyer." Everyone burst into laughter at my pronunciation.

What did Mrs. Delaney accomplish? Did she make me pronounce *lawyer* correctly? No. I say *attorney.* I never say *lawyer.* In fact, I've found substitutes for every word my tongue can't get around and for all the rules I can't remember.

For years I've played word cop on myself. I stop what I'm saying to think, "Objective or subjective case? Do I need *I* or *me* here? Hmmm. There's a *lay* coming up. What word can I substitute for it? *Recline?*"

And I've studied this stuff. After all, I've been an English teacher for almost fifteen years. I've gone through all of the *Warriner's* workbook exercises. I even found a lie/lay computer program and kept it in my head until I needed it in speech and became confused again.

Thanks to Mrs. Delaney, I learned early on that in our society language classifies me. Generosity, warmth, kindness, intelligence, good humor aren't enough—I need to speak correctly to make it. Mrs. Delaney taught me that the "melting pot" was an illusion. The real version of the melting pot is that people of diverse backgrounds are mixed together, and when they come out, they're supposed to look like Vanna White and sound like Dan Rather. The only diversity we celebrate is tacos and chop suey at the mall.

It wasn't until a few years ago that I realized grammar was an indication of class and cultural background in the United States and that there is a bias against people who do not use language "correctly." Even the terminology "standard" and "nonstandard" reflects that one is less than the other. English teachers are urged to "correct" students who speak or write in their home language. A friend of mine, whose ancestors came over on the Mayflower, never studied any of the grammar texts I keep by my side, but she can spot all of my errors because she grew up in a home where Standard English was spoken.

And I didn't, so I've trained myself to play language cop. The problem is that every time I pause, I stop the momentum of my thinking. I'm no longer pursuing content, no longer engaged in trying to persuade or entertain or clarify. Instead, I'm pulling *Warriner's* or Mrs. Delaney out of my head and trying to figure out how to say something.

"Ah, but this is good," you might say. "You have the rules and Mrs. Delaney to go back to. This is what our students need."

But it doesn't happen that way. I try to remember the rule or the catchy phrase that is supposed to etch the rule in my mind forever like "people never get laid," but I'm still not sure if I used it correctly. These side trips cost a lot of velocity in my logic.

Over the years my English teachers pointed out all of my errors—the usage errors I inherited from my mother's Bandon, Oregon, dialect, the spelling errors I overlooked, the fancy words I used incorrectly. They did this in good faith in the same way that, years later, I "corrected" my students' "errors" because I wanted them to know the rules. They were keys to a secret and wealthier society I wanted them to be prepared to enter, just as my teachers wanted to help me.

And we should help kids. It would be misleading to suggest that people in our society will value my thoughts or my students' thoughts as readily in our home languages as in the "cash language" as Jesse Jackson calls it. Students need to know where to find help, and they need to understand what changes might be necessary, but they need to learn in a context that doesn't say, "The way you said this is wrong."

English teachers must know when to correct and how to correct—and I use that word uneasily. Take Fred, for example. Fred entered my first-year class last year unwilling to write. Every day during writing time I'd find Fred doodling pictures of Playboy bunnies on his Pee Chee. When I sat down and asked him why he didn't write, he said he couldn't.

I explained to him that in this class his writing couldn't be wrong because we were just practicing our writing until we found a piece we wanted to polish, in the same way that he practiced football every day after school but played games only on Fridays. His resistance lasted for a couple of weeks. Around him, other students struggled with their writing, shared it with the class on occasion, and heard positive comments. Certainly, the writing of his fellow students was not intimidating. At that point this class was tracked—and Fred was in the lowest track.

On October 1, after reading a story by Toni Cade Bambara (1972) about trusting people in our lives, Fred wrote for the first time: "I remember my next door neighbor trusted me with some money that she owed my grandmother. She owed my grandmother about 25 dollars." Fred didn't make a lot of errors. In this first piece of writing it looked as if he had basic punctuation figured out. He didn't misspell any words. And he certainly didn't make any usage errors. Based on this sample, he appeared to be a competent writer.

However, the biggest problem with Fred's writing was the fact that he didn't make mistakes. This piece demonstrates his discomfort with writing. He wasn't taking any risks. Just as I avoid *lawyer* and *lay*, he wrote to avoid errors instead of writing to communicate or think on paper.

When more attention is paid to the *way* something is written or said than to *what* is said, students' words and thoughts become devalued. Students learn to be silent, to give as few words as possible for teacher criticism.

Students must be taught to hold their own voices sacred, to ignore the teachers who have made them feel that what they've said is wrong or bad or stupid. Students must be taught how to listen to the knowledge they've stored up but which they are seldom asked to relate.

Too often students feel alienated in schools. Knowledge is foreign. It's about other people, in other times (Bigelow 1990) [sic]. At a conference I attended recently, a young woman whose mother was Puerto Rican and whose father was Haitian said,

> I went through school wondering if anyone like me had ever done anything worthwhile or important. We kept reading and hearing about all of these famous people. I remember thinking, "Don't *we* have anyone?" I walked out of the school that day feeling tiny, invisible, unimportant.

As teachers, we have daily opportunities to affirm that our students' lives and language are unique and important. We do that in the selections of literature we read, in the history we choose to teach (Bigelow 1989), and we do it by giving legitimacy to our students' lives as a content worthy of study. One way to encourage the reluctant writers who have been silenced and the not-so-reluctant writers who have found a safe and sterile voice is to encourage them to recount their experiences. I sometimes recruit former students to share their writing and their wisdom as a way of underscoring the importance of the voices and stories of teenagers. Rochelle, a student in my senior writing class, brought a few of her stories and poems to read to my first-year students. Rochelle, like Zora Neale Hurston, blends her home language with Standard English in most pieces. She read the following piece to open up a discussion about how kids are sometimes treated as servants in their homes but also to demonstrate the necessity of using the language she hears in her family to develop characters:

"I'm tired of washing dishes. Seems like every time our family gets together, they just got to eat and bring their millions of kids over to our house. And then we got to wash the dishes."

I listened sympathetically as my little sister mumbled these words.

"And how come we cain't have ribs like grownups? After all, ain't we grown?"

"Lord," I prayed, "seal her lips while the blood is still running warm in her veins."

Her bottom lip protruded farther and farther as she dipped each plate in the soapy water, then rinsed each side with cold water (about a two second process) until she felt the majority of suds were off.

"One minute we lazy women that cain't keep the living room half clean. The next minute we just kids and gotta eat some funky chicken while they eat ribs."

. . . Suddenly it was quiet. All except my little sister who was still talking. I strained to hear a laugh or joke from the adults in the living room, a hint that all were well, full and ready to go home. Everyone was still sitting in their same spots, not making a move to leave.'

"You ought to be thankful you got a choice."

Uh-oh. Now she got Aunt Macy started. . . .

After reading her work, Rochelle talked about listening to her family and friends tell their stories. She urged the first-year students to relate the tales of their own lives—the times they were caught doing something forbidden, the times they got stuck with the dishes, the funny/sad events that made their first year in high school memorable. When Rochelle left, students wrote more easily. Some were afraid of the stories because as Rance said, "It takes heart to tell the truth about your life."

But eventually they write. They write stories. They write poems. They write letters. They write essays. They learn how to switch in and out of the language of the powerful, as Rochelle does so effortlessly in her "Tired of Chicken" piece.

And after we write, we listen to each other's stories in our read-around circle where everyone has the opportunity to share, to be heard, to learn that knowledge can be gained by examining our lives. (See Shor 1987, Shor and Freire 1987.) In the circle, we discover that many young women encounter sexual harassment, we learn that store clerks follow black students, especially males, more frequently than they follow white students, we find that many parents drink or use drugs, we learn that many students are kept awake by the crack houses in their neighborhoods.

Before we share, students often understand these incidents individually. They feel there's something wrong with them. If they were smarter, prettier, stronger, these things wouldn't have happened to them. When they hear other students' stories, they begin to realize that many of their problems aren't caused by a character defect. For example, a young man shared a passionate story about life with his mother who is a lesbian. He loved her but felt embarrassed to bring his friends home. He was afraid his peers would think he was gay or reject him if they knew about his mother. After he read, the class was silent. Some students cried. One young woman told him that her father was gay, and she had experienced similar difficulties but hadn't had the courage to tell people about it. She thanked him. Another student confided that his uncle had died from AIDS the year before. What had been a secret shame became an opportunity for students to discuss sexual diversity more openly. Students who were rigidly opposed to the idea of homosexuality gained insights into their own homophobia—especially when presented with the personal revelations from their classmates. Those with homosexual relatives found new allies with whom they could continue their discussion and find support.

Sharing also provides a "collective text" for us to examine the social roots of problems more closely: Where do men/women develop the ideas that women are sexual objects? Where do they learn that it's okay for men to follow women or make suggestive remarks? Where is it written that it's the woman's fault if a man leers at her? How did these roles develop? Who gains from them? Who loses? How could we make it different? Our lives become a window to examine society.

But the lessons can't stop there. Fred can write better now. He and his classmates can feel comfortable and safe sharing their lives or discussing literature and the world. They can even understand that they need to ask "Who benefits?" to get a better perspective on a problem. But still, when they leave my class or this school, some people will judge them by how their subjects and verbs line up.

So I teach Fred the rules. It's the language of power in this country, and I would be cheating him if I pretended otherwise (Delpit 1988). I teach him this more effectively than Mrs. Delaney taught me because I don't humiliate him or put down his language. I'm also more effective because I don't rely on textbook drills; I use the text of Fred's writing. But I also teach Fred what Mrs. Delaney left out.

I teach Fred that language, like tracking, functions as part of a gatekeeping system in our country. Who gets managerial jobs, who works at banks and who works at fast-food restaurants, who gets into what college and who gets into college at all are decisions linked to ability to use Standard English. So how do we teach kids to write with honesty and passion about their world and get them to study the rules of the cash language? We go back to our study of society. We ask: Who made the rules that govern how we speak and write? Did Ninh's family and Fred's family and LaShonda's family all sit down together and decide on these rules? Who already talks like this and writes like this? Who has to learn how to change the way they talk and write? Why?

We make up our own tests that speakers of Standard English would find difficult. We read articles, stories, poems written in Standard English and those written in home language. We listen to videotapes of people speaking. Most kids like the sound of their home language better. They like the energy, the poetry, and the rhythm of the language. We determine when and why people shift. We talk about why it might be necessary to learn Standard English.

Asking my students to memorize the rules without asking *who* makes the rules, *who* enforces the rules, *who* benefits from the rules, *who* loses from the rules, *who* uses the rules to keep some in and keep others out legitimates a social system that devalues my students' knowledge and language. Teaching the rules without reflection also underscores that it's okay for others—"authorities"— to dictate something as fundamental and as personal as the way they speak. Further, the study of Standard English without critique encourages students to believe that if they fail, it is because they are not smart enough or didn't work hard enough. They learn to blame themselves. If they get poor SAT scores, low grades on term papers or essays because of language errors, fail teacher entrance exams, they will internalize the blame; they will believe they did not succeed because they are inferior instead of questioning the standard of measurement and those making the standards.

We must teach our students how to match subjects and verbs, how to pronounce *lawyer,* because they are the ones without power and, for the moment, they have to use the language of the powerful to be heard. But, in addition, we need to equip them to question an educational system that devalues their lives and their knowledge. If we don't, we condition them to a pedagogy of consumption where they will consume knowledge, priorities, and products that have been decided and manufactured without them in mind.

It took me years to undo what Mrs. Delaney did to me. Years to discover that *what* I said was more important than *how* I said it. Years to understand that my words, my family's words weren't wrong, weren't bad—they were just the words of the working class. For too long, I felt inferior when I spoke. I knew the voice of my childhood crept out, and I confused that with ignorance. It wasn't. I just didn't belong to the group who made the rules. I was an outsider, a foreigner in their world. My students won't be.

Jefferson High School
Portland, Oregon 97211

Works Cited

Bambara, Toni Cade. 1972. *Gorilla, My Love.* New York: Random.
Bigelow, William. 1989. "Discovering Columbus: Rereading the Past."
   Language Arts 66.6: 636–43.
———. In press. "Inside the Classroom: Social Vision and Critical
   Pedagogy." *Teachers College Record.*

Delpit, Lisa. 1988. "The Silenced Dialogue: Power and Pedagogy in Educating Other People's Children." *Harvard Educational Review* 58.3: 280–98.

Shor, Ira. 1987. *Freire for the Classroom.* Portsmouth, NH: Heinemann.

Shor, Ira, and Paulo Freire. 1987. *A Pedagogy for Liberation.* South Hadley, MA: Bergin.

Thinking and Writing Questions

1. Explain the process whereby certain voices get associated with ignorance. Give an example of this association that you have observed or experienced.
2. The magazine in which this article first appeared, *English Journal*, is written for high school English teachers: Christensen's audience. What is her purpose in this piece? What impact does Christensen want her writing to have on teachers? How do you know this? What choices about content and structure does she make to achieve her purpose?
3. Christensen tells us the story of Fred's refusal to write. Thinking about Fred, review the pieces in Chapter Two on the practice of writing to identify what might help Fred to get started? Would these practices work? Why or why not?
4. Some writing teachers believe that students should not be allowed to use their voices of home in the classroom, that students should be using the voices of the academic community, so they will succeed in the world of work. Other teachers, like Christensen, believe that we must allow students' voices of home into the classroom. What do you think teachers should do? Why?

Flipping the Script: Exploring the Relationship between Form and Content in Teen Writing

Nora McCarthy

Writer and editor Nora McCarthy is currently the editor of Rise, *a magazine produced by Youth Communication and written by and for parents who have been involved with child welfare systems nationwide. Begun in 1980 in New York City, Youth Communication "helps teenagers develop their reading and writing skills so they can acquire the information they need to make thoughtful choices about their lives.* " *Youth Communication trains teens to write and then publishes their writings in three magazines:* New Youth Connections, *a general interest magazine with a readership in New York City of 200,000;* Represent *written by and about youth in foster care with a national readership of 12,000; and* Rise *with a national readership of 14,000. McCarthy has reported for* Newsday, Child Welfare Watch *and the* Voice. *She is a graduate of the Medill School of Journalism at Northwestern University in Evanston, IL, and has been working with teens at Youth Communication for nine years. McCarthy supports writers to "develop their skills [and] own their voices" (McCarthy). In "Flipping the Script," McCarthy recounts her experience of working with a teen writer who explores what she wants to say about her experiences in foster care and constructs voices to say it.*

—————— ✦ ——————

In her first story for *Represent*, a magazine by and for teens in foster care that I edit, Natasha Santos wrote with a charming blend of sassiness, introspection, and insecurity. Her story described not having friends to sit with during junior high school lunch.

"In the cafeteria, Natasha sees the different groups at their tables, talking away," Natasha wrote using the third person to describe herself. "Natasha stands there thinking, 'Where do I sit?' The problem is Natasha can't conform. 'Can't or won't?' her brain asks. Sometimes it makes her feel really low to be an alien to everyone around her. It gets hard to remember who she is: A young woman, not a rebel, but not a follower either. She's Natasha, and that won't change."

That story showcased Natasha's strength and survivor instinct. She turned a depressing and isolating experience into a funny, knowing article where she depicted herself as an iconoclast rather than a loser.

But in early drafts of her next story, tough and sassy Natasha was gone. "This story is going to be about love," she told me, and named the story on the computer "love.doc." In fact, the story was about whether Natasha had ever truly been loved by her drug-addicted mother or by her vindictive foster mom, who required Natasha to eat only from her own plate and spoon, so she would not contaminate the family's kitchenware. The draft was a dreary catalogue of abuses, ending with the conclusion that she definitely had not been loved.

I felt unsure how to handle her story. Like all of us in youth media, I know that satisfying personal stories, whether conveyed through radio, film, or writing, must go beyond simply ranting or rehashing painful experiences. I believe those writing for a teen audience have a responsibility to show how teens take charge of their lives, even if they've taken only the smallest steps. I also consider it my job to help writers recognize their strengths and to acknowledge that strength in their stories.

Evidence of my writers' resiliency is usually not hard to find. Writing a personal essay about a taboo subject like abuse is in itself an act of taking charge and resisting victimization. When a writer's instinct is to dwell on the pain of an event, I push her to shift the focus of the story to show instead how she handled that pain. Reframing a story to more heavily stress a young person's strengths and abilities affects not only their stories, but their self perceptions.

But Natasha seemed insistent that her story was solely about how she'd been victimized. She disregarded questions I wrote in the margins about the caring adoptive home she was now living in, or how she managed to achieve excellent grades despite all she'd been through. Instead, she handed in long drafts that burned with fury. Then one day she saw her story on my desk with the words "Anger Story" penciled on top.

"Why does it say 'Anger Story' on mine?" she asked me.

"Oh, just because that's what it's about," I said, not thinking.

"What about anger?" she asked.

"I don't know," I said, "It seems like it's about how you have all this anger from your past that you don't know what to do with. And you're trying to deal with it but you don't know how."

Something switched in Natasha during that exchange. She took her story to her computer and began writing. This time, her beaten-down voice was gone. "This is the story of a girl, born in the projects, neglected by her parents and tormented by memories of families she's no longer a part of. It's a story that I must tell so that I can move on," she wrote. That led to a story about Natasha's quest to acknowledge the pain of her past without succumbing to depression. Shifting the focus of her "love" story in this way helped Natasha reframe her worldview as well. She began to see that her painful sense of rejection as a child did not need to define her, and she could have a more hopeful future.

I was lucky to stumble across a way to help Natasha rethink her story. But, like all editors, I have a few tools that usually do the trick, that can work with young people producing personal stories in just about any medium, whether it be radio, film, or writing.

In most cases, focusing a story on a writer's strengths is just a matter of being encouraging and asking blunt questions that redirect a writer from detailing what happened to her to explaining what she did in response. When one student said she wanted to write about being raped, I asked, "What do you want the readers to take from your story?"

"I want to let them know to tell someone right away, because I waited four years and I shouldn't have," she said. I asked her to begin by describing the day she told her mom, and she wrote a powerful piece about how she began to recover once she asked for help.

Other times I have to actively sniff out evidence of resilience to help my writers see ways they resisted allowing their voices to be silenced. Scrutinizing the grammar and style a young person uses to tell her story often helps me figure out why the writer's voice seems to go passive or fall flat in certain stories. Every writer has a signature grammatical pattern. Some put "too much tinsel on the tree" by being too descriptive, others hit the reader with their points like a jackhammer.

Often, those grammatical patterns reflect how my writers view themselves and their relation to the world. When writers are uncomfortable or uncertain about what they're saying, their signature patterns get worse. Flowery prose turns purple.

One of my writers, Pauline, often hides behind adjectives and lots of dreamy metaphors. Sentences that clearly show Pauline taking action can be rare. In early drafts of a personal essay partly about surviving her father's physical and sexual violence, pauline seemed to disappear entirely. Very few of her sentences began with "I," and those that did were often in the passive voice. So many sentences began with "he" that it was as if, even in her retelling the story, her father had succeeded in dominating her.

We turned the story back around by searching for Pauline. I'd say, "Pauline, I don't see too much 'I' in this section. What were you doing?" It turned out that Pauline fiercely resisted her father and protected her sister. Pauline yelled for her mentally ill mother to intervene. She nudged her grandmother to take her on trips out of the house and encouraged her sister to come along. She spoke up when social workers visited her house.

When we shifted the focus from "what happened to Pauline" to "how Pauline responded," her story blossomed with "I" and active verbs, and Pauline was able to recognize and appreciate how courageously she had fought for her own well-being.

Natasha's signature writing style, on the other hand, sometimes veers too far into an angry, know-it-all tone, facilitated by tons of short sentence fragments. Describing a few well-off teens Natasha had interviewed during a field trip we took to a suburban school, Natasha wrote:

"Then there was Jesse and Jessica. The wealthy ones in the group. Jessica lived in the wealthiest community in Norwalk. And Jesse lived in the second wealthiest. Their answers may have been considered standard by someone else. But for me they were useless. Too sheltered and clouded to be of any real substance."

In the draft, Natasha wanted to convey that she felt only scorn for those naïve suburban teens. In truth, visiting that school in the suburbs had also made her feel jealous and cheated of a tranquil childhood. Her anger shined through those choppy sentences. I needed to help Natasha shift her story from a simplistic "Teens in the suburbs don't know about life," to a more thoughtful, "The teens I met in the suburbs seemed more hopeful than the teens in my ghetto neighborhood." Simply by requiring her to write full sentences, I figured I could draw out a more thoughtful response.

I sat Natasha down with this story, all the fragments underlined. I asked, "Do you know what a fragment is?" She surprised me by saying yes.

"What do you think all these millions of fragments are about?" I asked, and jokingly began to read them out loud in an annoyed, almost snotty voice: "The wealthy ones in the group . . . Too sheltered and clouded to be of any real substance."

"You sure want to get your point across!" I said, laughing. Natasha knows herself well, so she began laughing too. I told her that she needed to learn to use fragments only for emphasis, and to choose what to emphasize. Not everything is so important it needs to be highlighted, I explained.

"Ok, ok, I get it," she told me, and took the paper to her computer. Thirty minutes later she'd smoothed out every fragment, which took a lot of the defensive, snotty tone out of her writing. "I want to leave the last fragment," she told me, "for emphasis."

I put her on "Fragment Watch" after that, and the next draft she wrote almost knocked me over: Four paragraphs and not a single fragment. Then I felt pretty stupid. If I'd pointed out those fragments three years ago, when I'd first started working with Natasha, I could've saved myself a lot of time!

Or maybe Natasha needed to be ready to correct her own grammar. Since the way a person tells her own story is often so entangled with her worldview, maybe Natasha just needed to grow up before she felt confident enough to turn the volume down.

Thinking and Writing Questions

1. McCarthy discusses the teaching process she undertakes with several writers, including Natasha. What kind of tools does McCarthy use in her teaching? How effective are they? How do you know this?

2. McCarthy uses dialogue throughout this piece. Why? How might the piece change without the dialogue? Based on McCarthy's audience of young people who have been in foster care, which way is likely to be more effective? What makes you think so?

3. McCarthy and Craig Vetter, in "Bonehead Writing," Chapter One, speak about working with young, novice writers; however, each presents a different angle of vision. In *The Allyn and Bacon Guide to Writing*, Ramage, Bean and Johnson describe angle of vision as a writer's commitment "to a particular view of a subject that emphasizes some facts and values and de-emphasizes others" (80). Identify the angles from which McCarthy and Vetter view novice writers. What gets included and excluded by each author? If they were to talk with each other, what would they agree and disagree about? What else do you see that both of them are leaving out?

4. When you are told you need to revise, how do you like to be approached? Would McCarthy's ways be effective with you or do you need notes in your margins? A long note at the end of your paper? A meeting with the teacher? What's the best way to help you move forward with your revisions?

5. In McCarthy's essay, two definitions of voice arise: voice as the presence or personality a piece presents through choices a writer makes about words, sentence structure, and topic; and voice as the presence of power and agency that is exhibited by the writer. How does McCarthy relate these two concepts of voice? Does her portrayal of voice fit with what others from this chapter say?

A Plagiarism Pentimento
REBECCA MOORE HOWARD

Writer and teacher Rebecca Moore Howard is currently Visiting Professor of Writing and Rhetoric at Binghamton University and is the former writing program administrator at Syracuse, Texas Christian, and Colgate Universities. Howard has published extensively about literacy education in general and plagiarism in particular in College English *and* Computers and Composition. *Her book* Standing in the Shadow of Giants: Plagiarists, Authors, Collaborators *(1999) focuses on how writing instructors' view of plagiarism can circumvent the education that she regards as instrumental in individual development and essential for a democratic society. In "A Plagiarism Pentimento" Howard argues that a type of plagiarism in which students "patch" the words and voices of writers they are reading into their prose is a process used by student writers to understand and write about new ideas and texts they encounter in college.*

--- ◆ ---

> Two different acts are considered plagiarism: (1) borrowing someone's ideas, information, or language without documenting the source and (2) documenting the source but paraphrasing the source's language too closely, without using quotation marks to indicate that words and phrases have been borrowed. (Hacker 507)

I take issue with the definition of plagiarism offered in Diana Hacker's *Bedford Handbook for Writers.* That I nevertheless use this handbook in all my classes presents no paradox, for the *Bedford* innocuously reproduces accepted wisdom on plagiarism, its definition concurring in substance with those offered by all the other handbooks.

Because we teachers innocuously accept this definition and act upon it, we persecute students for crimes they did not commit. Worse, our adherence to the received definition of plagiarism blinds us to the positive value of a composing strategy which I call "patchwriting": copying from a source text and then deleting some words, altering grammatical structures, or plugging in one-for-one synonym substitutes. By failing to recognize patchwriting as a valuable composing strategy in which the writer engages in entry-level manipulation of new ideas and vocabulary, we fail to support our students in their efforts to assimilate the constructs of unfamiliar discourse. Instead we classify patchwriting as plagiarism and offer the remedy of instruction in source-attribution—how to quote, footnote, and construct a Works Cited page. Although students must learn these mechanical skills, they have a much more central need to learn how to manipulate new academic language.

One type of instruction that responds to the pedagogical value of patchwriting is the teaching of summary. Because its role in facilitating entry into academic discourse has not been recognized, though, summary has been disdained by some scholars as a pointless and mind-deadening exercise.

PATCHWRITING, NOT PLAGIARISM

In Spring 1986, while engaged in the familiar task of responding to students' papers, I encountered the loathsome apparition of plagiarism—or what at that time I believed was plagiarism. I believed, too, that I knew the best way to deal with it. In General Education 101, a core course required of all first-year students at Colgate University, I had asked the students to read a brief excerpt from R.L. Davidson's *Genesis 1–11* and to consider its implications not only for a reading of Genesis but also of Plato's *Phaedo*. The following sentence in one student's paper, though, transgressed the boundaries of academic ethics:

> Specifically, story myths are not for entertainment purposes, rather they serve as answers to questions people ask about life, about society and about the world in which they live. [Student 3]

Its similarity to the original text, Davidson's Genesis 1–11, was too close to be acceptable:

> Such 'story myths' are not told for their entertainment value. They provide answers to questions people ask about life, about society and about the world in which they live (Davidson 10).

The student writer, I assumed, had been insufficiently educated in the handling of sources. But then I read another paper whose author had the same problem:

> Story myths provide answers to philosophical questions about life, society and the world. [Student 6]

Soon I was faced with a veritable flood of plagiarism. Some of the students had documented the source, some had not; but nine of the twenty-six writers in my class had failed to summarize, paraphrase, or quote from the Davidson text. Instead, they had appropriated Davidson's words wholesale, making cosmetic changes:

> Davidson explains that story myths answer questions people ask about life, about society and about the world that we live in. [Student 5]
> The first type of story myths, which are used to explain a principle or answer a question about life, society, and the world. [Student 4]
> It provides answers to questions people ask about life, about society, and about the world in which they live. [Student 9]
> He says it can either answer questions people ask about life, society and the world in which they live or it can be the literary creation of a teacher to help others learn the meaning of life. [Student 5]
> The story myth will be discussed in the following context: story myths provide answers to questions people ask about life, society, and the world in which they live; these stories can be handed down within the community or by a conscious literary creation of a teacher whose concern is to help others share his insight of the meaning of life. [Student 7]

When recapitulating the source material, these writers "borrowed" phrases, patched together into "new" sentences; they "borrowed" whole sentences, deleting what they consider irrelevant words and phrases; and they "borrowed" a hodgepodge of phrases and sentences in which they changed grammar and syntax, and substituted synonyms straight from *Roget's*. Some provided footnotes, attributing the source of the theft; others did not. The samples reproduced above represent only a portion of the plagiarism that was rife in the prose of one-third of the class.

I responded to all the plagiarism in what seemed at the time a sensible manner, one that I have since found supported in published recommendations for responding to plagiarism: I gave them all "F's," delivered a lecture on source-attribution, and allowed the students to rewrite the paper for a better grade.

Yet I could not lay the episode to rest. What did it mean, that one-third of the first-year students in a class at a prestigious liberal-arts college—the CEO's of tomorrow—had blandly stumbled into plagiarism? Did it mean that a substantial number of well-prepared first-year college students did not know the basics of attributing sources? Did it mean that a substantial number of first-year college students who were aimed at careers in influential positions were cheaters? Or did it mean that I should search for a better paradigm than plagiarism for interpreting their textual strategies?

I embarked on the course of examining my own assumptions, and I emerge with deeply changed ideas about the composing strategy that in 1986 I classified as plagiarism. My original judicio-moral paradigm was gradually nudged aside by a cognitivist approach, which in turn gave way to social construction and finally to postmodernism. The result is a kind of plagiarism pentimento, in which the traces of my successive interpretive frameworks remain evident. As Lynn Worsham explains the way in which *l'ecriture feminine* can critique composition studies, she defines Lillian Hellman's pentimento, "which [Hellman] describes as a form of repentance that occurs when a painter changes his or her mind and redraws the lines expressing an artistic conception. When the paint ages and becomes transparent, it is sometimes possible to see the original lines and the initial conception still etched in the memory of paint and canvas. Pentimento is 'a way of seeing,' Hellman writes, 'and then seeing again'" (Worsham 85).

In the current canvas of my plagiarism pentimento, the "borrowings" of the 1986 General Education students were not plagiarism at all (in the sense that plagiarism involves an ethical transgression, whether committed by a calculating or a naive writer). Rather, they were "patchwriting," a composing phenomenon that may signal neither a willing violation of academic ethics nor ignorance of them, but rather a healthy effort to gain membership in a new culture. That this effort involves a transgression of the values of that culture is indeed an irony, for patchwriters, far from being unethical plagiarists, often strive to observe proper academic conventions. Four of the General Education patchwriters acknowledged sources with signal phrases like "Davidson says," and seven of the nine used footnotes, endnotes, or parenthetical documentation. They demonstrated a well-developed awareness of the need to acknowledge sources. Yet, in the words of the Bedford Handbook, they "paraphras[ed] the source's language too closely."

For the most part, this too-close paraphrase did not involve straightforward copying: only three times did any of students make exact copies of extended passages of the source material. All nine of the patchwriters saw a need to make changes in Davidson's language; for example:

> Davidson explains ritual myths as concepts that are illustrated through spoken words but are also accompanied by the performance of religious ceremonies. (Student 8)

The writer is using deletion, synonymy (substitution), and changes in grammar to reproduce Davidson's text:

> The world of the Ancient Near East, however, was familiar with myth of a rather different kind, myth as the spoken word which accompanied the performance of certain all-important religious rituals. (11)

The writer deletes Davidson's adjective phrase "certain all-important" and employs synonymy in changing "rituals" to "ceremonies." Grammatical changes appear in the switch from the singular "word" to "words" and the active "which accompanied" to the passive "are accompanied."

Substitution is a frequent tactic of patchwriting, occurring 18 times in the prose of these nine students. Changes in grammar or syntax occur 11 times. The most frequently employed strategy, though, was deletion, which accounted for 22 of the changes made in the patchwritten passages. The patchwriting strategy that occurred only once was rearrangement.

INTERPRETATIONS OF PATCHWRITING

Published scholarship on plagiarism offers statistics on the frequency of cheating, opinions on the threat that plagiarism poses to academic culture, and suggestions for instructing students so that they will not plagiarize; but it does not explain why the nine General Education students plagiarized. A plausible explanation does appear, however, in research on summary-writing conducted by Brown, Day, and Jones and by

Carol Sherrard. These studies suggest that the students didn't plagiarize at all. Instead they engaged in a summary technique characteristic of writers in difficulty, or writers in relatively early stages of cognitive development. I find these studies illuminating; and as I have increasingly come to interpret my world in the learner-external framework of social constructionism or postmodernism rather than the learner-internal framework characteristic of empirical research, I translate the application of cognitive studies to patchwriting into a social interpretation of why my students plagiarized. (As Carol Berkenkotter has argued, cognitive and social paradigms are not necessarily mutually exclusive.)

Brown, Day, and Jones' description of the "copy-delete" method of summary-writing explains the most frequent strategy used by the patchwriters in my class:

> The components of this strategy are (a) read text elements sequentially, (b) decide for each element whether to include or to delete, and (c) if inclusion is the verdict, copy the unit more or less verbatim from the text. . . . Fifth and seventh graders were diagnosed as using the copy-delete strategy in that the majority of the units included in their summaries were verbatim or near verbatim and occupied essentially the same temporal sequence as they had in the text. (974)

Writers of mature summary, say Brown, Day, and Jones, use their own words to rearrange and recast the ideas presented in the original source. Mature summary was demonstrated by the eleventh-graders and first-year college students in their study. Brown, Day, and Jones assert that "the ability to provide an adequate written summary of a lengthy text is a late-developing skill that continues to be refined throughout the school years" (Brown, Day, and Jones 977).

Applying their research to my General Education class would suggest that my patchwriters were not cheating but employing a strategy of summary writing. But according to the Brown, Day, and Jones taxonomy, the strategy they chose placed them at a fifth- or sixth-grade level! This, too, seems implausible. I was teaching students who were admitted on a very competitive basis to a prestigious college.

Yet Carol Sherrard's research adduces similar findings. Whereas Brown, Day, and Jones' first-year college students engaged in "mature summary" of narrative texts, all ten of the undergraduates in Sherrard's study resorted to copy-deletion when summarizing expository texts.

Why were Brown, Day, and Jones' college students writing mature summary, whereas all of Sherrard's and one-third of mine were resorting to copy-deletion? One possible explanation is that Brown, Day, and Jones' students were summarizing narrative texts, while Sherrard's and mine were facing the more cognitively difficult challenge of summarizing exposition. As Joseph M. Williams has noted, students' control over basic skills exhibited in narrative writing has been demonstrated to break down under the greater cognitive burden of producing expository writing (253). A similar continuum might prevail in the reading of narrative and expository texts.

Another possible explanation is that the students in Sherrard's study and my class were summarizing texts employing unfamiliar vocabulary and concepts. Since neither Brown, Day, and Jones nor Sherrard included the summarized text in their report of research, I cannot speculate on this possibility with regard to what they call their "subjects." But I know that my General Education students were, indeed, in foreign discourse territory. None of the concepts contained in Davidson's text had been previously introduced or discussed in class.

Copy-deletion, or what I prefer to call "patchwriting," may be a preliminary way of participating in unfamiliar discourse, of finding a way into it. Clifford Geertz argues that the academic disciplines are so discontinuous as to render cross-disciplinary communication difficult or even impossible, and that key terms are the locus of that discontinuity (160–1). If we faculty have difficulty comprehending and manipulating the languages of the various academic cultures, how much more difficult a task do undergraduate students face as they are presented with a bewildering array of discourse, none of which resonates with the languages of their homes and secondary schools? Keith D. Miller's argument that Martin Luther King, Jr., was engaged in "voice merging" also illuminates the patchwriting practices of undergraduate writers. Miller's account attributes King's "plagiarism" (a word which does not appear in Miller's essay) to the oral traditions of the community of which King was a member. Similarly, my account attributes students' patchwriting to issues of community membership—but in this case it is the target community, not the community of which the students are members, that precipitates the textual strategy. Kathryn T. Flannery, recapitulating Susan Miller, explains, "Students are always caught 'intertextually'—they are never inventing a new language out of nothing, but patch together fragments of the multiple texts, the multiple voices (as Bakhtin would put it) that are already available to them" (707). If, however, students are working in discourse so foreign that the only voice available is the one which they are reading, the eclectic "patching" that is such a natural, normal resource for composing becomes limited to the text at hand. The writers have no choice but to patch monologically from that text.

If that is the case, their patchwriting is a positive rather than negative trait. It is not "immature summary"; it is the outsider's membership application, a way of acquiring the language of the target community. The target community, the academy, will not accept the application, will not find it sufficient. Valued members of the academic community do not patchwrite.

THE SUMMARY RESPONSE

But it is the task of teachers to help outsiders gain entry, and the professor must devise pedagogy that responds to the larger cultural motivation for the patchwriting. This pedagogy would recognize patchwriting as an occasion for teaching. Teaching the rules of plagiarism or source-attribution, however, is an insufficient and perhaps peripheral response. On instrumentalist criteria alone, it has been demonstrated ineffective, as Frank J. McCormick has noted: instruction in the rules of plagiarism does not prevent students from transgressing.

Teaching the rules of plagiarism or source-attribution fails because it does not address the motivation for patchwriting. It does not respond to students' need for a set of latch-keys that might unlock new discourse communities. The rules of plagiarism help mark and bound the academy, identifying its insiders and outsiders, disciplining its participants. But although the applicant does need to know what the boundaries are, that identification does not carry with it the knowledge of how to enter the hermetic circle. Summary-writing, in contrast, represents one of the latch-keys by means of which an outsider might traverse the boundaries and become a participant.

Yet summary-writing has earned a bad name in composition studies. David Bartholomae believes it perpetuates students' status as outsiders:

> Much of the written work that students do is test-taking, report or summary—work that places them outside the official discourse of the academic community, where they are expected

to admire and report on what we do, rather than inside that discourse, where they can do its work and participate in a common enterprise. This, however, is a failure of teachers and curriculum designers, who speak of writing as a mode of learning but all too often represent writing as a 'tool' to be used by an (hopefully) educated mind. (144)

Similarly, Russell K. Durst's research suggests that students who are writing in the analytic mode engage in "metacognitive, self-regulatory behaviors," whereas they approach the task of writing summary in a much more superficial way (373). (Durst does demur, however: "the paucity of higher-level thinking we saw in summary writing is due in part to the nature of the specific task students were given in this study, which was to summarize a narrative") (374).

Harry Edward Shaw, in contrast, places a positive value on summary-writing: "Encourage students to paraphrase if they must rehearse an author's arguments: paraphrasing well usually requires them to understand a passage" (126). Sandra Stotsky waxes much more specific in her recommendations:

Another way to conceptualize new vocabulary in writing is through various forms of precis or summary writing, although this particular value of precis writing has not been mentioned in discussions of precis writing. Summary writing requires selection and generalization in order to reduce passages to a given proportion of words. Sometimes the key words in a passage must be retained; at other times a more general term for specific ideas must be found. Basic writing teachers might consider guiding their students by suggesting beforehand some of the key words they want their students to use in writing the summary of a particular passage. (340)

A learner-external paradigm might characterize summary-writing as a potential means of providing a novice with requisite vocabulary for entering a discourse community, for participating in its meaning-making. By struggling through and then beyond patchwriting in the effort to summarize difficult prose, students can assimilate new concepts and new vocabulary to the extent that they might move beyond the cut-and-paste of patchwriting and learn to manipulate that vocabulary in their own discussion of the concepts.

Summary writing has a variety of additional benefits. Applying the principles of Young, Becker, and Pike, John C. Bean declares, "[A] systematic program of summary writing may be a particularly effective tool for helping students overcome egocentrism" (344). Alice Drum also advocates the cognitive benefits of summary. Like Frank D'Angelo, she offers pedagogical techniques that emphasize matters stylistic.

My own classes now undertake to reanimate summary writing, in the highly structured mode of Behrens and Rosen's *Writing and Reading Across the Curriculum*. I review (and in some cases introduce) the whole congeries of skills that Brown, Day, and Jones say students must acquire in order to summarize academic expository prose successfully (977). I encourage my students to make use of summary not just when it is overtly assigned but also as an aid to their own studies—though I caution them to judge their texts carefully to determine which ones warrant the rigors of formal summary (see McGinley and Tierney). While acknowledging the complexities of the task, I tell students that they must read—and talk—until they understand; that only then will they be able to summarize successfully. I tell them that while they are drafting summary, they should not be looking at the original text. I tell them they could even go so far as to allow an hour to elapse between the time they read the original and the time they write about it.

But at the same time that I teach the learner-internal "skills" of summary-writing, I also engage my students in collaborative oral summaries of assigned readings, inquiry of the type described by Mariolina Salvatori: inquiry not so much into the text of the assigned reading as into the text produced by the student who is attempting to understand it. At the beginning of class, I call upon students to recount whatever they can remember of the assigned reading. I act as secretary, writing their recollections on the board. Other class members make their own contributions, and we piece together a summary of the assignment, with the entire class offering revisions. The silences in this collaborative text, the things they have collectively forgotten, usually turn out to be the difficult passages of the assignment, the parts where, if I have assigned written summary, they have patchwritten; and we turn to these passages and enter them together in a spirit of questioning, supplementing, and wondering. The students learn summary-writing as a means not just of understanding texts but of interrogating them, and they learn that through this interrogation, each reader produces her own text.

The students groan under the burden but celebrate the results: the composition class taught at the intersection of patchwriting, synonymy, and learning produces students who can comprehend and synthesize sources, learners who are empowered not at the "merely cognitive" level of knowing that they should do it (see Maimon et al., xvii-xix) but also at the metacognitive level of knowing how—and why. And the "why" is not "because you must not steal or lie" nor "because you must obey the rules," but rather "because you can join the people who understand, talk about, and change these ideas." In this pedagogy, incidents of patchwriting signal efforts to appropriate the discourse of the new community rather than an occasion for adjudication. And instruction in summary-writing turns students not into rote recipients of others' ideas but into members of a community who meet, challenge, modify, and perhaps even replace its constructs.

Works Cited

Bartholomae, David. "Inventing the University." In *When a Writer Can't Write: Studies in Writer's Block and Other Composing-Process Problems.* NY: The Guilford P, 1985. 134–165.

Bean, John C. "Summary Writing, Rogerian Listening, and Dialectic Thinking." *College Composition and Communication* 37 (October 1986): 343–45.

Behrens, Laurence, and Leonard J. Rosen. *Writing and Reading Across the Curriculum.* 3rd ed. Glenview IL: Scott, Foresman, 1988.

Berkenkotter, Carol. "Paradigm Debates, Turf Wars, and the Conduct of Sociocognitive Inquiry in Composition." *College Composition and Communication* 42 (May 1991): 151–169.

Brown, A.L., J.D. Day, and R.S. Jones. "The Development of Plans for Summarizing Texts." *Child Development* 54 (August 1983): 968–79.

D'Angelo, Frank J. "The Art of Paraphrase." *College Composition and Communication* 30 (October 1979): 255–59.

Davidson, Robert. *Genesis 1–11.* Cambridge: Cambridge UP, 1973.

Drum, Alice. "Responding to Plagiarism." *College Composition and Communication* 37 (May 1986): 241–43.

Durst, Russell K. "Cognitive and Linguistic Demands of Analytic Writing." *Research in the Teaching of English* 21 (December 1987): 347–76.

Flannery, Kathryn T. "Composing and the Question of Agency." Rev. of *Writing as Social Action*, by Marilyn Cooper and Michael

Holzman; *Reclaiming Pedagogy: The Rhetoric of the Classroom,* ed. Patricia Donahue and Ellen Quandahl; *Rescuing the Subject: A Critical Introduction to Rhetoric and the Writer,* by Susan Miller; *Expecting the Unexpected: Teaching Myself—and Others—to Read and Write,* by Donald Murray; and *The Presence of Thought: Introspective Accounts of Reading and Writing,* by Marilyn Sternglass. *College English* 53 (October 1991): 701–13.

Geertz, Clifford. *Local Knowledge.* New York: Basic Books, 1983.

Hacker, Diana. *The Bedford Handbook for Writers.* 3rd ed. Boston: Bedford Books, 1991.

Maimon, Elaine P., Barbara F. Nodine, and Finbarr W. O'Connor, eds. *Thinking, Reasoning, and Writing.* New York: Longman, 1989.

McCormick, Frank. "The *Plagiario* and the Professor in Our Peculiar Institution." *Journal of Teaching Writing* 8 (Fall/Winter 1989): 133–146.

McGinley, William, and Robert J. Tierney. "Traversing the Topical Landscape: Reading and Writing as Ways of Knowing." *Written Communication* 6 (July 1989): 243–69.

Miller, Keith D. "Composing Martin Luther King, Jr." *PMLA* 105 (January 1990): 70–82.

Salvatori, Mariolina. "Pedagogy: From the Periphery to the Center." *Reclaiming Pedagogy: The Rhetoric of the Classroom.* Ed. Patricia Donahue and Ellen Quandahl. Carbondale: Southern Ill UP, 1989. 17–34.

Shaw, Harry Edmund. "Responding to Student Essays." In *Teaching Prose: A Guide for Writing Instructors.* Ed. Fredric V. Bogel et al. New York: W.W. Norton, 1984. 114–54.

Sherrard, Carol. "Summary Writing: A Topographical Study." *Written Communication* 3 (July 1986): 324–43.

Stotsky, Sandra. "Teaching the Vocabulary of Academic Discourse." *Journal of Basic Writing* 2 (1970): 15–39. Rpt. in *A Sourcebook for Basic Writing Teachers.* Ed. Theresa Enos. NY: Random House, 1987. 328–347.

Williams, Joseph M. "The Problem of Finding the Right Metaphor." In *Thinking, Reasoning, and Writing.* Ed. Elaine P. Maimon, Barbara F. Nodine, and Finbarr W. O'Connor. New York: Longman, 1989. 245–55.

Worsham, Lynn. "Writing against Writing: The Predicament of *Ecriture Feminine* in Composition Studies." *Contending with Words: Composition and Rhetoric in a Postmodern Age.* Ed. Patricia Harkin and John Schilb. New York: MLA, 1991. 82–104.

Thinking and Writing Questions

1. What is patchwriting? Why, according to Howard, do writers end up plagiarizing the work of others by way of patchwriting?

2. Howard writes "A Plagiarism Pentimento" in first person. Both Bryant, in "Sexual 'Voices' in English 101," and Christensen, in "Teaching Standard English: Whose Standard,?" write in first person. Why would three academics who are writing for professional audiences use first person and tell personal stories? What impact do these authors achieve using first person?

3. Howard mentions Keith Miller's study of Martin Luther King, Jr.'s use of undocumented sources; from King's experiences of folk preaching, he "learned techniques of delivery, the practice of borrowing from oneself and others, and voice merging" (Miller "Composing" 78). Howard claims that King's "voice merging" "illuminates the patching practices of undergraduate writers" (121). As you read or reread "Redefining Plagiarism: Martin Luther King's Use of an Oral Tradition" by Keith Miller, note how Dr King's story sheds light on the process of patchwriting. How did Dr. King use patchwriting to develop his voice?

4. Examine how Howard summarizes and quotes the work of others. For what purposes does she include the words, voices, and ideas of others in "A Plagiarism Pentimento"? How does she integrate the words and ideas of others into her own prose? Does Howard "practice what she preaches"?

5. Outline your experience of learning how to work with the ideas and words of others in your prose. You might begin by remembering when you began to read and then summarize or write about the works of an author. Were you taught how to summarize? Did you create index cards that had the documentation information for your sources and significant quotes? Did you practice patchwriting? Why? What else do you need to learn about crafting prose that smoothly integrates the words and ideas of others?

Redefining Plagiarism: Martin Luther King's Use of an Oral Tradition

KEITH D. MILLER

Keith D. Miller teaches writing at Arizona State University in Tempe, AZ, where he has served as Associate Chair of the Department of English and as director of the first-year writing program. He frequently teaches in interdisciplinary Learning Communities for first-year undergraduates. Miller is an expert in the rhetoric and songs of the civil rights movement. He is the author of Voice of Deliverance: The Language of Martin Luther King, Jr., and Its Sources. *His essays on Martin Luther King, Jr., Malcolm X, Jackie Robinson, Frederick Douglass, and others have appeared in journals such as* College English, College Composition and Communication, *and* Journal of American History. *He is finishing a book tentatively titled* Martin Luther King's Biblical Epic: His Final and Greatest Speech. *"Redefining Plagiarism" is taken from* The Chronicle of Higher Education, *a publication for faculty and administrators in higher education. Miller explores how Dr. King developed his speaking style and writing voice by using passages from other speeches and essays. Miller encourages the academic community to reconsider its traditional definition of plagiarism.*

--------------- ✦ ---------------

Many people know that Martin Luther King, Jr., plagiarized large portions of his doctoral dissertation. Fewer realize that King used unacknowledged sources throughout his entire public career. He mined others' words for key passages in his famous "I Have a Dream" speech, in his "Letter From Birmingham Jail," in his lecture accepting the Nobel Peace Prize, in several of his books, and in literally scores of published and unpublished addresses and essays. Because these works electrified millions of people and helped transform American race relations, they are enormously more important than King's esoteric dissertation, which, as I write these words, remains unpublished and little read.

Just as King's academic writing raises ethical issues, so does his later, thoroughly characteristic use of unacknowledged sources. Simply put, we face a contradiction: We wish to lionize a man for his powerful language while decrying a major strategy that made his words resonate and persuade. How could such a compelling leader commit what most people define as a writer's worst sin? This contradiction should prompt us to rethink our definition of plagiarism. In much of King's public career, he drew on an oral tradition, forged during slavery, that rarely acknowledged sources. Is this plagiarism? Or should we accept different standards for oral presentations and for work intended for general, rather than academic, audiences?

I literally stumbled on these issues nine years ago in my father's ministerial study. Working on a dissertation about King's language, I casually picked up a well-thumbed collection of sermons and was surprised to find a sermon with a title similar to the title of one of King's speeches. Written by Halford Luccock in 1952, the homily began with an illustration—Rip Van Winkle sleeping through a revolution—that King employed in the 1960's. Knowing that a friend had made a similar discovery earlier, I scoured the library at Texas Christian University and, sure enough, located other texts with language that overlapped King's. Most were written by Harry Emerson Fosdick, Luccock, and other luminaries of the liberal Protestant pulpit—both black and white—a generation or two older than King.

In 1986, two years after finishing my dissertation, I began publishing scholarly essays about King's use of sources without acknowledgment throughout his career. Apart from a few curmudgeonly letters to editors, these essays drew little response.

In late 1990, *The Wall Street Journal* reported that the team of scholars editing King's papers at Stanford University had discovered King's repeated appropriation of others' language in his graduate essays and doctoral dissertation. News outlets relayed the story across the nation. My research was mentioned in the *Journal* story and in several other accounts, but the press concentrated on King's wooden and obscure graduate essays. Struggling to finish my book on King's sources and fearing piecemeal, sensationalized journalism, I refused to talk to reporters at length until my own findings were complete and in print. King deserved the best, most comprehensive account of his language that I could muster—not sentences blurted over the phone to a reporter.

When my book, *Voice of Deliverance: The Language of Martin Luther King, Jr., and Its Sources* (Free Press, 1992), did appear, it included the substantive material from my dissertation and essays. It also laid out—for the first time—lengthy sources for King's Nobel Prize lecture, "Letter From Bitmingham, Jail," and literally dozens of his other addresses and essays.

Although I was lucky enough to garner several reviews, interviews, and feature stories, few reporters treated my disclosures as news. They said: "We've heard this before." But King's public language raises issues about plagiarism and copyright as important—or more important—than those surrounding his academic discourse.

Probing King's rich, often borrowed language, I spent years attempting to fathom his father's folk preaching, which King heard as a child and adolescent. I studied available folk sermons and interviewed his father, his mentors, colleagues, and older members of his boyhood church. The ancient parchment voice and bright memories of King's third-grade Sunday school teacher, the Rev. J. H. Edwards, proved particularly helpful.

Mr. Edwards and others taught me that folk preachers—who were not formally trained—often swapped sermons. Legally forbidden to read and write, slaves had created a highly oral religious culture that treated songs and sermons as shared wealth, not private property. During and after slavery, African-American folk preachers gained stature by merging their identities with earlier, authoritative bearers of the Word. In this context, striking originality might have seemed self-centered or otherwise suspect. While growing up, King absorbed this tradition, hearing religious themes and metaphors that originated during slavery.

SEMINARY-TRAINED WHITE PREACHERS—both workaday ministers like my father and famous ones like Fosdick—also borrowed and adapted sermons. I traced many of King's themes, illustrations, quotations, and metaphors through collection after collection of Protestant homilies. King's sermon "Antidotes to Fear" had more than a dozen precedents in print, and the title and structure of his sermon "What Is Man?" (based on Psalms 8:4) date back at least to John Wesley in the 18th century.

Even though white preachers often borrowed from each other, professors in seminaries and the ministers themselves registered a deep ambivalence about the practice. Their confusion rose as clergy published sermons, funneling their oral messages into the contrasting container of print. The copyright strictures on publication developed because print enables the tracing of words and their antecedents. In an oral culture, beyond broad themes and metaphors, such tracing is difficult even to conceive because nothing is written down.

The designers of copyright protections assume that noteworthy language springs from a writer's individuality. By contrast, preachers strive to deliver the same Gospel message, not an original world view. Unable to resolve the conflict between oral religious practices and those of print, leading white professors and ministers sometimes castigated borrowing and other times accepted or even encouraged it. One famous pastor told preachers never to borrow, but then published a collection of illustrations for their sermons—drawn from other people's sermons.

Just as that minister attempted to do, we must decide how to define plagiarism within the context of an oral tradition. Whatever we may wish, King used unacknowledged sources habitually. The "Let freedom ring!" conclusion of his "I Have a

Dream" speech came from an address by Archibald Carey, a black pastor in Chicago. Failing to understand King's source means failing to understand King's speech and its roots in the black pulpit. Once we attend to King's sources; however, do we condemn him as a plagiarist, grant him (and some other groups such as preachers) a dispensation from the rules of copyright, or rethink plagiarism?

The questions raised by the conflicting demands of oral and print cultures reverberate far beyond King and other preachers. For example, a lawyer asked me for advice in defending a Native American student charged with plagiarizing papers in law school. The student came from an oral culture, he explained, and could not immediately understand or obey the rules of written English. Tutors at our writing center tell me that some international students confront a similar dilemma. King's example thus is not an isolated case. While we must teach students to avoid plagiarism, we also need to appreciate the difficulties that some may have in negotiating the boundaries between oral and print traditions.

With respect to copyrighted materials, we need to understand the dilemma of those whose voices have historically been excluded. They may experience a huge problem in attempting to sound like themselves while still reaching a mainstream audience. If they speak entirely in their own voices, as Malcolm X did, they may risk being marginalized by the majority, as he was. To guarantee that they will be heard by Middle America, they must take pains to insure that they sound like majority speakers. When the mainstream culture is alien, that problem can be formidable.

Clearly, we need to re-examine our definition of plagiarism. That will be a long and difficult process, but scholars can take a first step toward doing so by recognizing that some groups, for example preachers, will continue to share discourse, whatever copyright restrictions are imposed upon them. Other people will struggle as well to conduct rhetorical transactions between the sometimes conflicting, sometimes overlapping universes of oral and print communication. I am convinced that the process of securing fundamental human rights—such as those King championed—outweighs the right to the exclusive use of intellectual and literary property. I hope scholars will join in discussing new guidelines to address these issues.

Simply put, the offense of plagiarism is much more complex and much more ethically relative that we have wanted to admit.

Thinking and Writing Questions

1. Lay out Miller's argument for redefining plagiarism. What is his reasoning for suggesting such a review of this sensitive topic? Write an outline identifying the main points of Miller's argument.

2. Why does Miller begin with listing Dr. King's academic offences? What purpose does this serve? How does it enhance his ultimate argument? Or does it? What choice might you make if you were addressing *The Chronicle of Higher Education*'s audience?

3. When Miller talks about the Native American student accused of plagiarism, the defense was that "the student came from an oral culture . . . and could not immediately understand or obey the written rules of English" ("Redefining" 131). Could one view this student as being in the process of constructing a voice as argued by Bryant? Defend or refute this idea using Bryant's piece to support your ideas.

4. Study two or three of Dr. King's speeches to identify the voices that Miller is writing about. You might begin by rereading Miller's essay to make a list of the voice elements that you will be looking for. Another piece by Miller has been added in the Works Cited. You might want to add to your list of voice elements by checking your writing textbook. Then apply these elements to the works of Dr. King. *YouTube* has a few of his speeches.

Chapter 3: Thinking and Writing Questions

1. How has your voice developed? You might begin to answer this question by collecting as many pieces of past writing as you can: journals, diaries, letters, poems, speeches, elementary and high school writings. Study the types of words and sentences you chose to use, the topics you wrote about, and the attitudes you portrayed toward your topics: your angle of vision (Ramage, Bean and Johnson, 80). What personalities have you created with these choices? If we were to meet the person whose persona is shining through your words, how would we describe him or her? Serious? Sarcastic? Funny? Is your voice different in different types of texts? What conclusions can you draw about how you have constructed and reconstructed your voices? What facilitated these changes? Write a report for your classmates and teacher that explains your findings.

2. Many stories in *Essays on Writing* recount examples of writers' voices being judged, altered, and quieted. At times, teachers directly tell student writers to alter their voices. Christensen tells us about this in "Teaching Standard English: Whose Standard?" Other times, teachers silence our voices indirectly. Liz tells the story of Ms. Caldwell in the introduction to Chapter One about the teacher that told her she needed to learn how to write. And, there are times when the writer can't construct the needed voice. Harrington tells us about

General Apache's struggle to tell his story. bell hooks struggled to construct a voice to tell her autobiography. Make a list of the times that your voices have not spoken.

In Chapter Three, Bryant, Christensen, McCarthy, and Howard write about teaching that supports student writers and their voices. Reread the pieces noting how each approaches the students' struggles, comparing and contrasting their teaching strategies. Now, apply their teaching strategies to the examples you identified above. Which strategies would be most effective with you? Why? Write an evaluation of these different approaches using your examples as test cases.

3. Does plagiarism as a crime exist outside of the academic and professional worlds? Outside of the academic world, is it important to let others know that you are using the voice and ideas of another artist? Dr. King plagiarized his dissertation and continued to use the voices of other preachers in his speeches and sermons after he left the academy and began his work as the leading civil rights leader of our time. Assistant Professor of Finance Chris Dussold was fired from his position at Southern Illinois University for plagiarizing his teaching philosophy statement (McGrath). Glenn Poshard, President of Southern Illinois University, has been accused of plagiarism in his doctoral dissertation (Powers).

The practice of sampling in the music industry could also be seen as plagiarism. Take for example the story of white rapper Vanilla Ice's fall from popularity after he inserted clips of Queen's and David Bowie's song, "Under Pressure," in his hit "Ice Ice Baby" without acknowledging the sampling or paying for permission to use the sample. What about Bob Dylan's practice of creating "information collages" in his lyrics (Pareles). Investigate the stories of a few of these musical artists. Don't forget Puff Daddy's or P. Diddy's or Sean Combs' sampling. Research the group Negativland, an "experimental music and art collective" which has been sued for copyright infringement (Jenkins). Negativland's webpage reports that the band "re-arranges" parts of material taken from mass media that is owned by corporations "to make [these parts] say and suggest things that they never intended to say and suggest things they never intended to suggest."

Is there ever a time when plagiarism is acceptable? Write a narrative essay that records your exploration of this quandary of using other's words and ideas without permission or acknowledgement. Record your thinking as you explore this issue. You might decide to take a side or you might not.

4. How do we construct and reconstruct our voices to serve different purposes? Does your voice change when you beg forgiveness or when you ask your parents for money? When you tell a professor what he wants to hear to get a good grade on a paper? When you're looking for a boyfriend on the web like Heather Hunter does in "Traveling the Too-Much-Information Highway"? When crafting an identity on paper that allows you to tell your

story like bell hooks does in "writing autobiography"? When promoting a social cause to change the world? When politicking to become president?

Find an example of a public figure whose voice changed in different venues. You might examine the different voices of presidential candidate Barak Obama. On *YouTube*, find his speech at the 2004 Democratic National Convention, find his January 2008 speech at Dr. King's Ebenezer Baptist Church in Atlanta for Dr. King's birthday, and find the video done by Will.i.am of Obama's speech, "Yes We Can." Compose an analysis of how Obama's voice or the voice of the public figure you chose changed and why.

Works Cited

Halask, Kay. *A Pedagogy of Possibility: Bakhtinian Perspectives on Compositions Studies.* Carbonale, IL: Southern Illinois University Press, 1999.

Jenkins, Mark. "In Negativland's Plus Column; The Group's Victory Changes the Rules on Sampling." *The Washington Post* 20 (September 1998), G4.

McCarthy, Nora. Re: Rise mag. etc. E-mail to Liz Bryant. 5 March 2008.

McGrath, David. "Did Glenn Poshard's Dog Eat His Bibliography?" *EdNews.* 15 October 2007. http://www.ednews.org/articles/18426/1/Did-Glenn-Poshards-Dog-Eat-His-Bibliography-SIU-Presidents-Claims-and-the-Need-for-MLA-Reform/Page1.html, 9 March 2008.

Miller, Keith D. "Composing Martin Luther King, Jr." *PMLA* 105 (January 1990): 70–82.

"Negativland Bio." http://www.negativland.com/riaa/negbio.html. 9 March 2008.

Pareles, Jon. "Plagiarism in Dylan, or a Cultural Collage?" *New York Times.* 12 July 2003. www.nytimes.com/2003/07/12/arts/music/12DYLA.html?ex=1373428800&en=621a73700da7c178&ei=5007&partner=USERLAND, 7 March 2008.

Powers, Elia. "Southern Illinois President Cleared of Plagiarism" *Inside Higher Ed.* 12 October 2007. http://www.insidehighered.com/news/2007/10/12/siu, 9 March 2008.

Pratt, Mary Louise. 1991. "Arts of the Contact Zone." *Profession.* 33-40. New York: MLA.

Ramage, John D., John E. Bean, and June Johnson. *The Allyn and Bacon Guide to Writing.* 4th ed. New York: Pearson Longman, 2006.

CHAPTER 4

Technology and Integrity

Technology has changed the world. We air brush lumps from models. We mend pop stars' voices. We create avatars to match, or perhaps bend, our online identities. Most universities have systems in place for you to register for your classes, to have synchronous class discussions on line, and to check your grades. Your writing class might be in a computer lab where you research topics, compose drafts, and send them to classmates for review. You use spell check, grammar check, cut and paste, and other tools that are simply not as easy to perform when you put pen to paper.

According to a December 2007 study by Pew Internet and American Life Project, 33% of teens create or work on webpages or blogs for others, and 39% share their own artwork, photos, stories or videos (Lenhart et.al. i). Most interestingly, the study finds that "email continues to lose its luster among teens as texting, instant messaging, and social networking sites facilitate more frequent contact with friends" (iv).

Technology is part of our everyday writing. From emails and texting to term papers and online courses, technology plays a huge role in the way we approach writing and our writing processes.

Writing teachers have begun to sit up and take notice of this trend. In "Technology Transforms Writing and the Teaching of Writing," Wendy R. Leibowitz reports a conversation among several writing instructors as they lay out the pros and cons of technology and student writing. These instructors claim that student writing is longer—in quantity—and that students' pieces look better with graphics and design. They also find, however, that student writing lacks the quality of precise, critical thinking.

Technology also gives us another avenue to express ourselves: posting to discussion boards, MySpace, Facebook, and personal blogs. In "Traveling the Too-Much-Information Highway," Heather L. Hunter comments on the impact of sharing too much information (TMI). Hunter posts a love story on her blog, thinking this a "relatively safe" venue that would hide her identity (143). No longer is a love story written in a diary and shown to virtually no one. In this brave new world of technology, a blog is out there for the world—and possibly significant others—to see. She discovers the drawbacks to having TMI. Navigating these issues of identity and ownership becomes more and more difficult as technology continues to infiltrate our everyday lives and writing.

This ever-growing information highway has opened opportunities for students to buy and sell their writing. Websites that sell term papers abound, adding a series of ethical choices to busy students' lives. Websites claim to have your best interests at heart as they guarantee well-written pieces that are not plagiarized—pieces that guarantee your success in school. In "Adventures in Cheating," Seth Stevenson reviews several online term paper stores. He collected ten papers that were evaluated by three judges. Stevenson's goal is to help his readers figure out how to "do it right"—that is how to cheat (148). His study found that you don't always get what you pay for; sometimes you get less.

Nicole Kristal examines the scenario of buying and selling term papers from a different perspective. In "'Tutoring' Rich Kids Cost Me My Dreams," Kristal explains her position as an "academic prostitute" (153), a term she coined while writing papers for students in order to make ends meet. Kristal looks at the cost of this industry to the people who do the work and thinking for others. Her identity as an author was lost, handing over her "self-respect to rich losers" (155).

In "Of Plagiarism, Paper Mills and the Harried, Hurried Student," Maureen Hourigan posits reasons for plagiarism and discusses the consequences of plagiarism. She focuses on plagiarism from the perspective of the University and the instructor. In her research, Hourigan found that universities such as Rutgers are getting stringent in their punishment of plagiarism. Teachers are required to report plagiarism to University officials no matter the situation. Hourigan lays out the consequences of plagiarism even looking at how the honest student is penalized when some students turn in papers that are plagiarized.

As you read these pieces, contemplate your relationship with technology and the information highway. What impact is technology having on you and your writing? Are you writing more prose that is less insightful? Are you creating new personas online? Have you been using shortcuts in your text messaging and emails that have slipped into your academic writing? Are you beguiled by term paper sites that promise you more time to play and a good grade on your paper? What path are you taking along the information highway?

Technology Transforms Writing and the Teaching of Writing

WENDY LEIBOWITZ

Attorney and journalist Wendy R. Leibowitz is a graduate of the Columbia School of Journalism and Stanford Law School. She has written about technology and law for The National Law Journal *and* The American Lawyer. *She practiced criminal defense law with* The Legal Aid Society *before joining an intellectual property firm and then leaving the law for journalism. She is currently the associate editor of* Big Builder Magazine. *In "Technology Transforms Writing and the Teaching of Writing," which first appeared in* The Chronicle of Higher Education, *Leibowitz examines how technology has both helped and hindered students' writing abilities.*

✦

Ever since the days when students wrote in chalk on slates, or dipped quills into ink pots, technology and writing have been closely connected. But computers are affecting students' writing in ways unlike any other technology in the memory of their instructors.

Professors say students come to college accustomed to writing in the unstructured, chatty style of e-mail discussions, but not in formal prose. Students submit essays that are longer but not better written than those in years past. Worse, many students do not revise or even proofread their work, relying instead on software to check spelling and grammar.

"Computers make everyone write a lot more, and a lot longer. But they're absolutely not making them write better," says April Bernard, who teaches literature at Bennington College.

For students' writing, faculty members say, the new technology presents both perils and possibilities.

The perils are clearer. "Students will tinker endlessly with the text and forget that their paper doesn't have a thesis," says Kathleen Skubikowski, an assistant professor of English who directs the writing program at Middlebury College.

"I receive immaculately word-processed documents that are just terrible," says David Galef, an associate professor of English at the University of Mississippi.

The possibilities are exciting, but their effectiveness is largely unproved, say faculty members who teach writing. Many of the professors are looking for ways to make good use of the tools that students are already using.

Drafts of papers can be e-mailed to professors, and sensitive critiques can be delivered the same way, in a medium that is conducive to private "conversations." In computer-equipped classrooms, assignments can be easily distributed among students or posted in a collective electronic space. Students' work can be published on the World-Wide Web, attracting feedback from readers elsewhere who may be neither peers nor professors—and exposing the students to a wider variety of opinions.

"The one good thing that everyone always says" about technology, says Sven Birkerts, a lecturer in writing at Mount Holyoke College, "is that it seems to reduce the initial intimidation factor in writing itself.

"It's easier to get students to generate quantitative amounts of prose—and if you don't look too closely, that's a plus," says Mr. Birkerts, who describes himself as a "techno-skeptic." But on closer examination, he says, it is really a minus. "Where writing is concerned, quantity and quality are in an inverse relation. The very nature of technology generates a vast amount of prose and discourages the next step, which would be to prune, winnow, consolidate it. Give it texture and depth. That can't be done by the machine."

Students' unwillingness to revisit words that have scrolled off their screen may be the computer's most unfortunate literary legacy. "There is [a] tendency to write and never look back, alas," says Roslyn Bernstein, a professor of English and journalism at Baruch College of the City University of New York. "This means that students use a conversational voice, and that they do not proofread or copy-edit their writing. I generally make it clear to students that I expect carefully written prose, and I circle each and every problem area on the first paper."

She then requires a second draft. In fact, students send her drafts of their papers via e-mail throughout the semester. She emphasizes structure and organization, as well as transitions between ideas.

Rewriting, which many professors say is the essence of writing, is a slow process, and the computer culture encourages speed. Some writing professors are responding by trying to teach students how to slow down. "I try to build assignments around revision," says Mr. Birkerts. "A week or so will go by, and then I'll require them to look at their work, so the psychological distance is there."

He prefers a total rewrite. "It's easy with computers to say, 'Lines four, five, and six are fine,' and make quick, local changes." But, he acknowledges, "I'm battling a serious tendency" against slow, considered writing. "I can't claim any big success rate."

Revision is hardly the only issue. Good writers must be good readers, but students glued to the screen are neither, say faculty members. "They read more casually. They strip-mine what they read" on the Internet, says Mr. Birkerts. Those casual reading habits, in turn, produce "quickly generated, casual prose," he says. "They do not enter very deeply into either the syntax or the ideas" of an article.

What's more, writing on a computer has altered the process of composition, says Leslie C. Perelman, director of writing across the curriculum and an associate dean of undergraduate education at the Massachusetts Institute of Technology. When using a pen or a typewriter, writers usually think out the entire sentence before committing it to paper, he notes. "Otherwise, you end up crossing out a lot. It gets very messy. But on a computer, no one does that. People will start a sentence and then go back and move things around, because our computer screen is elastic. Therefore, the composing process has become very elastic."

Middlebury's Ms. Skubikowski says she notices an "additive style" in students' writing, in which sentences and thoughts pour out with all the structure of a small child's speech: "And this happened. And then that. And so then this." Such a style might work in an on-line discussion, where remarks cascade and build on each other. It is wonderful for brainstorming, she says. But such a collage of thoughts can translate into poor structure in a formal essay.

Ms. Skubikowski says she has learned to focus on what is essential to writing: precise thinking. "The tools will always change. We must teach what won't change. That's the connection between critical thinking and critical writing. At the center is precise thinking—the ability to articulate what you know."

Ms. Bernard, of Bennington, says students who want to articulate their thoughts clearly may, over time, even return to pen-on-paper outlines. "E-mail is here to stay, and certain types of computer conversations are here to stay, but I'm optimistic that they will wind up being adjunct to traditional forms of writing. I encourage students not to write their first drafts on a computer, so they might actually think before putting words on the page."

Elizabeth McCracken, a visiting faculty member at the University of Iowa Writers' Workshop, combats wordiness by asking students to print out their work. "If you don't print something out, you can forget how long it is, because all you can see is what you see through the keyhole of the screen," she says.

However, Diane Davis, a professor of rhetoric at Iowa, is enthusiastic about the combination of technology and writing. She encourages her students to publish their writing on the Web as a way of expanding their understanding of who the reader is.

"I haven't seen any evidence of student writing getting sloppier in print, even after they spend time in electronic writing spaces where slang, misspellings, and creative shorthand are the norm," she says. "On the contrary, my students seem to develop a kind of rhetorical savvy about this very quickly. What you can get away with in e-mail is a no-no in an essay."

Publishing her students' work on line improves their writing at all stages, Ms. Davis argues. "I've noticed that when students realize their work is going on line, in a Web journal or something similar, they tend to work harder." When students can receive e-mail responses to their posted writings from anywhere in the world, they pay more attention to how they can best express their ideas, and they worry about how poorly written prose may look to their readers, she says.

Telling students that their professor and their classmates will read their work does not have the same effect, says Ms. Davis. "They know that when it comes down to it, the real audience is the teacher—and the teacher is not a very interesting audience. But when I say, 'You're going to put this work on the Web, offer your e-mail address, and submit it to search engines,' students get excited."

The same technology that makes written works accessible to readers from across the world can also let students work more closely with classmates across the campus. E-mail and electronic bulletin boards let them exchange critiques 24 hours a day.

David Brown, provost of Wake Forest University and dean of the International Center for Computer-Enhanced Learning there, says it's "extremely useful" if students use collaborative tools to comment on each others' essays. "There is simply more communication, more collaboration, more accountability in the system" with high-tech tools, he says.

Indeed, many students have become so unused to the physical act of writing at length with pen and paper that M.I.T. no longer herds entering students into classrooms to produce writing samples on paper in the placement process for required writing courses. Now they submit the samples over the Web before arriving on the campus, says Mr. Perelman, the associate dean. "We allow them to use an on-line thesaurus, the grammar checkers and spell checkers, because in the real world people are allowed to use those tools," he says. "Most grammar checkers hurt more than they help, and we tell them that." The goal is to help students write as they will at M.I.T. and later in the professional world. "The move to the Web has been a major success," he says. "The technology has changed the way people write."

As students and professors alike strive for "electracy"—a neologism coined by Gregory Ulmer, an English professor at the University of Florida, to mean fluency in the new digital media—Iowa's Ms. Davis says electronic writing is taking its place alongside oral and print literacy.

"The Web is where we're all going," says Robert Coover, a professor of English at Brown University. "It is now the dominant medium of expression and communication. My own workshops make extensive use of it. The digital revolution and the rush to the Internet that followed on its heels seem, from this *fin-de-siecle* vantage point, irresistible and to be with us indefinitely. It has, more or less overnight, become a fundamental element of literacy."

The ability to write effective e-mail messages, for example, has become so important in the business world that M.I.T. now has a credit course on e-mail writing. "E-mail is an entirely different form" from other kinds of writing, says Mr. Perelman, who teaches the course. It will soon be required of all M.I.T. students.

"Be sure the [subject] header indicates very specifically what you're talking about," he tells students. "Have a short introductory sentence that summarizes what you're going to say in the body, because people get many e-mails a day."

Not everyone is a fan of e-mail. Mr. Galef, the English professor at Mississippi, says student prose is more emotional now than it used to be, which he thinks might be an outgrowth of e-mail culture. "On e-mail, people call up an address and just pour out anything they're thinking. It's anal-expulsive rather than anal-retentive."

But professors from many disciplines notice that many students who are quiet in the classroom will speak up in cyberspace, participating in e-mail discussions, posting on message boards, or asking questions during "e-office hours," when professors respond to e-mailed questions. Writing teachers in particular notice the new voices. "I had one international student tell me that he doesn't have an accent on line," says Ms. Skubikowski.

Many professors say computers also call into question the extent to which writing is a physical act as well as an intellectual one. "The real loss, students tell me, is the physical attachment to their writing—pressing down on the pen, thinking and feeling the word as your hand writes it out," says Ms. Skubikowski.

That slow, manual process touches the soul, she says. "Students who write essays on screen say they would never write a poem on screen."

Thinking and Writing Questions

1. Wendy Leibowitz claims that writing with technology can have both positive and negative consequences. Generate a list of these consequences. Pick at least one positive and one negative consequence, make a few notes about how these consequences have been manifested in your writing career, then tell your writing partner about your experiences.

2. This article is clearly written from an educator's perspective with quotes from eleven college professors. How might the article have to change to be written for students? Rewrite a section of the essay for an audience of college students.

3. Leibowitz reports that technology has encouraged students to produce more prose that lacks critical thought. The pieces in Chapter Two on the processes of writing address the need for writers to develop their ideas. Donald Murray calls this internal revision in which writers construct, refine, and develop the content of their writing. How can teachers employ technology to help students improve quality in their writing? How can teachers use a blog, a PowerPoint presentation, or other technology to teach internal revision?

4. Leibowitz reports that computers have also added to students' inability to read. Students "strip mine what they read" (139). What does this mean? Do you do this type of reading? Why do you read this way?

Traveling the Too-Much-Information Highway
HEATHER HUNTER

Heather L. Hunter is a technical writer living in New York City. Her thoughts can be found on her blog "This Fish Needs a Bicycle" at http://thisfish.ivillage.com. Hunter began this blog to complain about a romantic relationship. Because many enjoyed it, she continued the blog, and iVillage asked Hunter to move her blog to their website for a salary. In "Traveling the Too-Much-Information Highway," which first appeared in the New York Times, *Hunter examines the impact of sharing TMI online.*

✦

I AM a blogger. An emotional exhibitionist. On a daily basis I make my Dear Diary entries available online to the general public. A few years ago, I began writing my Web log to vent about a particularly difficult relationship.

It was therapeutic, relatively safe and vastly preferable to, say, slashing my boyfriend's tires. To my faceless Internet audience, I could express raw, sometimes grossly undignified aspects of my day-to-day life without fear of being judged, misunderstood or rejected (at least not to my face).

Love-scorned and willing to share every gory detail, albeit anonymously, I had, within my first year of blogging, effectively vilified my ex-boyfriend to the Web-surfing masses (2,000 daily readers, at last count). Sex sells. Apparently, so does angst. But these days, while I am hardly shy about revealing juicy details of romantic encounters with foreign tourists, I have become much less inclined to tell the whole, sordid truth. I have learned the hard way that there can be such a thing as too much information.

My story begins in the fall of 2003, when I met the Musician— or, I should say, I met his blog. I was immediately drawn to the openness of his writing, and we soon developed a close friendship through e-mail and instant messages. Long before we met in person, he knew about my compulsive housecleaning, trust issues and addiction to Ben & Jerry's cookie dough ice cream. In turn, I knew about his fears of flying and commitment, and his grand passion for aviator sunglasses.

When we finally got together one cold night in late November, the resulting romance became an intriguing addition to my blog. From our snowy weekend at a cozy Connecticut inn to our frenzied moments in the bathroom stall of a seedy Brooklyn bar, I taunted readers with the details of our spicy affair.

During the summer I began to see less of him. In fact, weeks and then months passed when I did not see him at all, unless I happened to pay the cover charge to attend one of his performances. He was always glad to see me and was as charming and affectionate as ever, but he hadn't asked me to meet for coffee, catch a movie or take one of our walks by the river in ages.

He said he was busy, and I empathized. After all, his blog looked like an extraordinarily complex to-do list: documentaries, marathon training, concerts, family obligations. Rather than appear needy, and knowing quite well that pushing for "face time" would send him reeling in the opposite direction, I settled for keeping up via hasty instant messages and the occasional e-mail, and by checking his blog.

One afternoon, after finding his entry to be nothing more than a dull account of rehearsal schedules and late-night dinners ("Healthy Choice turkey, potatoes and vegetables"), I started clicking through some of the newer blog links on his site and quickly found myself caught up with one in particular, the diary of a young photographer. Accompanied by striking photos of its pretty Web mistress were scandalous tales of her Manhattan dating life: bizarre one-night stands, the indiscretions of B-list celebrities, hot and steamy cab rides. I was immediately hooked. I was also struck by an odd feeling of familiarity while reading about this girl's social engagements. And then, I saw it: the Musician's name—my musician—mentioned as her date for the previous evening.

Oh. I see.

While I'd known he was dating other people (I hadn't exactly turned a blind eye to the mascara smudge I'd seen on the collar of his jacket one night), I never expected to be privy to the actual play-by-play. My face grew warm as I read about their candlelit dinner (lamb was on the menu) and night out at swanky clubs in the meatpacking district (she had worn falsies). My God, he'd even kissed her good night in full view of her doorman—this, the same guy who had told me of his fierce objection to public displays of affection. Kissing! In front of her doorman! I had to fight the overwhelming urge to flee to the ladies' room and hurl my Starbucks iced mocha.

Because the Musician and I had met through our respective Web logs—and thus always understood that oversharing was an inherent risk—our relationship had never been terribly traditional. We didn't seem to spend time wondering what the other person was thinking. In my case, I figured I'd just write about it anyway.

But unlike me, the Musician rarely wrote about his dating habits. He had conspicuously failed to blog about our own relationship, and so I was blissfully ignorant of other women in his life. Suddenly, with the discovery of the Young Photographer's blog, that bliss was gone. Gone also were the days when I assumed night-vision goggles would be necessary to stalk a lover. All I had to do was open my Internet Explorer. Although good sense told me that blog-stalking my lover's lover wasn't the healthiest approach to the situation, compulsion trumped reason, and I stalked freely.

It wasn't long before I knew about her preferred sexual position (her toes had to be pointed), her birth control (the pill) and her cup size (34C). And the more I read, the more I was convinced that she was more stylish, more intelligent and more charming than I could ever be. If she wrote about applying a "contouring duo" eye shadow before one of her dates with the Musician, my mind raced: Did I even own a contouring duo, much less know how to use one? If she mentioned wearing vintage Chanel to a press junket, I became painfully aware of the conspicuous lack of silk, vintage or otherwise, in my wardrobe. I bought more silk.

Still, it remained: my shoes weren't expensive enough, my social engagements not nearly as glamorous, and my freckles not half as lovable. Despite knowing that he didn't expose his love life in his blog, I began combing through the Musician's daily entries for any mention of her and for any unthinkable indication that he might like her more than me.

I had been in nonexclusive relationships before and had demonstrated my ability to share perfectly well with others. In fact, I had found I preferred being the other woman to being the woman in most cases. But idly wondering what the object of my affection was up to, and knowing what he was up to, were two different matters. I did not get on well with the second.

Despite my earlier instincts not to crowd the Musician, I began lobbying for more time together, and soon we were sharing a dinner or two and a few nights on the town, but I remained on edge. His behavior toward me had changed, or so it seemed in subtle ways that perhaps only I noticed. If he neglected to take my arm while crossing the street, I was painfully aware. I found myself snapping at him, baiting him and getting upset over the smallest miscommunications. I wrote long, pouting posts on my blog, blaming work or other stresses for my anxiety.

The Musician, perhaps sensing that my bout of unhappiness was not work-related and maybe even suspecting his own role in my mood, appeared at my apartment early one evening and offered to buy me a drink. A few minutes later, sitting in the dim light of an Upper East Side pub, he asked, "Should I be worried about you?"

"No, it's just stress."

He sipped at his pint of Stella. "Is there more to it?"

"No."

"Would you tell me if there was?"

"No." That was as honest as I would get that night.

Maybe I was waiting for him to ask the right question, or maybe I was hoping the wine would make me bold enough to tell the truth. But neither happened, and it was very clear that our relationship colored by too much information had suddenly become one of not nearly enough. I didn't know what he was thinking and he didn't know what had been obsessing me. We were reaping all of the consequences of a blogging relationship and none of the benefits.

And then, a few weeks later, I was jolted by a new entry in the Young Photographer's blog: she'd broken off her relationship with the Musician, after learning about his complex love life through his links to other blogs—maybe mine, maybe even another girl's. "I hate the incestuous nature of blogs," the Photographer wrote. "I hate learning things about people in blogs, reading about some-one I know in a blog."

It turns out the Photographer didn't like stumbling upon details of the Musician's racy exploits any more than I did. All this time I'd thought she and I were adversaries. Now I felt a sense of solidarity with her.

Only after time had dulled the agony of my own experience did I finally find the nerve to tell the Musician the true nature of my insecurities. And once I'd done so, our relationship began to improve. Our e-mails became friendly and flirtatious again, and our time together was tension-free. My confidence was restored. The Musician even became a regular character in my writing again.

So when I received a bitter, anonymous e-mail message one day from SmugontheUWS, calling me out as "nothing more than the Musician's groupie," I had the uneasy but not altogether unpleasant feeling that I had come full circle. Instinct told me that it was from someone he was dating and that the same insecurities that had driven me were now driving her.

I also knew if she was anything like me—and let's face it, she probably was—she had her own blog. But there was also a major difference between us; I had never sent a nasty e-mail to the Young Photographer. I'd never sent her any e-mail, nor would I. I had to wonder: who was this smug Upper West Sider whose bitterness knew no bounds?

I was tempted to ferret her out, to learn her story. Very tempted. It would only take the click of a mouse and a simple Google search to satisfy my curiosity. But this time, I'm happy to report that reason trumped compulsion—I knew I had to close and permanently delete the e-mail, and I did. My sanity required it.

Thinking and Writing Questions

1. Would you consider Heather Hunter's actions cyber snooping or was it fine for her to "Google" the person she was interested in dating? How did "too-much-information" affect the relationship?

2. What purpose is Hunter trying to achieve in this piece, being that it is published in the *New York Times* rather than her blog? How does publishing in different venues affect a writer's purpose?

3. Compare and contrast Hunter's piece with bell hooks' piece, "writing auto-biography." What might hooks say about Hunter's decision to publicly air her private issues?

4. Why is Hunter "less inclined to tell the whole, sordid truth" after this incident (143)? How can there be "too much information"?

5. Do you blog on MySpace, Facebook, or some other website? What is the purpose of your blog? How does your identity and persona change when you blog? Why does it change? How does blogging compare to writing in a diary or journal? If you don't blog, why not?

Adventures in Cheating
SETH STEVENSON

Seth Stevenson is a contributing author for Slate.com *magazine where he writes the "Ad Report Card" as well as features on travel, sports, and pop culture. In his column, "Ad Report Card,"*

Stevenson evaluates the effectiveness of ads. He was a staff writer for Newsweek *and has also written for the* New York Times Magazine, Rolling Stone, *and* Readers Digest. *In "Adventures in Cheating," which first appeared at Slate.com, Stevenson evaluates various websites that sell term papers.*

———————— ✦ ————————

Students, your semester is almost over. This fall, did you find yourself pulling many bong hits but few all-nighters? Absorbing much Schlitz but little Nietzsche? Attending Arizona State University? If the answer is yes to any or (especially) all these questions, you will no doubt be plagiarizing your term papers.

Good for you—we're all short on time these days. Yes, it's ethically blah blah blah to cheat on a term paper blah. The question is: How do you do it right? For example, the chump move is to find some library book and copy big hunks out of it. No good: You still have to walk to the library, find a decent book, and link the hunks together with your own awful prose. Instead, why not just click on a term paper Web site and buy the whole damn paper already written by some smart dude? *Que bella!* Ah, but which site?

I shopped at several online term paper stores to determine where best to spend your cheating dollar. After selecting papers on topics in history, psychology, and biology, I had each paper graded by one of my judges. These were: *Slate* writer David Greenberg, who teaches history at Columbia; my dad, who teaches psychology at the University of Rhode Island (sometimes smeared as the ASU of the East); and my girlfriend, who was a teaching assistant in biology at Duke (where she says cheating was quite common). So, which site wins for the best combination of price and paper quality? I compared free sites, sites that sell "pre-written papers," and a site that writes custom papers to your specifications.

FREE SITES

A quick Web search turns up dozens of sites filled with free term papers. Some ask you to donate one of your own papers in exchange, but most don't. I chose one from each of our fields for comparison and soon found that when it comes to free papers, you get just about what you pay for.

EssaysFree.com

From this site I chose a history paper titled "The Infamous Watergate Scandal." Bad choice. This paper had no thesis, no argument, random capitalization, and bizarre spell-checking errors—including "taking the whiteness stand" (witness) and "the registration of Nixon" (resignation). My judge said if they gave F's at Columbia, well . . . Instead, it gots a good old "Please come see me."

BigNerds.com

Of the free bio paper I chose from this site, my judge said, "Disturbing. I am still disturbed." It indeed read less like a term paper than a deranged manifesto. Rambling for 11 single-spaced pages and ostensibly on evolutionary theory, it somehow made reference to Lamarck, Sol Invictus, and "the blanket of a superficial American Dream." Meanwhile, it garbled its basic explanation of population genetics. Grade: "I would not give this a grade so much as suggest tutoring, a change in majors, some sort of counseling . . ."

OPPapers.com

This site fared much better. A paper titled "Critically Evaluate Erikson's Psychosocial Theory" spelled Erikson's name wrong in the first sentence, yet still won a C+/B- from my dad. It hit most of the important points—the problem was no analysis. And the citations all came from textbooks, not real sources. Oddly, this paper also used British spellings ("behaviour") for no apparent reason. But all in all not terrible, considering it was free. OPPapers.com, purely on style points, was my favorite site. The name comes from an old hip-hop song ("You down with O-P-P?" meaning other people's . . . genitalia), the site has pictures of coed babes, and one paper in the psych section was simply the phrase "I wanna bang Angelina Jolie" typed over and over again for several pages. Hey, whaddaya want for free?

SITES SELLING PRE-WRITTEN PAPERS

There are dozens of these—I narrowed it down to three sites that seemed fairly reputable and were stocked with a wide selection. (In general, the selection offered on pay sites was 10 times bigger than at the free ones.) Each pay site posted clear disclaimers that you're not to pass off these papers as your own work. Sure you're not.

AcademicTermPapers.com

This site charged $7 per page, and I ordered "The Paranoia Behind Watergate" for $35. Well worth it. My history judge gave it the highest grade of all the papers he saw—a B or maybe even a B+. Why? It boasted an actual argument. A few passages, however, might set off his plagiarism radar (or "pladar"). They show almost too thorough a command of the literature.

My other purchase here was a $49 bio paper titled "The Species Concept." Despite appearing in the bio section of the site, this paper seemed to be for a philosophy class. Of course, no way to know that until after you've bought it (the pay sites give you just the title and a very brief synopsis of each paper). My judge would grade this a C- in an intro bio class, as its conclusion was "utterly meaningless," and it tossed around "airy" philosophies without actually understanding the species concept at all.

PaperStore.net

For about $10 per page, I ordered two papers from the Paper Store, which is also BuyPapers.com and AllPapers.com. For $50.23, I bought "Personality Theory: Freud and Erikson," by one Dr. P. McCabe (the only credited author on any of these papers. As best I can tell, the global stock of papers for sale is mostly actual undergrad stuff with a few items by hired guns thrown in). The writing style here was oddly mixed, with bad paraphrasing of textbooks—which is normal for a freshman—side by side with surprisingly clever and polished observations. Grade: a solid B.

My other Paper Store paper was "Typical Assumptions of Kin Selection," bought for $40.38. Again, a pretty good buy. It was well-written, accurate, and occasionally even thoughtful. My bio judge would give it a B in a freshman class. Possible pladar ping: The writer seemed to imply that some of his ideas stemmed from a personal chat with a noted biologist. But overall, the Paper Store earned its pay.

A1Termpaper.com (aka 1–800-Termpaper.com)

In some ways this is the strangest site, as most of the papers for sale were written between 1978 and '83. I would guess this is an old term paper source, which has recently made the jump to the Web. From its history section, I bought a book report on Garry Wills' *Nixon*

Agonistes for $44.75, plus a $7.45 fee for scanning all the pages—the paper was written in 1981, no doubt on a typewriter. Quality? It understood the book but made no critique—a high-school paper. My judge would give it a D.

I next bought "Personality as Seen by Erikson, Mead, and Freud" from A1 Termpaper for $62.65 plus a $10.43 scanning fee. Also written in 1981, this one had the most stylish prose of any psych paper and the most sophisticated thesis, but it was riddled with factual errors. For instance, it got Freud's psychosexual stages completely mixed up and even added some that don't exist (the correct progression is oral-anal-phallic-latency-genital, as if you didn't know). Showing its age, it cited a textbook from 1968 and nothing from after '69 (and no, that's not another Freudian stage, gutter-mind). Grade: Dad gave it a C+. In the end, A1 Termpaper.com was pricey, outdated, and not a good buy.

With all these pre-written papers, though, it occurred to me that a smart but horribly lazy student could choose to put his effort into editing instead of researching and writing: Buy a mediocre paper that's done the legwork, then whip it into shape by improving the writing and adding some carefully chosen details. Not a bad strategy.

PAPERS MADE TO ORDER

PaperMasters.com

My final buy was a custom-made paper written to my specifications. Lots of sites do this, for between $17 and $20 per page. PaperMasters.com claims all its writers have "at least one Master's Degree" and charges $17.95 per page. I typed this request (posing as a professor's assignment, copied verbatim) into its Web order form: "A 4-page term paper on David Foster Wallace's *Infinite Jest*. Investigate the semiotics of the 'addicted gaze' as represented by the mysterious film of the book's title. Possible topics to address include nihilism, figurative transgendering, the culture of entertainment, and the concept of 'infinite gestation.' "

This assignment was total hooey. It made no sense whatsoever. Yet it differed little from papers I was assigned as an undergrad English major at Brown.

After a few tries (one woman at the 800 number told me they were extremely busy), my assignment was accepted by Paper

Masters, with a deadline for one week later. Keep in mind, *Infinite Jest* is an 1,100-page novel (including byzantine footnotes), and it took me almost a month to read even though I was completely engrossed by it. In short, there's no way anyone could 1) finish the book in time; and 2) write anything coherent that addressed the assignment.

I began to feel guilty. Some poor writer somewhere was plowing through this tome, then concocting a meaningless mishmash of words simply to fill four pages and satisfy the bizarre whims of a solitary, heartless taskmaster (me). But then I realized this is exactly what I did for all four years of college—and I paid them for the privilege!

When the custom paper came back, it was all I'd dreamed. Representative sentence: "The novel's diverse characters demonstrate both individually and collectively the fixations and obsessions that bind humanity to the pitfalls of reality and provide a fertile groundwork for the semiotic explanation of addictive behavior." Tripe. The paper had no thesis and in fact had no body—not one sentence actually advanced a cogent idea. I'm guessing it would have gotten a C+ at Brown—maybe even a B-.(Click here to read the rest of the paper.) If I were a just slightly lesser person, I might be tempted by this service. One custom paper off the Web: $71.80. Not having to dredge up pointless poppycock for some po-mo obsessed, overrated lit-crit professor: priceless.

Thinking and Writing Questions

1. In the opening paragraph, Stevenson says that college students who drink too much, do illegal drugs, and attend low quality universities are the ones who plagiarize their term papers. Is this your preception? In your educational careers, what students plagiarize, cheat, and buy term papers online? What reasons do students give for cheating?

2. Who is the audience for this piece? How can you tell? Underline key sections of the text that speak to Stevenson's intended audience. Explain to your writing partner what decisions and choices Stevenson made to direct the piece to his intended audience.

3. Stevenson calls this act of submitting someone else's work as your own cheating but downplays it with, "Yes, it's ethically blah blah blah to cheat on a term paper blah" (148). He rationalizes that students are short on time, and the goal is to figure out how to cheat correctly. Websites that sell term papers

also address students' busy lives, "AcaDemon recognizes that you have a hectic schedule and tight deadlines to meet." Another site, "Un-censored and Unbelievable Facts about . . . Term Paper Writing!," guarantees that their site is not selling plagiarized papers: "100% original and Non-Plagiarized Term Paper Writing Services." Many sites claim that their goal is to make you successful, "Term papers in our Store are intended for RESEARCH PURPOSES ONLY. We were established to help you, not to let you cheat" (AcaDemon). How do these websites and Stevenson build their argument that buying a term paper on line is acceptable?

4. "Adventures in Cheating" is a review essay in which Stevenson evaluates ten papers from seven websites. Based on his findings, would you trust your course grade and career to the papers he describes? What quality in the papers brought them a more positive assessment by the judges? A negative assessment?

"Tutoring" Rich Kids Cost Me My Dreams

NICOLE KRISTAL

Singer-songwriter and author Nicole Kristal graduated with a degree in journalism from the University of Oregon. Her first book, The Bisexual's Guide to the Universe, *was published in 2006. She has also written for* Newsweek, Premiere *magazine,* Back Stage West *newspaper, and websites such as* BiCafe *and* Ostrich Ink. *She is currently a staff-writer for a weekly newspaper in Los Angeles and is in the process of recording a new album. In "'Tutoring' Rich Kids Cost Me My Dreams," which was first published in* Newsweek, *Kristal explains how she prostituted her mind to write papers for rich students.*

---------------------- ✦ ----------------------

FOR THREE YEARS, I WAS AN academic prostitute. I ruined the curve for the honest and ensured that the wealthiest, and often stupidest, students earned the highest marks. I was a professional paper-writer.

It all started when I quit my journalism job in order to pursue my dream of being a singer-songwriter. I snagged a job tutoring inner-city foster children, but it didn't pay the bills. One day, I found a TUTORS WANTED flier on the UCLA campus. A small tutoring agency that serviced affluent families hired me.

"Just sit at her computer and type for her," my boss advised me with my first client, a private-high-school student. But as I typed her name at the top right corner of the screen, she slithered onto her bed to watch "Are You Hot?" I asked her what she remembered about Huxley's "Brave New World."

"She's a slut," my client said with a sigh, referring either to the character of Lenina or the woman on TV. After a handful of three-word responses like that, I realized she didn't care. I was hired to do the thinking. The parents knew it. So did my boss.

Welcome to the world of professional paper-writing, the dirty secret of the tutoring business. It's facilitated by avaricious agencies, perpetuated by accountability-free parents and made possible by self-loathing nerds like me. For three-hour workdays, the ability to sleep in and the opportunity to get paid to learn, I tackled subjects like Dostoevsky while spoiled jerks smoked pot, took naps, surfed the Internet and had sex. Though some offered me chateaubriand and the occasional illicit drug, most treated me like the help. I put up with it because I feared working in an office for $12 an hour again.

Six months into the job, my boss sent me on a problem-solving mission for $10 more per hour than I was already making. He had earned C's and D's on papers for Evan (not his real name), a USC freshman my boss described as a "typical surfer retard." Evan's parents had hired "tutors" to compose their son's papers since he was 12 because he "wasn't going to be a writer anyway." They were furious.

In Evan's penthouse, surfers carved across the screen of his 51-inch television, next to a poster of "Scarface." The former clothes model handed me his assignment: to describe utopia. "I couldn't ask for a better life. I mean, —— was my soccer coach," Evan said, naming a famous studio head.

Despite living in utopia, during the session Evan purchased an ounce of weed and a bag of Xanax. His WASPy girlfriend washed down a pill with some Smart Water and offered me one. I declined. Evan sent me home with his $3,000 PowerBook to write his paper because he was "too busy" to work. Before I left, his girlfriend hired me to write her paper on "Do the Right Thing." I drove home at midnight, once again missing my chance to hit the music scene and battle my stage fright.

No matter. After I scored an A on Evan's paper, he promised to pass my demo on to a legendary music producer—a family friend. He also promised a few leftover pairs of designer jeans. He never mentioned either again, and I knew I'd been played. The only help Evan offered came in the form of new clients, such as his roommate, who had one-night stands with strippers and said things like "Why should I care about some little black girl?" in regard to Toni Morrison novels.

When my streak of A's ended after I scored a B-minus on Evan's paper about clanship in "My Big Fat Greek Wedding," I never heard from him again. His teenage sibling, for whom I composed countless high-school English papers, revealed that Evan had replaced me with a classmate.

That summer break, my boss referred me to a junior at a private Christian university who couldn't spell "college." Come fall, the kid leased my brain three hours a day, five days a week. Depressed, I lounged around in my bathrobe until he finished class, then waded through rush-hour traffic to demoralize myself. One day, my Ford Bronco lost all power on the freeway and I could have died. I hadn't played a gig for seven months. I could barely pay my bills because I refused to take on more paper-writing clients.

Last spring, two months shy of my client's graduation date, I snapped while staring at a term-paper assignment on Margaret Thatcher. "I can't do this anymore," I mumbled. I had completed nearly two years of college for him. He replaced me with a teacher about to earn his Ph.D. who charged $15 less per hour than I did.

Despite my intellect, I handed over my self-respect to rich losers. I allowed myself to be blinded by privilege and the hope that some of it would rub off on me and help my flailing music career. Ultimately, trading my morals for money cost me the confidence I needed to turn my dreams into reality. Unemployment was a small price to pay to restore my fractured dignity.

Thinking and Writing Questions

1. How did Kristal's experience of "tutoring" rich kids cause her to lose her self-respect and integrity?

2. Examine the persona that Kristal creates in her essay. How does she characterize herself in the essay? As a writer, what techniques does she use to create this presence? What purpose does Kristal accomplish with her reader by creating this persona?

3. Both Stevenson, in "Adventurers in Cheating," and Kristal characterize students who buy term papers as beer-drinking druggies who aren't too bright.

What if a student had three children, worked forty hours per week, and had to visit her grandmother in the nursing home? Would it be "okay" for this student to buy term papers? Write a clear paragraph that states your position, including the rational for your position.

4. Kristal asks us to think about the costs of buying and selling term papers and the ideas of others. Make a list of the costs that Kristal covers. Working with your writing partner, add to this list, including costs to the student, the school, the hired writers, and society.

5. Some students with money are able to buy their way out of having to think and work. Should their money exempt them from the hard work that is required of others? Why? Why not?

Of Plagiarism, Paper Mills, and the Harried Hurried Student
MAUREEN HOURIGAN

Professor Maureen Hourigan has taught writing since 1964. She received her Ph.D. from the University of South Florida and her MA from State University of New York at Buffalo. She directed the first-year writing program at the University of Nevada at Las Vegas and retired from Kent State Trumbull in 2005. In her first book, Literacy as Social Exchange, *Hourigan examines how class, race, ethnicity, and gender play in students' learning to negotiate the conventions of academic discourse. She has also published on policies of grading writing, ethical issues in composition studies, Chaucer, and Jane Austin. Hourigan wrote "Of Plagiarism, Paper Mills, and the Harried Hurried Student" for this collection. She lays out the consequences of plagiarism from the perspective of the university and the instructor.*

---◆---

When was the last time you checked your university's or college's undergraduate catalog for its official policies on plagiarism? Do your course syllabi include a general statement about plagiarism and the penalties for "getting caught"? Usually these are found toward the end of a syllabus, following the course description, objectives, materials, expectations. Do you know what these policies are? You should.

Long before the advent of the Internet, students were adept at presenting someone else's work or ideas as their own. In the 1960s, when I was a college student, fraternity and sorority houses kept files of graded papers on hand for brothers and sisters too busy, too indifferent, or too lazy to compose their own. Some students paid or begged other students to write their papers for them; some copied huge chunks of material from books or articles, changed every third word or so with some help from Roget's Thesaurus, and claimed it as their own. Still others purchased entire papers from paper mills that, ironically, advertised in the student newspapers. When I directed the writing program at a large Southwestern university, I was a regular patron of these services: I would order each new edition of available paper titles to keep on hand for instructors who suspected the ideas in a student's term paper had been "stolen" from someone else. Of course some students got caught—and some got punished.

Students plagiarize for many reasons, the majority of which apply to both the pre- and post- Internet age. Students have always been busy. The traditional aged college student of forty years ago had to juggle the demands of the standard load of five or six courses, extracurricular clubs, and perhaps a part-time job; today's students must oftentimes juggle the demands of school, a full-time job, and perhaps a family. Furthermore, students have always had the pressure of getting good grades, either from parents or from employers who will reimburse proportionally (or not at all) depending upon the grade earned in a course. And yes, students have always grumbled about assignments that seem to have no inherent value to their chosen majors or careers and sometimes submitted work that was not their own to free up time for assignments in other classes. On the face of it, the most significant impact the Internet would seem to have had on plagiarism is the instant availability of texts on line. Admittedly, it is far less time consuming to "borrow" texts online than it was to find texts in the library to "borrow" from some forty years ago.

IN A PANIC OVER PLAGIARISM

Whether or not easy access to a profusion of sources and papers on the Internet has caused an increase in student plagiarism is a subject of debate among academics. But common academic wisdom suggests that it has. For example, citing several studies, including one conducted in 2001 where 41% of undergraduate students admitted to one or more instances of cut and paste Internet plagiarism, Neil Granitz and Dana Loewy conclude that the Internet has "created an explosion in student plagiarism" (293). While the Internet makes plagiarism easier for students, ironically, it makes the detection of it easier for professors as well. "Cheaters Amok," a Primetime Thursday special (29 April 2004), explored the use of such plagiarism detection devices as Turnitin as a solution to the problem of detecting Internet plagiarism. Along with the availability of these devices, claims James Purdy, has arrived the current "fervor to eradicate plagiarism—or at least to capture and punish those who plagiarize" (277). As a result, academic institutions now take "drastic actions . . . to avoid being labeled as tolerating plagiarism—or any behavior closely akin to it" (Purdy 275).

A search of *The Chronicle of Higher Education* (a must-read for academics) for recent articles on "plagiarism" underscores Purdy's claims about an increased "fervor to eradicate plagiarism." Indeed, there seems a "stampede to fight what the *New York Times* calls a 'plague' of plagiarism" (Howard "Forget"). The widely publicized case of a plagiarism scandal at the University of Southern California involving Elizabeth Paige Laurie, heir to the Wal-Mart billions (see *New York Times* ["Rebuff For Wal-Mart Heiress"] and *USA Today* ["College Removes Name of Wal-Mart Heiress on Arena"]), receives attention in *The Chronicle* as well. An article in the December 2004 *Chronicle* reports that the University of Missouri at Columbia voted to change the name of its sports arena when it was discovered that Laurie, whose parents had paid $25-million to name the arena for their daughter, had allegedly paid ex-roommate Elena Martinez $20,000 over three and a half years to write term papers and other assignments for her at USC (Carlson and Suggs). According to a University of Missouri spokesperson, "[O]fficials heard from every part of the university that some action had to be taken."

Michael Jackson, Vice-President of Student Affairs at USC, in an interview with Mandalit del Barco on *All Things Considered*, stated that if Martinez's allegations of cheating were true, it was "pretty diabolical" and "of a serial nature." Curiously, while Laurie did not get her papers from an Internet service, Jackson looks to the Internet as an explanation for a "level of alleged cheating" that he had never seen in his twenty-five years as an educator: "I do think that the advent of the Internet and all these paper mills have created more temptation for people than ever before." Moreover, he opines, "There is something deeper going on that has to do with 'Me first'; 'I should get what I want when I want it'; and 'It doesn't matter'; and 'As long as I don't get caught, it's OK.'" While Laurie's parents consistently maintained that her college record was a private matter, a year after Martinez decided to tell her story on *20/20* in the hopes that "maybe people will see what's going on in our schools" and "maybe there will be some change" ("Big Cheats on Campus"), Laurie returned her University of Southern California degree ("Heiress Returns Her Degree"). How fortunate for Nicole Kristol's "rich kid" at USC that she decided to withhold his real name ("'Tutoring' Rich Kids" 153).

ACADEMICS GET SERIOUS ABOUT PLAGIARISM

A sea change in attitudes toward plagiarism on college campuses? Perhaps. Rebecca Moore Howard, a leading researcher on this issue, observes that "all the attention now lavished on the figure of the student plagiarist" has motivated both faculty and administrators "to reconsider previous pedagogy and policy." ("Understanding" 12). A search for "plagiarism polices" on the MSN search engine in the summer of 2007 produced more than 25,000 hits. At the top of the list, was a revised plagiarism statement for the department of Sociology, Anthropology, and Criminal Justice at Rutgers University, Camden, one that is linked to several other universities' plagiarism policy sites (http://www. sociology.camden.rutgers.edu/curriculum/plagiarism.htm). Let us consider, vis-à-vis Rutgers' revised plagiarism policy, the "priceless" feeling Seth Stevenson experienced ("Adventures in Cheating") after having purchased a paper on David Foster's *Infinite Jest* to hand into a "po-mo obsessed, overrated lit-crit professor" in 2001 (152). In unembellished language, rarely found in more esoteric statements of plagiarism, Rutgers' policy identifies "cutting and pasting paragraphs from different websites" and "handing in a paper downloaded from the internet" as plagiarism, a serious academic offense that can lead to expulsion from the university. Moreover, the policy warns students that "all Rutgers professors have access to *Turnitin.com*, a very effective resource for catching plagiarism." Thus, should Stevenson's professor uncover the true source of the paper (and as we shall see in a few paragraphs that it is quite likely he will), the "priceless" feeling of "[n]ot having to dredge up pointless poppycock" will likely give way to one of trepidation when the "real price" of plagiarizing becomes known (152).

In language intended to resonate with students who may see a college degree as little more than a means to a larger paycheck or a ticket to graduate or professional school, Rutgers' policy statement illustrates that being accused of plagiarism has become a big deal. Not only is a notation of plagiarism placed on the student's transcript, but perhaps more importantly, "University faculty and administrators knowledgeable of academic dishonesty infractions are ethically bound to report such incidences" to educational institutions and prospective employers in letters of recommendation requested by a student. (http://www.camden.rutgers.edu/RUCAM/info/Academic-Integrity-Policy.html#plagiarism). Not so "priceless" a feeling anymore, I would suspect.

THE SPECIAL CASE OF INTERNET PAPER MILLS

"Term-paper and essay-writing services have joined prostitutes, firearms dealers, and hacking sites in Google's forbidden-advertising zone," a *Chronicle of Higher Education* article announced in June 2007 (Fischman A29). Ah yes, it's not just universities and colleges who perceive on-line paper mills as troubling purveyors of purloined goods. In truth, academics regard purchasing a paper on line as "one of the more egregious forms of plagiarism," argues Kelly Ritter, "perhaps because it is often viewed as a less complicated problem in the context of larger, more 'forgivable' acts such as the visible rise of cut and paste . . . plagiarism" ("Buying In" 25). Howard, too, who has frequently been taken to task by fellow academics for being soft on plagiarism takes a hard line on the subject of papers purchased from an Internet paper mill: "Now, a downloaded paper is something that no professor should tolerate. It has to be punished. . . . We have to protect education; we have to demand that our students learn" ("Forget").

But Ritter contends that a student's decision to purchase a paper on line may be more complicated than most academics have allowed. She argues that students turn to paper mills because of their "disengagement from academic definitions of authorship; their overreliance on consumerist notions of ownership . . . [and their] lack of confidence in their own writing and research skills" ("Buying In" 26). In other words, because students don't see themselves as "authors" who own ideas, when they purchase a paper from an online service, they see it not as unethically "stealing" some one else's ideas and words, but as purchasing a document that is theirs to own. Importantly, she makes the case that "the idea of ownership versus authorship when determining ethical use of a paper, especially a purchased one, is less clear in many students' minds" than it is in the minds of the faculty (Ritter "The Economics" 614).

To test Ritter's assertion that Internet paper mills purposely exploit a naïve student's consumerist attitude toward paper ownership, I decided to examine in some detail the TermPaperRelief.com site. This site is interesting for two reasons. First, when Josh Fischman reported on Google's decision to no longer accept ads from paper mills, he contacted Sandra Brown, a spokesperson for Term Paper Relief, for comment ("'We're not doing anything wrong here,'" she sniffed). Second, Charles McGrath uses this site as a prime example in a two-part 2006 *New York Times* exposé on Internet paper mills ("Outsourcing Homework: At $9.95 a Page, You Expected Poetry?" and "Term Paper Project, Part II").

In accessing http://www.termpaperrelief.com/, what immediately caught my eye on this text laden first page is the picture of four students at the top of the page, grinding about term papers in comic strip bubbles that drift above their heads. Depicted here, we find four classic cases of hurried, harried students: the social butterfly ("Damn! I'll have to cancel my Saturday night date to finish my term paper before Monday's deadline."), the grade-pressured student ("Dad's going to take away my car if I fail again this term."), the overextended student ("How can I attend my ballet rehearsal? I'm two days short of my deadline"), and the apathetic student ("Man, another term paper!"). Also, at the top of the page, in large blue and hot pink lettering, students who patronize Term Paper Relief are promised "A-grade term papers" that are "custom-written on your specified topic, completely non-plagiarized, written by our experienced writers, and delivered before your deadline." At the bottom of the page, and stated twice, however, is the disclaimer that "termpaperrelief.com provides custom term paper writing/rewriting services inclusive of research material, for assistance purposes only. The term papers should be used with proper reference."

Clicking on the "why you should buy from us" link, students discover that Term Paper Relief does "things that others only promise." Indeed, if you "trust [them] with your problems and let [them] help you" (by ordering a "custom term paper," of course), you are promised "no more screwed up social life; no more pain and frustration over a demanding deadline; and no more rejected term papers because of insufficient data, inadequate research, or ineffective writing style." Even more important, Term Paper Relief promises that "the custom term papers we provide will be 100% original, written specially for you. You can be absolutely certain that your term paper will pass through all plagiarism detection software successfully." Why would a student, who has ostensibly purchased the paper for assistance only, be worried about its passing through Turnitin's software program, you might ask? Kevin Smith, a co-founder of Asian Grade, a free Internet paper site, freely admits that while his site, like Term Paper Relief, is intended only to assist students with their research, "'We can't control what they do with it afterwards'" (qtd. In McGrath "Term Paper"). And curiously, for all Smith's claims that Asian Grade is not intended to help students plagiarize, for a fee, it will remove a paper from its data base to "prevent your professor from find-ing your original source, as well as making sure other students in your class don't submit a similar paper to your own'" (qtd. In McGrath "Term Paper"). Brown's insistence that Term Paper Relief is "not doing anything wrong" and Smith's claim that Asian Grade exists to "provide students with research help" are echoed by Anna Popielarz, owner of CustomPapers.com. Interviewed by *20/20*, she claimed "her company is providing a service for stu-dents, not helping them cheat. They don't have to turn the paper in as their own. They can just use it as the model paper . . . You can't really blame me for students cheating.'" "Yes, I can," replied the *20/20* host ("Big Cheats on Campus").

Ritter argues that students' "overreliance on consumerist notions of ownership" accounts for their confusion about the eth-ical use of term papers purchased whole from Internet papers mills. Students are confused, she reasons, because "the paper-for-sale floats in cyberspace like so many other products, on sites quite similar to those selling legitimate products to the same eighteen-to-twenty-five-year-old target demographic" ("The Economics" 619). I find myself not entirely convinced by her argu-ment that naïve students are duped into believing that the paper "products" they purchase from Internet paper mill sites are theirs to do with as they please. But my examination of the Term Paper Relief site has persuaded me to reconsider. One of the things that struck me was the site's answer to the question, "Who will own the final right to my term paper?" "Any term paper you order from our site would bear your ownership," proclaims the site. Furthermore, it states, "It is the policy of Term Paper Relief that a term paper

once sold is the property of the owner and would not be reproduced or sold in any form." Nowhere does the site caution its
patrons that once they affix their names to their purchased prop-
erties, they are guilty of a serious breach of academic integrity.

BEYOND "GOTCHA!"[i]

Believe it or not, professors do not delight in playing the
"Gotcha!" game. We would much rather spend our time
commenting on your ideas than running your papers through a
software detection program or plugging a few apt phrases into
an Internet search engine.[ii] But professors are diligent in ferreting
out plagiarists because plagiarists cheat the honest student.
Nicole Kristal was not exaggerating when she claimed that she
"ruined the curve for the honest" (153). By means of example,
Bear Braunmoeller and Brian J. Gaines discovered that the great
majority of their students would have been disadvantaged had
they not "engaged in [plagiarism] monitoring activities" (838).
The two conducted an experiment in an introductory political
science course to determine the effect plagiarized papers would
have on a grading curve. Unbeknownst to the students, and after
extensive warnings not to plagiarize, Braunmoeller and Grimes
ran the first set of papers through EVES, a Turnitin-like
plagiarism detection device. All papers were ultimately awarded
two grades. The first was the grade the paper would have received
if it had had not contained "significant amount of uncited or
unreferenced material." If it did, its second, "discounted" grade
was based upon the amount of undocumented material it
contained. Therefore, if a paper had originally been awarded a
grade of 88% but was found to be 50 percent unoriginal, the
grade was reduced to 44% (838). As for the honest student, his or
her grade was improved once the grading curve had been
adjusted for penalties. Thus, "an honest student who had initially
received a B on the paper would have received a B + once the
grading curve had been adjusted" (836). All in all, "the net result
of penalizing problematic papers was an average increase of one
third of a grade for all papers not deemed problematic" (836). Not
surprisingly, student reaction to the professors' experiment was
mixed; moreover, only one "quite clearly problematic" paper
showed up in the second set of papers (836).

But there's more to the issue than just not getting caught.
When you purchase a paper from an online site you are cheating

yourself by not gaining the writing and thinking skills the assigned paper was designed to foster. And you are probably getting ripped off by the paper mill to boot. As a case in point, in September 2006, the *New York Times* conducted an experiment on online paper mills. According to Charles McGrath, a *Times* editor ordered three papers on typically assigned subjects for English literature classes, one from *Superior Papers.com*, one from *Term Paper Relief.com*, and a third from *Go Essays.com*. The results? One never arrived on time (Superior Papers); the second (Go Essays) earned a D + grade from the professor, a self-described "'soft touch,'" who volunteered to grade it; and the third (Term Paper Relief) would have merited a "'come and see me'" from a different professor/volunteer reader ("Outsourcing Homework.")

But even more interesting is what happened when the *Times* decided to test the paper that it purchased from Term Paper Relief for plagiarism. Remember this claim? "The custom term papers we provide will be 100% original, written specially for you. You can be absolutely certain that your term paper will pass through all plagiarism detection software successfully." When the *Times* submitted the paper to Turnitin for a check, it discovered that "every single paragraph of the essay was borrowed from material already floating on the Internet or Nexis." Whole chunks of the paper "were included in a paper turned in by a student in Helenvale State High School in Queensland, Australia, in November 2002" ("Term Paper"). When the Times contacted Term Paper Relief with evidence of plagiarism in the purchased paper, they offered to redo the entire assignment but declined to offer a refund. So much for Term Paper Relief's vaunted promise of "no more pain and frustration over a demanding deadline." After failing to receive papers as promised and after finding rampant plagiarism in supposed plagiarism-proof papers, not to mention the abysmal quality of papers that did arrive, the *Times'* McGrath was forced to conclude: "The whole experience suggests that. . . . you might as well do the work yourself" ("Term Paper").

Plagiarism, representing someone else's ideas as your own, is dishonest and a serious breach of academic integrity, the foundation upon which education rests. Intentional plagiarism is unethical, and as Granitz and Loewy demonstrate in an article in the *Journal of Business Ethics*, "unethical behavior in school can lead to unethical behavior in business and to financial ruin" (294). Indeed, in a survey conducted by Donald McCabe, professor of management and global business at Rutgers, MBA students had the highest levels of self-reported cheating among graduate students. Chillingly, they felt themselves above the rules because they believed cheating was an accepted practice in business ("The Honest Truth about Cheating"). In passing off someone else's work as your own, you cheat yourself of learning experiences, cheat fellow students of fair evaluation of their work, diminish trust between student and teacher, and undermine the value of a degree from your institution. Rutgers has it right: "Avoid plagiarism at all costs."

CODA[iii]

As I was composing this piece, a position for "Dissertation Advisors" appeared in The Chronicle of Higher Education":

> Online education site [*Dissertation Advisors.com*] needs retired or part-time faculty to assist graduate students during the thesis/dissertation writing process. NOTE: This is NOT a paper mill. Advisors assist students using the same ethical guidelines as faculty advisors. You may not do the student's work (e.g., data collection, ghostwriting).
>
> Applicants must pass our scholarly writing/English fluency test (approx. 30 minutes of time investment) and will take a short copyediting test. Preference will be given to applicants who are willing to commit long-term and who have online teaching experience. Graduate student advising/committee experience is REQUIRED for the freelance advising network.
>
> Consultants set their own rates.
>
> Range: $35 -$55 per hour.

I have all the credentials needed to apply. Should I choose to do so, will I tread the same path as Nicole Kristal when she applied to the **TUTORS WANTED** flier on the UCLA campus? To borrow the closing words of many student essays I have graded over the years, "What do you think?"

Notes

    i. I'm indebted to Margaret Price for this heading. See "Beyond 'Gotcha!'": Situating Plagiarism in Policy and Pedagogy.' *College Composition and Communication*, Vol. 54, No. 1. (Sep., 2002), pp. 88–115. Stable URL: http://links.jstor.org/sici?sici=0010-096X%28200209%2954 %3A1%3C88%3AB%22SPIP%3E2.0.CO%3B2-Q

ii. That's not to say that catching students plagiarizing isn't always without some humor, generally quite unintended. I am thinking, for instance, of a student who strode into my office, angrily complaining about the unfairness of her teacher's grading scale. She was particularly exercised by the "C" she had received on the paper she was holding in her hand. "Both my roommate and I handed in the same paper, and she got a '"B" and I got a 'C,'" she fumed. Of course, by the time she exited my office, she and her roommate had indeed earned the same grade for "their" work—an "F."

iii. I have always admired the "coda" conclusion Lynn Bloom has in so many of her scholarly articles and decided to incorporate it here.

Works Cited

"Big Cheats on Campus." *20/20*. ABC. 19 November 2004. http://abcnews.go.com/2020/story?id=264646 1 September 2007.

Braunmoeller, Bear, and Brian J. Gaines. "Actions Do Speak Louder than Words: Deterring Plagiarism with the Use of Plagiarism-Detection Software". *PS: Political Science and Politics* 34.4(2001): 835–39.

Carlson, Scott, and Welch Suggs. "U. of Missouri Rechristens Sports Arena in Wake of Cheating Accusations Against Walton Heir." 10 December 2004. *Chronicle of Higher Education* http://chronicle.com/subscribe/login?url=/weekly/v51/i16/16a02202.htm, 1 September 2007.

"Cheaters Amok." *Primetime Thursday*. ABC. 29 April 2004. http:// www.softwaresecure.com/pdf/ABConCHeating_050404_.pdf, 15 August 2007.

"College Removes Name of Wal-Mart Heiress on Arena." *USA Today* 24 November 2004. http://www.usatoday.com/money/industries/retail/2004–11–24-walmart-heiress-arena_xtm, 1 September 2007.

"Consulting." *Dissertation Advisors*. N.d. http://www.dissertationadvising.com/consulting.shtml, 27 July 2007.

Faculty of Arts and Sciences and School of Business, "Academic Integrity Policy." *Rutgers, Camden*. 10 February 2004. Rutgers University, Camden. http://www.sociology.camden.rutgers.edu/curriculum/plagiarism.htm, 1 September 2007.

Fischman, Josh. "ONLINE." *Chronicle of Higher Education*. 1 June 2007. 53.39 (2007): A29. *Academic Search Complete*. 15 August 2007. AN25426926.

Granitz, Neil and Dana Loewy. "Applying Ethical Theories: Interpreting and Responding to Student Plagiarism." *Journal of Business Ethics* 72 (2007): 293–306.

"Heiress Returns Her Degree." *New York Times*. 20 Oct. 2005. http://query.nytimes.com/gst/fullpage.html?res=9E04E2D9123FF 933A15753C1A9639C8B63, 15 August 2007.

"Honest Truth about Cheating." *Weekend Edition Sunday*. NPR. 6 May 2007. http://www.npr.org/templates/story/story.php?storyId= 10033373, 30 September 2007.

Howard, Rebecca Moore. "Forget About Policing Plagiarism. Just Teach." The *Chronicle of Higher Education*. 16 November 2001: B24.

—. "Understanding 'Internet Plagiarism.'" *Computers and Composition* 24 (2007) 3–15.

Jackson, Michael. Interview. "USC Cheating Probe Focuses on Wal-Mart Heir. *All Things Considered*. NPR. 4 December 2004. http://www.npr. org./templates/story/story.php?storyID=4203407, 30 August 2007.

McGrath, Charles. "Outsourcing Homework: At $9.95 a Page, You Expected Poetry?" *New York Times*. 10 September 2006. http://www. nytimes.com/2006/09/10/weekinreview/10mcgrath.html?_r=1&oref= slogin, 18 September 2007.

—. "Term Paper Project, Part II." *New York Times*. 17 September 2006. http://www.nytimes.com/2006/09/17/weekinreview/17mcgrath.html, 18 September 2007.

"Plagiarism Policy." *Department of Sociology, Camden, Rutgers*. 23 July 2007. http://www.sociology.camden.rutgers.edu/curriculum/ plagiarism.htm, 1 August 2007.

Purdy, James P. "Calling Off the Hounds: Technology and the Visibility of Plagiarism." *Pedagogy: Critical Approaches to Teaching Literature, Language, Composition, and Culture* 5 (2005): 275–95.

"Rebuff for Wal-Mart Heiress." *New York Times*. 25 November 2004. http://query.nytimes.com/gst/fullpage.html?res=9E03E2D9153EF 936A15752C1A9629C8B63&partner=rssnyt&emc=rss, 30 August 2007.

Ritter, Kelly. "Buying In, Selling Short: A Pedagogy against the Rhetoric of Online Paper Mills. *Pedagogy: Critical Approaches to Teaching Literature, Language, Composition, and Culture* 6 (2006): 25–51.

—. "The Economics of Authorship: Online Paper Mills, Student Writers, and First-Year Composition." *College Composition and Communication* 56 (2005): 601–31.

Term Paper Relief. N.d. http://www.termpaperrelief.com/relief, 1 September 2007.

"USC Cheating Probe Focuses on Wal-Mart Heir." *All Things Considered*. NPR Radio. 4 December 2004. http://www.npr.org. /templates/story/story.php?storyID=4203407, 30 August 2007.

Thinking and Writing Questions

1. Why, according to Hourigan, do teachers and universities work so hard to guarantee that students submit their own writing and not the writing of others?

2. What purpose is Hourigan trying to achieve in this essay? Who is her intended audience? How can you tell? Where does she appeal to what she assumes are her audience's interests, attitudes, and beliefs?

3. Locate your institution's policy on plagiarism and compare it with Rutgers' newly revised one (http://www.sociology.camden.rutgers.edu/curriculum/plagiarism.htm). Consider similarities and differences in language, definitions, and penalties. What, specifically, are your institution's penalties for "getting caught"?

4. Hourigan quotes a study that reports 41% of undergraduates admitted to one or more instances of internet plagiarism. Do you believe that more students cheat today because of the easy accessibility of texts and papers on line? What evidence can you offer for your belief? Where could you find additional support?

5. Suppose you were one of the unwitting students in Braunmoeller and Gaines' political science class. Do you think it was fair of them to conduct the experiment and run the students' papers through EVES without the students' knowledge? If your grade had been discounted 50% because of "unreferenced material," how would you react? If your grade had been raised from a B to a B+ on the new curve, how would you react?

Chapter 4: Thinking and Writing

1. How far have you traveled down the information highway? Are you moving quickly in a Porsche? Stopping for coffee at every rest stop? Getting lost? Pedaling along on your tricycle stopping to get ice cream? Create an image of your information highway. A corridor with endless file cabinets? A fifty-lane highway with many toll booths? Compose a poem that makes vivid the image of you on this information highway.

2. Bart Simpson would probably buy a term paper online without hesitation and claim that it hurts no one. Lisa Simpson would probably say that buying a term paper rips at the very fiber of academic integrity. Write a speech in which you explain to your classmates which of the two you agree with and why. Use pieces from Chapter Four to support your position.

3. Kelly Ritter, whose research is cited by Hourigan in "Of Plagiarism, Paper Mills, and the Harried Hurried Student," claims that the sales pitch of online paper mills is like that of similar sites "selling legitimate products" that appeal to 15-to-25-year olds. Make a list of sites you visit to purchase products (music downloads come to mind). Examine at least one of these sites

and compare its rhetoric with that of at least one online paper mill site. Do the websites try to convince you how much better your life will be with their product? Do they use the testimonies of satisfied customers? What content, structure, design, and voice do they use to convince you to buy? Does your investigation support Ritter's conclusion? Explain.

4. How has technology and the media affected your life and influenced your work as a reader, writer, and thinker? If you are between the ages of twelve and seventeen, the 2007 study by the Pew Internet and American Life Project says that "the use of social media—from blogging to online social networking to creation of all kinds of digital material—is central" to your life. Ninety three percent of 12–17 year olds use the internet mostly as a "venue for social interaction—a place where they can share creations, tell stories, and interact with others." Teenagers are writing online: 28% created blogs in 2007, up from 19% in 2004; 55% have written profiles on social networking sites (Lenhart et al. i). And if you're not between the ages of twelve and seventeen—maybe thirty-five and returning to school—your experience with writing online might be different.

As you reread the pieces on technology in Chapter Four, list and reflect on the ideas that resonate with your connection to technology. Are you generating more prose that is not insightful and crafted like Leibowitz reports in "Technology Transforms Writing and the Teaching of Writing"? Do you get more response to your writing when you email it to your classmates and teachers, or post on *MySpace* or *Facebook*? Are you exposing too much information to the world like Hunter claims in "Traveling the Too-Much-Information Highway"? Has the ability to instantly purchase papers online left you unable to compose an essay? Also, look at "What Corporate America Can't Build: A Sentence" in Chapter Five. Has your expert use of email and text messaging led to cryptic messages and confusing prose in your work documents?

Develop a multi-genre piece that reflects how technology and media have or have not influenced your life. A multi-genre piece is composed of different genres that are carefully chosen and ordered to achieve your purpose. Websites are listed below that address multi-genre writing.

> Alexander, Jonathan and Margaret M. Barber. "Multi-Genre Research Projects." http://wps.ablongman.com/long_alexander_an_1/27/7031/ 1799968.cw/index.html, 2 February 2008.
>
> Flannery, Rip. "Guidelines for the Multi-genre Research Essay." http://www.emunix.emich.edu/~adlerk/multigenre_instructions.htm, 30 January 2008.
>
> "What is a Multi-genre Research Paper?" Griswold High School. http:// www.griswold.k12.ct.us/index.cfm?Menu=412&Id=7415, 2 February 2008.

Works Cited

AcaDemon Term Papers & Essays. http://www.academon.com/buy-term-papers.html, 5 February 2008.

Lenhart, Amanda, Mary Madden, Alexandra Rankin Macgill, and Aaron Smith. "Teens and Social Media." 19 December 2007. http://www.pewinternet.org/pdfs/PIP_Teens_Social_Media_Final.pdf, 2 February 2008.

Un-censored and Unbelievable Facts about . . . Term Paper Writing! December 2006. http://www.top-term-paper-sites.com/, 5 February 2008.

CHAPTER 5

Impact

When you were in elementary school did your teachers say to you, "You need to learn this because you will need it in middle school"? And in middle school, did they say to you, "You need to learn this because you will need it in high school"? And in high school, did they say to you, "You need to learn this because you will need it in"—yes, you got it—"college"?

Well, here you are in college. So now what? How many of you have asked yourselves, "Why do I have to take a writing class?" Liz often responds to that question with a snappy comeback, "If you don't know how to write, you certainly won't use it. However, if you can craft clear, insightful prose, you will be asked to do it, respected for it, valued for it, and paid well for it." Now that you're in college, our answer to your question, "Why learn to write?" is this: the influence writing can have on you and in your world. Your ability to produce clear prose that supports your position will influence your academic, professional, and community lives.

Many professions demand lots of writing. Charlene Spretnak reported in 1980 that engineers spend more than half of their work time on reading and writing tasks (133). In 1985, Lisa Ede and Andrea Lunsford reported on the writing of professionals in sciences, applied sciences, social sciences, information sciences, humanities, business, and government. These writers reported that they spend 44% of their professional time "in some kind of writing activity" (47). The National Commission on Writing reported in 2006, "Two-thirds of salaried employees in large American companies have some writing responsibility."

So, don't sell yourself short. If you write well, you can make a strong, positive impact, but if you write poorly, well—let's just say poor writing has an impact, too. Take, for example, the lawyer in the first article, "Judge Finds a Type-Prone Lawyer Guilty of Bad Writing." Adam Liptak reports on a judge in Pennsylvania who reduced a lawyer's fees by over $30,000 because his writing was so riddled with errors. Talk about consequences!

In "What Corporate America Can't Build: A Sentence," Sam Dillon explores the financial cost of poor writing to corporate America. Dillon gives us examples of this poor writing, reasons for the lack of clarity in much business prose, and what corporate America is paying to help their employees learn to write. Corporate America is paying big bucks for people who can write well.

Money, of course, is not the only thing lost due to confusing writing. In this excerpt, "Three Mile Island and the Billion Dollar Memo," from his textbook *Writing: A Guide for Business Professionals*, C.W. Griffin tells the story of the billion dollar memo which contributed to the nuclear accident at Three Mile Island in 1979 and caused a $1 billion cleanup cost. Griffin analyzes how the structure of the memo and its confusing sentences prevented its readers from understanding the severity of the message. Griffin suggests ways that writers can clean up muddied prose and prevent other disasters.

The act of writing can also have positive impacts. In "Healing through the Written Word," Karen Cangialosi reports how medical patients are writing to help themselves not only spiritually but also physically. Cangialosi sites studies that show "merely writing about past stressful life experiences results in symptom reduction among patients with asthma or rheumatoid arthritis" (188–189). She explains the power of the written word when used to vent feelings of fear, sadness, or loss.

Educator Carol Avery has also experienced the positive effects of writing. In "Laura's Legacy," she recounts the death of a student in her first grade classroom. Because Avery's students had written so much, Laura left behind many stories from which the students carried her memory. One of Avery's students points out, "It feels like Laura is right here with us, right now. We just can't see her" (197). Even in the first grade, writing has an impact.

Margaret Atwood expresses her ideas about the impact of writing in the poem "Spelling." She moves from the image of the daughter playing with "plastic letters,/red, blue & hard yellow" to create words to the image of the "the burning witch,/her mouth covered by leather/to strangle words" (199). Playing on the verb "spell," Atwood asks her readers to consider how they are learning to spell.

We end with Mary Pipher's *Writing to Change the World*. Pipher explains how "[g]ood writing connects people to one another, to other living creatures, to stories and ideas, and to action" (8). In the chapter we reprint, "Writing to Connect," Pipher offers many examples of writers whose stories push readers to understand the world in a different way. A new perspective reshapes how we see the world. And this new perspective calls for change.

As you read the following essays, consider how writing has had a direct and indirect impact on your life: from the essay you wrote to get a grant that sent you to college to the first amendment of the U.S. Constitution. Do these pieces in Chapter Five convince you that the skill, craft, and art of writing are worth your time? Does Laura's story convince you that writing is significant?

Maybe you didn't get much experience and practice writing in the first grade or in high school, but now's your chance. Ask yourself: Are you willing to focus on improving your writing as you move through college? Willing to invest time and energy in a writing education that will influence your life—not just to get a good grade? No matter what your attitude, your process, your voice, or your feelings about technology, writing influences our lives. Will you be a part of the conversation? What will be your impact?

Judge Finds a Typo-Prone Lawyer Guilty of Bad Writing

ADAM LIPTAK

Lawyer Adam Liptak is the National Legal Correspondent for the New York Times. *He has also written for* Rolling Stone, *the* New York Observer, *and* Business Week. *He teaches at the Journalism School of Columbia University in New York. Mr. Liptak received both a BA in English Literature and a JD from Yale University. In "Judge Finds a Typo-Prone Lawyer Guilty of Bad Writing," which first appeared in the* New York Times, *Liptak reports on a judge who punished a lawyer by lowering the fee for his services because of his poor writing.*

✦

A federal judge in Philadelphia, in prose suggesting barely suppressed chortles, reduced a lawyer's request for fees last month because his filings were infested with typographical errors.

The lawyer, Brian M. Puricelli, had offered this vigorous but counterproductive defense:

"Had the defendants not tired to paper plaintiff's counsel to death, some type would not have occurred. Furthermore, there have been omissions by the defendants, thus they should not case stones."

The judge was amused. But he was not moved. "If these mistakes were purposeful," Magistrate Judge Jacob P. Hart ruled, "they would be brilliant."

His decision was first reported in The Legal Intelligence[sic], a Philadelphia newspaper.

In the time-honored legal tradition, Magistrate Hart supported his ruling with evidence. "We would be remiss," he wrote, "if we did not point out some of our favorites."

In one letter, Mr. Puricelli had given the magistrate's first name as Jacon, not Jacob.

"I appreciate the elevation to what sounds like a character in 'The Lord of the Rings,'" Magistrate Hart wrote, "but, alas, I am only a judge."

In all of Mr. Puricelli's filings, moreover, he identified the Federal District Court in Philadelphia as the United States District Court for the Easter District of Pennsylvania.

But the magistrate was quick to add that in many ways Mr. Puricelli is a terrific lawyer, at least when he is on his feet at a trial.

"Considering the quality of his written work," the magistrate wrote, "the court was impressed with the transformation. Mr. Puricelli was well prepared, his witnesses were prepped, and his case proceeded quite artfully and smoothly."

Indeed, Mr. Puricelli won the case he tried before Magistrate Hart. He represented John DeVore, a former Philadelphia police officer, in a civil rights case against the city and several of its officials. Mr. DeVore said he had been fired in retaliation for reporting that his partner had stolen a cellphone. The jury awarded him $430,000, which Magistrate Hart reduced to $354,000.

The law under which Mr. DeVore sued allowed him to recover his legal expenses, too, and Mr. Puricelli sought more than $200,000. The defendants objected, saying the quality of the work had not been worth $300 an hour.

Magistrate Hart agreed, in part, awarding $150 an hour for the time Mr. Puricelli spent writing legal papers. Never mind the typos, he wrote. Mr. Puricelli's prose was "vague, ambiguous, unintelligible, verbose and repetitive."

"Mr. Puricelli's complete lack of care in his written product shows disrespect for the court," Magistrate Hart wrote. "Mr. Puricelli's lack of care caused the court and, I am sure, defense counsel, to spend an inordinate amount of time deciphering the arguments."

He reduced Mr. Puricelli's fee by $31,500, to $173,000.

Mr. Puricelli, in a telephone interview, said he regretted the mistakes but considered them minor.

"There was no intention to be disrespectful to the court," he said.

On the same day Magistrate Hart issued his decision, a Utah appeals court judge chastised another lawyer for textual malfeasance.

The judge, Gregory K. Orme, wrote in a dissent in a zoning case that he had been persuaded of the plaintiff's position in spite of rather than because of its filings. He chastised the plaintiff's lawyer, Stephen G. Homer, for his "unrestrained and unnecessary use of the bold, underline, and 'all caps' functions of word processing or his repeated use of exclamation marks to emphasize points in his briefs."

"While I appreciate a zealous advocate as much as anyone, such techniques, which really amount to a written form of shouting, are simply inappropriate in an appellate brief," Judge Orme continued. "It is counterproductive for counsel to litter his brief with burdensome material such as "WRONG! WRONG ANALYSIS! WRONG RESULT! WRONG! WRONG! WRONG!"

Mr. Homer declined to comment.

Bryan A. Garner, the editor of Black's Law Dictionary and the president of LawProse, a legal-writing consulting firm, said courts are becoming increasingly impatient with many lawyers' substandard writing skills.

"Lawyers are the most highly paid professional writers in the world," he said. "It's a good thing for judges to be more demanding."

Thinking and Writing Questions

1. What consequences does the author Adam Liptak address as a result of lawyer Puricelli's "complete lack of care in his written product" (175)?
2. Paragraphs 1–9 are one sentence. In the last fourteen paragraphs, seven are two sentences and seven are one sentence. Why might the author use one and two sentence paragraphs? What were you taught in high school about the number of sentences and types of sentences in paragraphs?

3. In "Internal Revision," Donald Murray delineates two "separate editorial acts involved in revision" (81): internal and external revision. In external revision, writers craft their ideas for the audience. Writers address "the conventions of form and language, mechanics, and style" (81). What might Donald Murray say to Attorney Puricelli about his writing?

4. The federal judge cut Attorney Puricelli's fee in half because of his "complete lack of care in his written product" (175). Does this seem fair? Why or why not? What action should teachers take when students' work shows a "complete lack of care"?

5. To what lengths should a writer go to get rid of errors? What strategies have you used to edit your prose? Does this strategy work for you?

What Corporate America Can't Build: A Sentence

SAM DILLON

Journalist Sam Dillon is a two-time Pulitzer Prize winner and a national correspondent for the New York Times. *In 1987, he was one of six reporters at the* Miami Herald *who won the Pulitzer Prize for their coverage of the Iran Contra Affair. From 1995 through 2000, he was the* New York Times *Mexico City bureau chief. In 1998, Dillon was one of the* New York Times *staff who won the Pulitzer Prize for international affairs for their coverage of the drug trade in Mexico. His book,* Opening Mexico: The Making of a Democracy, *2005, coauthored with Julia Preston, narrates Mexico's political changes since 1968. He is presently covering public schools and higher education for the* New York Times. *In "What Corporate America Can't Build: A Sentence," first published in the* New York Times, *Dillon reports on the education industry that has developed to teach business people to write.*

◆

BLOOMINGTON, Ill. - R. Craig Hogan, a former university professor who heads an online school for business writing here, received an anguished e-mail message recently from a prospective student.

"i need help," said the message, which was devoid of punctuation. "i am writing a essay on writing i work for this company and my boss want me to help improve the workers writing skills can yall help me with some information thank you".

Hundreds of inquiries from managers and executives seeking to improve their own or their workers' writing pop into Dr. Hogan's computer in-basket each month, he says, describing a number that has surged as e-mail has replaced the phone for much workplace communication. Millions of employees must write more frequently on the job than previously. And many are making a hash of it.

"E-mail is a party to which English teachers have not been invited," Dr. Hogan said. "It has companies tearing their hair out."

A recent survey of 120 American corporations reached a similar conclusion. The study, by the National Commission on Writing, a panel established by the College Board, concluded that a third of employees in the nation's blue-chip companies wrote poorly and that businesses were spending as much as $3.1 billion annually on remedial training.

The problem shows up not only in e-mail but also in reports and other texts, the commission said.

"It's not that companies want to hire Tolstoy," said Susan Traiman, a director at the Business Roundtable, an association of leading chief executives whose corporations were surveyed in the study. "But they need people who can write clearly, and many employees and applicants fall short of that standard."

Millions of inscrutable e-mail messages are clogging corporate computers by setting off requests for clarification, and many of the requests, in turn, are also chaotically written, resulting in whole cycles of confusion.

Here is one from a systems analyst to her supervisor at a high-tech corporation based in Palo Alto, Calif.: "I updated the Status report for the four discrepancies Lennie forward us via e-mail (they in Barry file) . . . to make sure my logic was correct It seems we provide Murray with incorrect information. . . . However after verifying controls on JBL - JBL has the indicator as B ???? - I wanted to make sure with the recent changes - I processed today - before Murray make the changes again on the mainframe to 'C'."

The incoherence of that message persuaded the analyst's employers that she needed remedial training.

"The more electronic and global we get, the less important the spoken word has become, and in e-mail clarity is critical," said Sean Phillips, recruitment director at another Silicon Valley corporation, Applera, a supplier of equipment for life science research, where most employees have advanced degrees. "Considering how highly educated our people are, many can't write clearly in their day-to-day work."

Some $2.9 billion of the $3.1 billion the National Commission on Writing estimates that corporations spend each year on remedial training goes to help current employees, with the rest spent on new hires. The corporations surveyed were in the mining, construction, manufacturing, transportation, finance, insurance, real estate and service industries, but not in wholesale, retail, agriculture, forestry or fishing, the commission said. Nor did the estimate include spending by government agencies to improve the writing of public servants.

An entire educational industry has developed to offer remedial writing instruction to adults, with hundreds of public and private universities, for-profit schools and freelance teachers offering evening classes as well as workshops, video and online courses in business and technical writing.

Kathy Keenan, a onetime legal proofreader who teaches business writing at the University of California Extension, Santa Cruz, said she sought to dissuade students from sending business messages in the crude shorthand they learned to tap out on their pagers as teenagers.

"hI KATHY i am sending u the assignmnet again," one student wrote to her recently. "i had sent you the assignment earlier but i didnt get a respond. If u get this assgnment could u please respond. thanking u for ur cooperation."

Most of her students are midcareer professionals in high-tech industries, Ms. Keenan said.

The Sharonview Federal Credit Union in Charlotte, N.C., asked about 15 employees to take a remedial writing course. Angela Tate, a mortgage processor, said the course eventually bolstered her confidence in composing e-mail, which has replaced much work she previously did by phone, but it was a daunting experience, since she had been out of school for years. "It was a challenge all the way through," Ms. Tate said.

Even C.E.O.'s need writing help, said Roger S. Peterson, a freelance writer in Rocklin, Calif., who frequently coaches executives. "Many of these guys write in inflated language that desperately needs a laxative," Mr. Peterson said, and not a few are defensive. "They're in denial, and who's going to argue with the boss?"

But some realize their shortcomings and pay Mr. Peterson to help them improve. Don Morrison, a onetime auditor at

Deloitte & Touche who has built a successful consulting business, is among them.

"I was too wordy," Mr. Morrison said. "I liked long, convoluted passages rather than simple four-word sentences. And I had a predilection for underlining words and throwing in multiple exclamation points. Finally Roger threatened to rip the exclamation key off my keyboard."

Exclamation points were an issue when Linda Landis Andrews, who teaches at the University of Illinois at Chicago, led a workshop in May for midcareer executives at an automotive corporation based in the Midwest. Their exasperated supervisor had insisted that the men improve their writing.

"I get a memo from them and cannot figure out what they're trying to say," the supervisor wrote Ms. Andrews.

When at her request the executives produced letters they had written to a supplier who had failed to deliver parts on time, she was horrified to see that tone-deaf writing had turned a minor business snarl into a corporate confrontation moving toward litigation.

"They had allowed a hostile tone to creep into the letters," she said. "They didn't seem to understand that those letters were just toxic."

"People think that throwing multiple exclamation points into a business letter will make their point forcefully," Ms. Andrews said. "I tell them they're allowed two exclamation points in their whole life."

Not everyone agrees. Kaitlin Duck Sherwood of San Francisco, author of a popular how-to manual on effective e-mail, argued in an interview that exclamation points could help convey intonation, thereby avoiding confusion in some e-mail.

"If you want to indicate stronger emphasis, use all capital letters and toss in some extra exclamation points," Ms. Sherwood advises in her guide, available at www.webfoot.com, where she offers a vivid example:

"Should I boost the power on the thrombo?

"NO!!!! If you turn it up to eleven, you'll overheat the motors, and IT MIGHT EXPLODE!!"

Dr. Hogan, who founded his online Business Writing Center a decade ago after years of teaching composition at Illinois State University here, says that the use of multiple exclamation points and other nonstandard punctuation like the :-) symbol, are fine for personal e-mail but that companies have erred by allowing experimental writing devices to flood into business writing.

He scrolled through his computer, calling up examples of incoherent correspondence sent to him by prospective students.

"E-mails-that are received from Jim and I are not either getting open or not being responded to," the purchasing manager at a construction company in Virginia wrote in one memorandum that Dr. Hogan called to his screen. "I wanted to let everyone know that when Jim and I are sending out e-mails (example- who is to be picking up parcels) I am wanting for who ever the e-mail goes to to respond back to the e-mail. Its important that Jim and I knows that the person, intended, had read the e-mail. This gives an acknowledgment that the task is being completed. I am asking for a simple little 2 sec. Note that says "ok", "I got it", or Alright."

The construction company's human resources director forwarded the memorandum to Dr. Hogan while enrolling the purchasing manager in a writing course.

"E-mail has just erupted like a weed, and instead of considering what to say when they write, people now just let thoughts drool out onto the screen," Dr. Hogan said. "It has companies at their wits' end."

Thinking and Writing Questions

1. To what do the speakers in Dillion's article attribute the fact that many professionals can't compose a sentence?

2. Contemplate the use of the word "drool." In the last sentence of the essay, Dillon quotes Dr. Hogan as saying, "people now just let thoughts drool out onto the screen"(180). What tone, defined as attitude toward the topic, does Dr. Hogan create with the use of "drool"? What tone does Dillon create by placing this word and quote at the end of his article?

3. What can you make of this "poor" writing in the corporate world based on the information given to you by Seth Stevenson, Nicole Crystal, and Maureen Hourigan on cheating and buying papers online?

4. Who is responsible for the fact that "a third of employees in the nation's blue-chip companies" write poorly? Should these companies have to spend $3.1 billion on remedial writing (177)? What suggestions can you offer for solving this problem of poor, unclear writing?

5. Dillon reports that many business persons who are asked to attend workshops and improve their writing are defensive and resistant. Why might this be? When a teacher asks you to work on and improve your writing, do you experience some resistance? Why? What can your teachers and peers do to help you overcome this resistance?

Three Mile Island and the Billion Dollar Memo

C. W. GRIFFIN

Professor C. W. Griffin directed the first-year writing program at Virginia Commonwealth University from 1970–1984. He received his Ph.D. from Indiana University, where he studied English. He is retired from Virginia Commonwealth University where he taught writing, Shakespeare, and business communication. He has published on teaching composition, business writing, writing across the curriculum, and teaching Shakespeare. In "Three Mile Island and the Billion Dollar Memo," which first appeared as part of a chapter in Writing: A Guide for Business Professionals, *Griffin explains how a poorly written memo contributed to a nuclear accident at the Three Mile Island nuclear plant.*

---- ◆ ----

A WRITING SITUATION

Some people call the memo that follows the billion dollar memo. Why? Because it was one link in a chain of mistakes and miscommunications that contributed to the 1979 accident at Three Mile Island, a nuclear facility located in Pennsylvania. The accident occurred because the water surrounding the nuclear core fell so low that the core was uncovered and began to heat up. Meltdown, a disaster of staggering potential, was only narrowly avoided. Costs to repair the resulting damages have been estimated at one billion dollars.

Actually, some people in the company that had built the facility knew months before the accident that unless certain procedures were changed, the possibility of uncovering the core existed. Yet because of faulty communications and bureaucratic slip-ups, the procedures were not changed. After you read the memo, you will understand why. Since its subject is a technical one, you may need the following summary to understand it:

- *Paragraph 1.* This paragraph states that the attached references recommend changing a particular procedure.

BABCOCK & WILCOX COMPANY
POWER GENERATION GROUP

TO: Manager, Plant Integration
FROM: Manager, Plant Performance Services
      Section (2149)
SUBJECT: Operator Interruption of High
         Pressure Injection (HPI)
DATE: August 3, 1978

References: (1) . . . to . . . , same
             subject, February 9, 1978

             (2) . . . to . . . , same subject,
             February 16, 1978

References 1 and 2 (attached) recommend a
change in B&W's philosophy for HPI system use
during low—pressure transients. Basically,
they recommend leaving the HPI pumps on, once
HPI has been initiated, until it can be
determined that the hot leg temperature is
more than 50° F below T_{sat} for the RCS pressure.

Nuclear Service believes this mode can cause
the RCS (including the pressurizer) to go
solid. The pressurizer reliefs will lift,
with a water surge through the discharge
piping into the quench tank.

[Continued]

- *Paragraph 2.* Nuclear Service, the department in the section that sent the memo, believes that such a change may result in problems.
- *Paragraph 3.* Therefore, it sets forth two questions that should be answered before the procedure is changed.
- *Paragraph 4.* The author of the memo notes that the attached references *do* suggest that the core may be uncovered if present procedure is not changed.
- *Paragraph 5.* The author asks that the Plant Integration Unit resolve the issue.

We believe the following incidents should
be evaluated:

1. If the pressurizer goes solid with one
   or more HPI pumps continuing to
   operate, would there be a pressure
   spike before the reliefs open which
   could cause damage to the RCS?

2. What damage would the water surge
   through the relief valve discharge
   piping and quench tank cause?

To date, Nuclear Service has not notified
our operating plants to change HPI policy
consistent with References 1 and 2 because
of our above—stated questions. Yet, the
references suggest the possibility of
uncovering the core if present HPI policy
is continued.

We request that Integration resolve the issue
of how the HPI system should be used. We are
available to help as needed.[1]

Now imagine that you are the Plant Integration manager who
receives this memo in the morning's mail. Read it quickly, just as
the manager did, and see whether you can understand what the
writer wants you to do.

---

[1]Stanley M. Gorinson and Kevin P. Kane, *Staff Report to the President's
Commission on the Accident at Three Mile Island: The Role of the Managing
Utility and Its Suppliers* (Washington, D.C.: U.S. Government Printing Office,
1979) 227.

The writer's major goal was to request that the Plant Integration manager resolve the question of whether procedures needed to be changed. Yet the manager didn't do it. In fact, apparently he didn't even notice the request. When he testified before the Nuclear Regulatory Commission after the accident had occurred, here is what he said about reading the memo.

> I don't recall ever really feeling the significance of what [he] was trying to communicate. It seemed to me that it was a routine matter; Nuclear Service was asking . . . two questions, and I sent it on, two of the questions [to be] answered in a rather routine manner.[2]

The important request to determine whether to change current procedures came at the end of the memo instead of the beginning. The Plant Integration manager therefore overlooked its significance and focused instead on the two questions in the middle.

THE COMPLEXITY OF CLARIFYING YOUR GOAL

The Babcock & Wilcox memo is a classic example of the kind of misunderstanding that can occur when a writer's major goal is not clear to his or her reader. But before we condemn its writer too harshly, we might speculate about the complexity of the situation he faced. He may, in fact, have had conflicting goals. On the one hand, he probably wanted to tell his reader about the recommended change in procedure and describe his reservations. On the other hand, he wanted to request that the manager decide whether the procedures should be changed and warn of the possible consequences of not changing them. He may never have decided which of these goals was the most important and which should therefore have been highlighted. The result was this confusing and costly memo.

You will have to deal with similar problems when you write on the job. You may hardly have the time to focus on your goal, especially if you have to get a report out in half a day. Or you may be interrupted and distracted by the telephone or by people dropping in with important questions. And some of your writing projects may be so complicated that you won't be able to clarify your major goal easily. You may even face a situation like the one just described, in which you have conflicting goals. Or you may begin

---

[2]Gorinson and Kane, 135.

a letter with one goal—perhaps to answer a client's question about a new system—and realize before you finish that your goal is really to persuade your client to buy the system.

HOW TO CHOOSE YOUR GOAL

Considering these kinds of constraints, how can you focus clearly on your major goal so that you can be sure of accomplishing it in any memo, letter, or report you write?[3] One way is to think of your major goal as the bridge between you and your readers. Your goal is how you want to affect your readers—what you want to happen to them as a result of what you have written. You may want them to feel good about a job well done, to be aware of a new company policy, to understand why a change was made, to be able to operate a new system, to buy a new piece of equipment, or to make a crucial decision.

Another way to picture your major goal in a particular situation is to see it as the "so that" of your writing—you are writing a memo *so that* your staff will follow a new procedure, a letter *so that* your client will be persuaded that you can solve his problem, a report *so that* your manager will understand exactly what's wrong with an antiquated system, or a manual *so that* an operator will be able to use a new system effectively. If you think about your major goal in this fashion, then you will have a way of continually clarifying it for yourself. Even if you lose sight of it because you become deeply involved in your subject, or if it changes as you progress through a document, or if you begin to sense that you are facing conflicting goals, you can always stop and say to yourself: "I am writing this document *so that* my reader will [be affected in this way]."

THE EFFECTS OF YOUR GOAL ON CONTENT AND ORGANIZATION

When you learn how to write particular documents later in this book, you'll see how a precise definition of your major goal can be particularly helpful as you decide what information to include and what to leave out. If, for instance, your major goal in a memo is to show an operator how to run a new system, you may decide

---

[3]By the way, when I use the term "goal," I mean the same thing someone else might mean by "purpose" or "intention." If you are more comfortable with one of these words, substitute it as you read.

not to bother to describe the system in great technical detail, since your reader doesn't need to know this. But if your major goal is to show a technician how to repair that same system, then you will have to give details.

You'll also see how a clear understanding of your major goal can affect the way you organize a document. If you are writing a memo to inform your staff about some new office procedures, you will probably organize your memo in a top-down pattern, putting the most important procedures at the beginning and then following with others. But if you realize that your goal is also to persuade your staff to adopt the new procedures readily, you may decide to begin the memo by describing how people will benefit from the new procedures before getting to the procedures themselves. For instance, when the writers revising the memo in Chapter 1 finally decided that their major goal in the flextime memo was to persuade employees to accept the new system, they put the system's benefits first.

THINK, THINK, THINK—THE KEY TO EFFECTIVE WRITING

If you were totally systematic and worked in an ideal world, you would begin every new writing task by carefully thinking about the major goal you wanted to accomplish. Unfortunately, you won't always be so systematic—you'll dash off a letter sometimes without thinking twice, and you'll probably begin some reports without knowing where you will end up or what you are really trying to do. And the world of work is far from ideal—you'll be interrupted as you write, have to meet impossible deadlines, and have a manager on your back if you don't write something in a certain way.

But if you can discipline yourself to clarify your major goal for a writing project (ideally when you begin but certainly before you finish), you will write more effectively. Get in the habit of thinking to yourself, "I am writing this document *so that* my reader will [be affected in this way]."

What would have happened if the writer of the Three Mile Island memo had read his memo over and decided to clarify his major goal? He might have said to himself, "I am writing this memo *so that* my reader will decide whether to change procedures or not. Since that's my major goal, I'd better begin with it." He might then have revised the first part as the memo on the right shows (changes are underlined), and the Three Mile Island accident might have been prevented.

```
BABCOCK & WILCOX COMPANY
POWER GENERATION GROUP


TO:   Manager,  Plant  Integration
FROM: Manager,  Plant  Performance
      Services Section (2149)
SUBJECT: Proper Use of HPI System
DATE: August 3, 1978


References: (1) B. M. Dunn to J. Taylor, same
               subject, February 9, 1978
               (2) B. M. Dunn to J. Taylor, same
               subject, February 16, 1978


This is to request that Plant Integration
decide the important question of how the HPI
system should be used. The attached
references suggest the possibility of
uncovering the core if present HPI policy is
continued.


References 1 and 2 (attached) recommend a
change in B&W's philosophy for HPI system use
during low-pressure transients. Basically,
they recommend leaving the HPI pumps on, once
HPI has been initiated, until it can be
determined that the hot leg temperature is
more than 50° F below $T_{sat}$ for the RCS
pressure. . . .
```

Thinking and Writing Questions

1. What part did this memo play in the accident at Three Mile Island?
2. This reading comes from a textbook. How is the design and structure different from the newspaper article, "Judge Finds a Typo-Prone Lawyer Guilty of Bad Writing"? Being that students are the audience for "Three

Mile Island and the Billion Dollar Memo," why is it designed and structured in this manner?

3. What might William Zinsser, author of "Simplicity," say to the authors of the Billion Dollar Memo?

4. The managers at Babcock & Wilcox Company who wrote this memo were educated professionals whose writing and reading had a significant impact on the people they were serving. Consider the profession you are planning to join. How could your writing and reading influence negatively and positively the constituency you will serve? How can you ensure positive impacts?

Healing through the Written Word
KAREN CANGIALOSI

Psychotherapist Karen Cangialosi works at Kaiser Permanente's Positive Choice Wellness Center in San Diego and runs a group called "Healing Through the Written Word" through the Creative Arts Therapy program. She uses writing in therapy with individual clients and is a published poet. Previously, she was a project manager for Microsoft Corporation. In "Healing through the Written Word," which first appeared in The Permanente Journal, *Cangialosi reports how writing can be used to decrease pain associated with physical illness.*

---◆---

Writing is not only a salve but often a tool that opens our minds and hearts to things that are deep inside us. The famous American poet, EE Cummings, said, "To be nobody-but-yourself—in a world which is doing its best, night and day, to make you everybody else—means to fight the hardest battle which any human being can fight . . . ."[1] I agree with EE Cummings that people need help to fight the battles of their lives, but first people must be aware of and accept these battles before they can move on to conquer them. As David Spiegel, MD, said in the April 14, 1999 issue of *JAMA*, " . . . Smyth and colleagues demonstrate that merely writing about past stressful life experiences results in symptom reduction among patients with asthma or rheumatoid arthritis."[2:1329] Reporting in *The MedServ Medical News* on the same study by Smyth and colleagues, Mara Bovsun concluded that "The simple act of writing about bad times can be a potent, and low cost, method of relieving pain and symptoms of chronic illnesses . . . ."[3] This research points out and supports the idea that emotions left unattended can change into symptoms that cause confusion when they present in physicians' offices. Through a weekly writing workshop offered by Kaiser Permanente's Positive Choice Wellness Center in San Diego, people become aware of their battles or issues, how to accept them, and how to move more fully into a personal healing process.

WRITING HAS THE POWER TO HEAL

In his book, *Opening Up*,[4] James W Pennebaker, PhD, documented his decades-long research into the healing effects of writing. Pennebaker proved what many people have found incidentally through keeping a journal or diary: If we can create a cohesive personal narrative of our lives and if we can link up our emotions with specific events, then we have the power to take control of how those emotions and events affect our lives.

Although many of us might be drawn to simply eliminate the pain in our lives, those who constructively learn how to use that pain are often far healthier than those who don't.[4,5] Pennebaker noted that the number of doctor office visits are reduced through the process of writing. In her *Medserv Medical News* article, Bovsun quoted Smyth and colleagues, "[a]lthough it may be difficult to believe that a brief writing exercise can meaningfully affect health, this study replicates what a burgeoning literature indicates in healthy individuals," and then points out that "[t]he scientists do not know why writing appears to help, but other research suggests that it may bolster immune function and enhance . . . ability to cope with painful incidents."[3]

May Sarton said that ". . . the only way through pain . . . is to go through it, to absorb, probe, understand exactly what it is and what it means . . . . Nothing that happens to us, even the most terrible shock, is unusable, and everything has somehow to be built into the fabric of the personality . . . ."[6] By using the different writing forms—fiction, nonfiction, poetry, journaling, list-making, and others—we can use the pain in our lives to further develop the "fabric of our personality."[6] Through writing, we try to find order in the things that have happened to us; to use our writing as a form of self-analysis; or to give form and sense to what has affected us. Whichever form our writing takes, it has the power to heal us and to help us grow.

Often we form destructive attachments by putting energy into certain activities that seem to give us either pleasure or relief. Writing helps us to understand who we are and where and why we have formed such attachments. Writing can then help us redirect our energy. Writing allows us to get in touch with what is often hidden from us—whether it be the reason behind our weight gain, a hard-to-understand addiction, a compulsion we fight daily, or a pain we wish would go away. Writing helps us to form connections with what is going on inside us and with others.

HOW DOES WRITING HEAL?

People simply start by writing about a specific event or situation or relationship that affected them. For example, a woman can begin by writing a letter to her mother or father (that does not get sent) telling the parent about the best and worst things the parent did for her. Or a man can begin by writing about how he experiences the emotion of anger or where in his body he actually feels the emotion of bitterness. People must write freely; ideally, the writing is continued for at least 20 minutes without stopping. People should not edit what they are writing; they shouldn't worry about grammar or punctuation or how things might sound. They simply need to write and see what comes out; and, according to Pennebaker, they must write about both the event and the emotions surrounding that event.[4]

Although the simple exercise of writing has actually been proven to decrease blood pressure and improve immune functioning,[4] reading the work aloud and processing it with others can itself further enhance the overall healing effects of writing. The ability to tell their own story often gives people the first chance to really understand that story. Many people have said that they didn't know what they were going to write until it was written; another way of describing this phenomenon is to say that the writing taps into their unconscious. Healing through the written word happens when people learn about themselves and open themselves to the healing power within.

For example, here are pieces written during the "Healing Through the Written Word" group at Positive Choice:

FROZEN IN TIME
By Diana Medlin[a]

When I was quite small I entered battle.
I did not have any weapons nor armor
To shield me.
All I had were my toys and my stuffed bear.
We created our own foxhole and waited
Out the night.
We did not dare sleep until it had stayed quiet
For a long time.
We held our breath together and looked out the window
Into the frozen midnight.
And when it was safe to breathe we would
Press our faces up against the glass and
Marvel at the fading impression.

EMPTINESS
By Santo Messina[b]

Emptiness stands,
Great breeze that tickles the skin,
Sounds give music harmony.
Seeing green that transforms into yellow
   and bursting in red
tranquilized by orange,
     then storming clouded haze gives way to
       bright shining streaks of rays that cut the clouds
    and warm the skin.
Calmed by water dropping over soft melted stones
bleached by sun and coming slow
     then fast
     then big
     then slow again
       and gone
         and quiet
     and lull
    and not
and fragrance breaks the quiet spell.

I meet tranquility and love breaks through
And wetness strikes from nowhere known
without a signal, without knowing
and flood my eyes with sadness-joy
and quiet want
as no one knows
my heart is deep and mended not
without a chance to consider why
as sudden chirp as feathers fly
and land on foot to sobbing heaves
as though the flying friend knew, what lies within
                              as I do not.

The shriek of voices that comes outside
to violently thrust my pain aside
and dew drops must be hid or else
creatures know and floods will flow.
I cannot stop this flowing yet
I need to hide
so again I smile and brush my hair and know not where to
    shroud my care.
I cannot stop
and still I hear the voice that comes outside
and is still afar.
I cannot stop
I will not stop.
The voice is louder and louder
not caring, it is slicing parts within me bleeding
and so I hear
      and so I hear
I do not want to stop but still
    I hear
and hear. . . . .

Each of these people has used writing as a way to get in touch with, understand, and begin to heal from painful events. Specifically, by writing about these experiences, these individuals are able to shift the power of the event from the event or experience itself into their own hands. As they write, they recreate the situation or event mentally and begin to work with it. They gain access to their own feelings, sometimes discovering feelings they didn't even know were there. People who discover or uncover these feelings can begin to work through them.

POSITIVE CHOICE WELLNESS CENTER INCLUDES WRITING WORKSHOPS

In the weekly writing group at KP's Positive Choice Wellness Center, each person has an opportunity to share her or his writing with others. Through empathetic listening and response, participants help each other gain ". . . sufficient honesty to look at the inner self . . . [and] enough objectivity to view a feeling or behavior pattern from another perspective . . . ."[7:p58] From this experience of sharing and reflection, people often gain the self-confidence to accept and understand their difficult issues and to process them more thoroughly than ever before.

RESEARCH SHOWS EFFICACY OF WRITING

In his 1990 book, *Opening Up*, James W Pennebaker, PhD, first published his findings about how expressing emotions through writing affects the immune system[4]. On the basis of what was to become years of research and study, Pennebaker showed that ". . . actively holding back or inhibiting our thoughts and feelings can be hard work. Over time, the work of inhibition gradually undermines the body's defenses. Like other stressors, inhibition can affect immune function, the action of the heart and vascular systems, and even the biochemical workings of the brain and nervous systems. In short, excessive holding back of thoughts, feelings, and behaviors can place people at risk for both major and minor diseases."[4:p2]

Before psychoneuroimmunology commanded the attention it does today, Pennebaker worked with the research team of Janice K Kiecolt-Glaser (a clinical psychologist) and Ronald Glaser (an immunologist) to use " . . . precise, state-of-the-art techniques to measure the action of T-lymphocytes, natural killer cells, and other immune markers in the blood."[4:p35] By taking blood samples before, immediately after, and six weeks after the writing experience, Pennebaker made inroads into measuring the effects of self-expressive writing on the immune system.

Pennebaker has conducted numerous studies to corroborate his original findings: "When disclosing deeply personal experiences, there are immediate changes in brainwave patterns, skin conductance levels . . . after confessions, significant drops in blood pressure and heart rate, as well as improvements in immune function, occur. In the weeks and months afterward, people's physical and psychological health is improved."[4:p56] Others (eg, Joshua M Smyth[5] at North Dakota State University) have expanded on Pennebaker's research to show that writing helps people who have chronic diseases, such as asthma and arthritis.

As a group facilitator, I take the lead in listening with empathy and understanding to help guide people through the often-difficult process of recognizing important emotions and events that have long been left unattended. By working with images and specific language that individuals use, I can often identify behavioral patterns and issues that surface. By gently probing into what their own writing uncovers, people often come to believe that change is possible. Although neither the group nor I try to tell people how they might change, we do create an environment in which change is possible. Emotional change in these groups has led to stress reduction and weight loss, both of which affect a person's health and well-being. In this way, writing about events and emotions and sharing these with others in a supportive environment is an example of how powerful the healing effects of writing can be.

For those not able to participate in the writing workshop facilitated by the KP Positive Choice Wellness Center in San Diego, the Web site www.journalingmagazine.com offers exercises, suggestions, and inspiration to those who want to write. In addition, many books are available, such as *Writing Your Way to Healing and Wholeness* by Robin B Dilley,[8] which invites people to write in a journal on a variety of topics; or *Writing as a Way of Healing* by Louise DeSalvo,[9] which shows how effective a tool writing has been and continues to be for people.

References

1. Cummings EE. A poet's advice to students. In: Cummings EE. A miscellany revised. New York: October House; 1965. p 335.
2. Spiegel D. Healing words: emotional expression and disease outcome [editorial]. JAMA 1999 Apr 14;281(14):1328–9.
3. Bovsun M. Writing relieves asthma, arthritis pain. MedServ Med News 1999 Apr 13. Available on the World Wide Web (accessed April 26, 2002): www.medserv.dk/health/1999/04/14/story01.htm.
4. Pennebaker JW. Opening up: the healing power of expressing emotions. New York: Guilford Press; 1997.
5. Smyth JM, Stone AA, Hurewitz A, Kaell A. Effects of writing about stressful experiences on symptom reduction in patients with asthma or rheumatoid arthritis: a randomized trial. JAMA 1999 Apr 14;281(14):1304–9.
6. Sarton M. Recovering: a journal. New York: Norton; 1980. p 13.

7. Hynes AM, Hynes-Berry M. Bibliotherapy: the interactive process: a handbook. Boulder (CO): Westview Press; 1986.
8. Dilley RB. Writing your way to healing and wholeness: simple exercises: exploring your past and changing your future. Glendale (AZ): Robin B Dilley, PhD, Ltd; 1999.
9. DeSalvo L. Writing as a way of healing: how telling our stories transforms our lives. Boston: Beacon Press; 1999.

Thinking and Writing Questions

1. Explain in writing to a friend who has never read this piece how medical professionals think that writing supports healing. How does putting our thoughts and feelings into words reduce the symptoms of asthma and rheumatoid arthritis as reported by Dr. David Spiegel?
2. Why does Karen Cangialosi quote doctors and their research in her piece? For what purpose does she use their research?
3. In "Laura's Legacy," Avery writes, "The last five weeks of school will be filled with memories of Laura as we work through our loss together" (197). How does the writing described in "Laura's Legacy" serve as healing to Laura's classmates and her teachers?
4. Try your hand at using writing to "develop the fabric of your personality" (190) Pick an incident to reflect on: a negative or positive incident—possibly the birth of a child, death of a friend, an illness. Remember that this writing can take many forms: poems, memoirs, a short story, a comic strip, etc. Use this writing "to give form and sense to what has affected us" (Cangialosi 190). If you compose a piece that you like, send it to us, so we can consider it for inclusion in the next edition of *Essays on Writing*. bryant@calumet.purdue.edu and hclark28@ivytech.edu

---

Laura's Legacy
CAROL AVERY

Educator Carol Avery is the author of . . . And With a Light Touch, a book on teaching language arts to first graders. She holds degrees in English, library science, elementary education, and writing. She has taught at the elementary, secondary, and college levels and also served as a school librarian. In 1997, Avery served as President of the National Council of Teachers of English. She consults in classrooms across the country, conducting demonstration lessons for

teachers on how to develop writing workshops. In "Laura's Legacy,"
first published in Language Arts, *Avery tells the story of students*
writing in her first grade classroom.

──────────── ✦ ────────────

MAY 8, 1987

We celebrate Mother's Day in our first grade classroom this
Friday afternoon. The children perform a play for their mothers
entitled "The Big Race," the story of the tortoise and the hare.
Laura is the "turtle" who wins the race.

A few minutes later Laura reads aloud the book she has
authored about her mother. The group laughs as she reads about
learning to count with her cousins when she was three years old.
Laura writes: "I was learning six. Then my Mom came in and asked
what we were doing. I said, 'I'm learning sex!'" Laura's mother was
delighted. The reading continues with a hilarious account of a family squabble between Mom and Dad over a broken plate. Laura
concludes the anecdote, "So then I just went in and watched TV."
Laura looks at me and smiles as she pauses, waiting for her audience
to quieten before she goes on. I wink at her; I know she is thinking,
"Wait till they hear the next part. It's the funniest of all." She reads
about a llama spitting in Mom's eye on a visit to the zoo. Laura's way
with words has brought delight to everyone. I remember a week
earlier when Laura and I sat to type her draft and she said, "This is
the best part. I put it last so that everyone will feel happy at the end."

MAY 9, 1987

Saturday night, around 11:45 P.M., a light bulb ignites fabric in a
closet outside Laura's bedroom. Laura wakes. She cannot get
through the flames and by the time firefighters reach her it is too
late. Laura dies. No one else is injured.

MAY 11, 1987

The children and I gather on our Sharing Rug in the classroom
on Monday morning. I have no plans. We start to talk. There are
endless interruptions until Michael says, "Mrs. Avery, can we shut
the door so people stop bothering us?" So Michael shuts the door.

"Are you going to read us the newspapers?" they ask. "Is that what you'd like?" "Yes," comes the unanimous response. The children huddle close; a dozen knees nuzzle against me. I read aloud the four-paragraph story on the front page of the *Sunday News* that accompanies a picture of our Laura sprawled on the lawn of her home with firefighters working over her. I read the longer story in Monday morning's paper that carries Laura's school picture. We cry. We talk and cry some more. And then we read Laura's books—writings which Laura determined were her best throughout the year and which were "published" to become part of our classroom library. These books are stories of Laura and her family, stories with titles such as *My Dad Had a Birthday* and *When My Grandmother Came to My House*. Laura's voice comes through loud and clear with its sense of humor and enthusiasm. We laugh and enjoy her words. "Laura was a good writer," they say. "She always makes us laugh when we read her stories." Then Dustin says, "You know, it feels like Laura is right here with us, right now. We just can't see her."

A short time later we begin our writing workshop. Every child chooses to write about Laura this day. Some write about the fire, some write memories of Laura as a friend. I write with them. After forty-five minutes it is time to go to art and there are cries of disappointment at having to stop. We will come back to the writing. There will be plenty of time. The last five weeks of school will be filled with memories of Laura as we work through our loss together. The children will decide to leave her desk in it's [sic] place in the room because, "It's not in our way and anyway, this is still Laura's room even if she's not really here anymore." Laura's mother and little brother will come in to see us. On the last day they will bring us garden roses that Laura would have brought. Laura will always be a part of us and none of us will ever be the same.

In the days immediately following Laura's death and in the weeks since then certain thoughts have been rattling around in my head: I'm glad that I teach the way I do. I'm so glad I really knew Laura. I know that I can never again teach in a way that is not focused on children. I can never again put a textbook or a "program" between me and the children. I'm glad I knew Laura so well. I'm glad all of us knew her so well. I'm glad the classroom context allowed her to read real books, to write about real events and experiences in her life, to share herself with us and to become part of us and we of her. I'm grateful for a classroom community that nurtured us all throughout the year and especially when Laura was gone. Laura left a legacy. Part of that legacy is the six little published books and the five-inch-thick stack of paper that is her writing from our daily writing workshops. When we read her words, we hear again her voice and her laughter.

Thinking and Writing Questions

1. Describe the legacy that Laura leaves for her classmates and for the readers of this essay. Does Laura's story convince you that it is important to be a writer?

2. What genre does Carol Avery use to tell Laura's story? What purpose does she accomplish with this genre?

3. In the first chapter of *Essays on Writing*, "Attitudes toward Writing," the authors speak about writing as a skill and as an art. How do you think this first grade teacher Carol Avery and her students would characterize the purpose of writing in their classroom? As a skill for practicing their spelling? As a tool they will need for second grade? As something else?

4. Avery comments on her teaching, "I'm glad that I teach the way I do. . . . I'm glad the classroom context allowed [Laura] to read real books, to write about real events and experiences in her life, to share herself with us and to become part of us and we of her" (197). How do you think Avery's classroom structure and content contributed to the way Laura and her classmates view writing?

Spelling

MARGARET ATWOOD

Writer Margaret Atwood has been labeled as a feminist and humanitarian due to the subject of gender issues in her writing and her interests in environmentalism and biotechnology. With over eleven novels, five children's books, and seventeen collections of poetry, Atwood is a prominent writer on the Canadian literary scene. She received her undergraduate degrees from the University of Toronto and her master's degree from Ratcliff. She has taught at New York University, the University of British Columbia, and the University of Alberta. In "Spelling," which was first published in True Stories, *Atwood demonstrates how spells can be cast with the spelling of words.*

✦

SPELLING
Margaret Atwood

My daughter plays on the floor
with plastic letters,
red, blue & hard yellow,
learning how to spell,
spelling,
how to make spells

*

and I wonder how many women
denied themselves daughters,
closed themselves in rooms,
drew the curtains
so they could mainline words.

*

A child is not a poem,
a poem is not a child.
There is no either/or.
However.

*

I return to the story
of the woman caught in the war
& in labour, her thighs tied
together by the enemy
so she could not give birth.

Ancestress: the burning witch,
her mouth covered by leather
to strangle words.

A word after a word
after a word is power.

*

At the point where language falls away
from the hot bones, at the point
where the rock breaks open and darkness
flows out of it like blood, at
the melting point of granite
when the bones know

they are hollow & the word
splits & doubles & speaks
the truth & the body
itself becomes a mouth.

This is a metaphor.

*

How do you learn to spell?
Blood, sky & the sun,
your own name first,
your first naming, your first name,
your first word.

Thinking and Writing Questions

1. What spell does Atwood cast on you as you read her poem? How do you respond to her images and ideas?
2. Atwood plays on the word "spell." Explain this play on words.
3. Examine Atwood's choice of the image of mainlining words. Women "closed themselves in rooms,/drew the curtains/so they could mainline words" (199). In this image how does Atwood characterize the reason for writing? How does her belief about writing compare to those of writers in the first chapter on attitudes?
4. Atwood writes "A word after a word/after a word is power" (199). How do words exert power over people? Give a few examples.
5. In the last stanza Atwood asks, "How do you learn to spell?" (200). Write a piece that speaks to Atwood. In prose or poetry, tell Atwood how you are learning to "spell."

Writing to Connect
Mary Pipher

Psychologist Dr. Mary Pipher is a professor at the University of Nebraska. She received her BA in Cultural Anthropology at University of California at Berkeley and her PhD in Clinical Psychology from the University of Nebraska. Pipher studies and writes about how American culture influences mental health. She has written seven non-fiction books and is best known for Reviving Ophelia, *about the struggle of adolescent girls to develop esteem. Three of her books have been on the* New York Times *best sellers list. Pipher travels the world sharing her ideas with community groups, schools, and health care professionals. In "Writing to Connect," a chapter from her new book* Writing to Change the World, *Pipher argues that we can write to share our stories, connect with each other, and influence some aspect of our world.*

---------------------◆---------------------

The first book to change my view of the universe was *The Diary of Anne Frank*. I read Anne's diary when I was a twelve-year-old, in Beaver City, Nebraska. Before I read it, I had been able to ignore the existence of evil. I knew a school had burned down in Chicago, and that children had died there. I had seen grown-ups lose their tempers, and I had encountered bullies and nasty schoolmates. I had a vague sense that there were criminals—jewel thieves, bank robbers, and Al Capone–style gangsters—in Kansas City and Chicago. After reading the diary, I realized that there were adults who would systematically kill children. My comprehension of the human race expanded to include a hero like Anne, but also to include the villains who killed her. When I read Anne Frank's diary, I lost my spiritual innocence.

In September 2003, when I was fifty-five years old, I visited the Holocaust Museum, in Washington, D .C., to view the Anne Frank exhibit. I looked at the cover of her little plaid diary, and at pages of her writing, at her family pictures. Meip Gies, Otto Frank's employee who brought food to the family, spoke on video about the people who hid in the attic. She said that Anne had always wanted to know the truth about what was going on. Others would believe the sugar-coated version of Miep's stories, but Anne would follow her to the door and ask, "What is really happening?"

The museum showed a short film clip of Anne dressed in white, her long hair dark and shiny. She is waving exuberantly from a balcony at a wedding party that is parading down the street. There are just a few seconds of film, captured by a film-maker at the wedding who must have been entranced by her enthusiasm. The footage is haunting. Anne's wave seems directed at all of us, her small body casting a shadow across decades.

At the end of the exhibit, attendees hear the voice of a young girl reading Anne's essay "Give," a piece inspired by her experience of passing beggars on the street. She wonders if people who live in cozy houses have any idea of the life of beggars. She offers hope: "How wonderful it is that no one has to wait, but can start right now to gradually change the world." She suggests action: "Give whatever you have to give, you can always give something, even if it's a simple act of kindness." And she ends with: "The world has plenty of room, riches, money and beauty. God has created enough for each and every one of us. Let us begin by dividing it more fairly."

Even though Anne Frank ultimately was murdered, she managed, in her brief and circumscribed life, to tell the truth and bequeath the gift of hope. She searched for beauty and joy even in the harsh, frightened world of the attic in which her family hid from the Nazis.

Her writing has lived on to give us all a sense of the potential largesse of the human soul, even in worst-case scenarios. It also reminds us that, behind the statistics about war and genocide, there are thousands of good people we have a responsibility to help.

All writing is designed to change the world, at least a small part of the world, or in some small way perhaps a change in a reader's mood or in his appreciation of a certain kind of beauty. Writing to improve the world can be assessed by the goals of its writers and/or by its effects on the world. Most likely, Mary Oliver did not write her poem "Wild Geese" to inspire environmental activists and yet environmentalists have found it motivational. Bob Dylan claims he had no intention of composing a protest song when he penned "Blowin' in the Wind," but it became the anthem for many of the causes of the last half of the twentieth century. On the other hand, musicians like Tori Amos, the Indigo Girls, and the band Ozomatli do hope to influence their listeners in specific ways, and they succeed. Looking back, Rachel Carson, in *Silent Spring*, satisfies both intent and effect: she wrote the book to stop the use of certain pesticides, and, following its publication, DDT was banned in the United States.

My dad told me about a rule he and other soldiers followed in the Pacific during World War II. It was called the Law of 26, and it postulates that for every result you expect from an action there will be twenty-six results you do not expect. Certainly this law applies to writing. Sometimes a book intended to have one effect has quite another. For example, Upton Sinclair wrote *The Jungle* to call attention to the exploitation of the immigrant labor force and their working conditions in factories, yet it led to an outcry over unsanitary conditions in the meat industry and helped establish uniform standards for beef processing and inspection nationwide.

ART/ARTFUL/PROPAGANDA

All writing to effect change need not be great literature. Some of it is art, of course, such as Walt Whitman's "I Hear America Singing" or Abraham Lincoln's Gettysburg Address. Some of it is relatively straightforward, such as *Rampage: The Social Roots of School Shootings* by Katherine Newman, David Harding, and Cybelle Fox. And some of it is both artful and straightforward. For example, in *The Age of Missing Information*, Bill McKibben has a clever idea that he executes beautifully: he compares what he learns from a week in the mountains to what he learns from watching a week's worth of cable television. On the mountaintop, McKibben experiences himself as small yet connected to something large and awe-inspiring. He comes down from the mountain calm and clear-thinking. Watching cable for a week, he hears over and over that he has unmet needs, that he is grossly inadequate, yet he still is the center of the universe, deserving of everything he wants. McKibben ended the week feeling unfocused, agitated, and alone.

Many effective writers are not stylists, but they manage to convey a clear message. Their writing is not directed toward sophisticates or literary critics. It is designed to influence cousin Shirley, farmer Dale, coworker Jan, Dr. Lisa, neighbor Carol, businessman Carl, or voter Sylvia. Expository writing for ordinary people calls for a variety of talents—storytelling skills, clarity, and the ability to connect. Whether they are working on an op-ed piece, a speech, or a poem, skilled writers exercise creativity and conscious control. They labor to make the important interesting, and even compelling, to readers.

Change writers hope that readers will join them in what Charles Johnson calls "an invitation to struggle." Whereas writers of propaganda encourage readers to accept certain answers, writers who want to transform their readers encourage the asking of questions. Propaganda invites passive agreement; change writing invites original thought, openheartedness, and engagement. Change writers trust that readers can handle multiple points of view, contradictions, unresolved questions, and nuance. If, as André Gide wrote, "Tyranny is the absence of complexity," then change writers are founders of democracies.

Good writing astonishes its writer first. My favorite example of this phenomenon is Leo Tolstoy's *Anna Karenina*. Tolstoy planned to write a novel that condemned adultery, and his intention was to make the adultress an unsympathetic character. But when he came to truly understand Anna as he wrote the book, he fell in love with her, and, a hundred years later, so do his readers. Empathy can turn contempt into love.

Socially conscious writers want authenticity and transparency to saturate every page of their work. They strive to teach readers how to think, not what to think. They connect readers to ideas and experiences that readers would not have on their own. Always, this kind of writing coaxes readers to expand their frames of reference, or, as the Buddhists say, to put things in bigger containers.

MORAL WRITING

You write in order to change the world, knowing perfectly well that you probably can't, but also knowing that literature is indispensable to the world. . . . The world changes according to the way people see it, and if you alter, even by a millimeter, the way people look at reality, then you can change it.

—JAMES BALDWIN

All kinds of writing can change the world by James Baldwin's millimeter. Recently, I read an article by horticulturalist Twyla Hansen that encouraged landowners to plant slow-growing shade trees, the kinds of trees that may not grow tall on our watch but will be beautiful for our grandchildren. After reading Hansen's article, I bought a sycamore.

For many years, I wrote "Urgent Action" letters for Amnesty International. I mailed them all over the world, to protest the torture and imprisonment of innocents, the curtailment of civil liberties, the oppression of women, and the harassment of journalists and others who worked for democracy. I am sure that many of my letters were simply tossed away; however, thanks to all those letters, a number of campaigns produced results. The Red Cross and Red Crescent were allowed into horrific prisons. Dissidents there were allowed access to their attorneys or even set free. And universities and presses have been allowed to reopen.

Examples of effective writing abound. President John Kennedy was so moved by Michael Harrington's *The Other America* that he launched the War on Poverty, later implemented by President Johnson. More recently, the state of New York was able to amend and soften the harsh Rockefeller drug laws instituted in the 1970s. A *New York Times* article credited this policy change to Jennifer Gonnerman's book *Life on the Outside*. which told the story of a woman detained for sixteen years for a single sale of cocaine.

Academics can be revolutionaries. Donella Meadows, Dennis Meadows, and Jorgan Randers in *The Limits to Growth* educated us about the future of the earth's resources. They plotted graphs showing that while the world's population is increasing, such natural resources as oil, water, and arable land are decreasing. Their work gave scientists, policymakers, and everyday citizens new ways to frame environmental, energy, and population issues. Dr. Paul Farmer, writing as a medical anthropologist, has revolutionized medicine in the developing world with such books as *AIDS and Accusation: Haiti and the Geography of Blame* and *Infections and Inequalities: The Modern Plague*.

Journalists can change the zeitgeist as well. Think of Bob Woodward and Carl Bernstein on Watergate, or of Seymour Hersh's recent writing on Iraq and Afghanistan. Reporters pick the stories to tell from the thousands of available ones. They call readers' attention to what they think is newsworthy. And readers respond. For example, Jim Barksdale, former Netscape CEO, offered to reward students in Mississippi up to ten thousand dollars of their college tuition if they did well in school. His generosity was inspired by an article he had read on the state's struggle to fund its educational system.

Many writers who have suffered great sorrows write memoirs for cathartic reasons. They also write to document their experiences, to express outrage at injustice and unnecessary suffering, and to help others to see and feel what can happen to people like themselves. They write to both bind up their own wounds and inspire others to care.

Most likely, Loung Ung's memoir, *Lucky Child*, was written for all of the above reasons. Ung tells the story of her family's experience of the genocide that took place in Cambodia. Both her parents and several of her siblings died, but Loung fortunately escaped to a refugee camp with an older brother and his wife. Later, they settled in the United States. *Lucky Child* compares Luong's life in the United States with the life of her younger sister who stayed behind in Cambodia. It shows readers the differences between living in a prosperous, yet stressed, democratic country and living in an impoverished, yet communal, autocratic country.

Song can be a powerful tool for connecting people to one another. Think of civil rights workers singing "We Shall Overcome."

Think of Woody Guthrie's "This Land Is Your Land," Curtis Mayfield's "People Get Ready," or Tracy Chapman's "Revolution."
Films often change the world. Morgan Spurlock's entertaining, witty, and solidly researched *Super Size Me* has Spurlock, a healthy young man, bravely eat nothing but McDonald's fast food for a month. With doctors monitoring him, he gained weight and suffered numerous health problems. His downhill slide into a dangerous medical condition was highly instructive for the rest of us, and it pushed McDonald's toward offering healthier choices.

Any form of writing can change the world. Your goal is to find the form that allows you to use every one of your talents in the service of what you consider to be your most important goals. You want to search for what you alone can say and then how you can say it most effectively.

Ordinary people can and do change the world every day. Yet even as I write, I hear a despairing voice inside me whisper that right now car bombs and nuclear weapons seem more powerful than words, that few people read serious writing, and that even those readers who do seem to read only to reinforce their established beliefs. Some days, I have to argue with myself for a long while before the urge to connect in me wins and sends me off to work.

Discouragement can stop us from doing our work, as can humility. Many writers silence themselves by thinking, Who am I to write? And who among us has not written letters to editors, corporations, or government officials that were simply ignored? I remember *The Lazlo Letters* by Don Novello, published years ago. It featured crazy letters written by one "Lazlo Toth, American." The twist was that Novello's fictional protagonist wrote to real government officials, real heads of universities, and real CEOs. Alongside Lazlo's silly letters were the actual replies he received. Most of the responses clearly showed that Lazlo's letters had not been carefully read, let alone considered. The book inspired laughter, but not a zeal for letter writing.

Another discouraging factor is that our relationship to the written word is changing. Fewer people are reading newspapers and serious magazines these days. Most adults consider themselves too busy to read. And children reared on television and PlayStation have shorter attention spans. Living in an atmosphere saturated by video games, junky writing, and stupid television and movies, we are finding it difficult to muster much optimism for what Carol Bly calls "the passionate accurate story." It is easy to think, Why even bother?

Yet, paradoxically, our discouragement can be the very impetus that motivates us to write. We may feel the need to be that voice crying out in the wilderness. We may feel compelled to shout "Fire!" or "Man overboard!" or simply "The emperor has no clothes!"

Writing turns out to be one thing we can control in a world where much feels beyond our control. Most of us will not be spearheading protest marches against the World Trade Organization, masterminding boycotts against sweatshops in China, or leading the charge against oil exploitation in Nigeria. We won't be building orphanages for children in South Africa. But we do what we can.

We write. Every day we witness the degradation of much that we value. We witness sorrowful examples of unfairness, ignorance, and cruelty. We see our children educated to want all the wrong things. And so we write. We write with a sense of urgency. We write because we discover that we have something we alone can say. And we struggle on because we still believe in the power of words, just as Anne Frank believed in goodness despite powerful evidence to the contrary.

Fyodor Dostoyevsky lived in a hopeless time and place, a world of pogroms, starvation, filth, and syphilis. His life was plagued by epilepsy, mental problems, and poverty. Yet he left us this message:

> Love all of God's creation, the whole of it and every grain of sand. Love every leaf, every ray of God's light! Love the animals, love the plants, love everything. If you love everything, you will perceive the divine mystery in things. And once you have perceived it, you will begin to comprehend it ceaselessly, more and more every day. And you will at last come to love the whole world with an abiding, universal love.

A few years ago, I visited a market on the Burmese border. It was a profoundly unsettling experience. I walked past frightened, impoverished people hawking Leonardo DiCaprio beach towels, dried fish, Nike knockoffs, and counterfeit cigarettes. Old women with no teeth sat behind piles of peppers or rice. Listless children with dead eyes lay on ragged blankets behind their parents' stalls or sat watching shoppers walk by. A skinny teenager was apprehended by soldiers, beaten, and thrown into the back of a black van, his mother running after him, screaming, pulling her hair. Everyone in this tawdry market seemed almost comatose with inertia and grief. Gradually, I realized the underlying cause of what I was witnessing: the total absence of hope.

However, one man was different. He squatted in the gutter, almost naked, selling children's Magic Slates. As I walked by, he quickly scrawled on his display pad "Freedom from Fear," which is the motto of Aung San Suu Kyi, who is the daughter of a former leader in Burma. A Western-educated exile, Kyi returned to Burma to work for the restoration of democracy. And while she currently is under house arrest there, her ideas have kept hope alive for the citizens of that beleaguered country.

I looked at the words the man had written on the little plastic slate and then into his eyes. He smiled at me—a fierce, desperate smile—and then he quickly erased what he had written. This man had almost been silenced. But he made a leap. He dared to make a connection with a westerner. He used heroic words to carve out a Magic Slate–sized piece of freedom, which he then shared with me. I have never felt more honored and more humbled. When I think of people writing to connect, I think of the man with the Magic Slate. I write for him.

Thinking and Writing Questions

1. Explain the difference between writing for change and propaganda.
2. Pipher uses many examples in this chapter, beginning with the story of Anne Frank. Why so many examples? How do you think she wants these examples to influence her reader?
3. Review the pieces in *Essays on Writing*. List the pieces that are an attempt to change the world. Share your list with a classmate and explain what the authors in three of these pieces are trying to change. How do these authors succeed?
4. Pipher refers to the Buddhists to explain expanding our "frames of reference." Socially conscious writers invite readers "to put things in bigger containers" (204) What do Pipher and the Buddhists mean by this?
5. What is it that you want the world to think about and to see in a different way? We want you to see writing in a different way, so we put this book together. Now it's your turn. Get started.

Chapter 5: Thinking and Writing Questions

1. In "Judge Finds a Type-Prone Lawyer Guilty of Bad Writing," Liptak characterizes "bad" writing as full of typos and errors. In "What Corporate American Can't Build: A Sentence," Dillon characterizes "bad" writing as chaotic and

incoherent with "long convoluted passages." In "Three Mile Island and the Billion Dollar Memo," Griffin analyzes "bad" writing in a memo that is not clear. In Chapter One, on attitudes toward writing, the authors characterize writing as a skill, an art, playing God, a struggle, agonizing, and growth. Chapter Two gives you advice on how to get your writing done. Yet, no one clearly describes "good" writing. Join this conversation about writing by adding your voice.

Write an essay in which you define "good" writing based on the pieces in *Essays on Writing*. Skim the book in order to extract characteristics of good writing. You might go so far as to say if "this" is considered bad writing then "that" must be good writing. As you reread, note the sections that relate to good writing. Then, synthesize the notes you have made to discern patterns and links.

2. In "Writing to Connect," Pipher mentions the writing of many authors that have influenced the world. She starts with the story of Anne Frank. Write a research report that documents the impact a piece of writing has had on the world. Reread "Writing to Connect" and make a list of the authors she mentions. Work with your classmates to add other documents that have changed the world. To get yourself thinking, try to remember documents you studied in history class. Choose a document and start your research. For example, Pipher mentions Bob Dylan's song, "Blowin' in the Wind," that became an anthem of the anti-Vietnam War and Civil Rights movements. To investigate the impact of "Blowin' in the Wind" you might start by reviewing the history of the song in a publication like *Rolling Stone*. Then, turn to texts and documents that exhibit the use of "Blowin' in the Wind" as part of the Civil Rights and anti-war movements.

3. *Essays on Writing* wants to convince you of the value of "good" writing, so you will commit yourself to producing well-crafted prose. Compose a newspaper editorial, speech, or letter to students at a local high school that convinces your audience they should invest time and energy in improving their writing. Review the pieces in *Essays on Writing* to gather data for your piece. After you have crafted, revised, and edited your piece, send it to your intended audience and to us. We might be able to include your essay in the next edition. *bryant@calumet.purdue.edu* and *hclark28@ivytech.edu*

4. Authentic writing has a purpose: an audience to influence and a writer who wants to influence that audience. In school, this authenticity can be difficult when students see themselves writing for the teacher to get a grade. What can high school teachers do to develop authentic writing situations? Rather than motivating students to write with the promise of good grades and success in the next level of English, can teachers motivate students to produce authentic writing?

Develop your own authentic, high school writing project. You might turn an old high school assignment into a project in which students produce a document, send it out, and wait for a reply. Write a proposal laying out your suggestions for an authentic writing activity along with the rationale for your proposal. Draw on what you have read in *Essays on Writing* and your experiences to develop the rational: the reasons for assigning authentic writing that influences the world. Document your resources using a system such as APA or MLA. Ponder how much convincing your audience of teachers will need and provide them with that. As you craft, revise, and edit your piece, decide in what venue you want your piece to appear: a magazine for English teachers, a website that posts writing assignments for teachers, a letter to the English Department at a local high school, the website at your former high school. Send your piece to its audience, and wait for a reply.

Works Cited

Ede, Lisa and Andrea Lunsford. *Singular Texts/Plural Authors: Perspective on Collaborative Writing*. Carbondale, IL: Southern Illinois University Press, 1990.

National Commission on Writing. "Writing: A Ticket to Work . . . or A Ticket Out: A Survey of Business Leaders." September 2004. http://www.writingcommission.org/prod_downloads/writingcom/writing-ticket-to-work.pdf, 16 September 2008.

Pipher, Mary. *Writing to Change the World*. Penguin Books: New York, 2006.

Spretnak, Charlene M. "Reading and Writing for Engineering Students." *JAC: Journal of Advanced Composition* 4 (1983): 133–37.

CREDITS

Chapter 1

Clark, Roy Peter, "I Won't Use Writing as Punishment. I Won't. . . . " Printed by permission of Roy Peter Clark

Harrington, Dick, "Writing about General Apache," *Teaching English in the Two-Year College*. Volume 16, Number 3, October 1989, pp.190–192. Copyright 1989 by the National Council of Teachers of English. Reprinted and used with permission.

Holt, John, "Making Children Hate Reading," *Redbook 30* (Nov. 1967): 50+. Rpt. In *The Underachieving School*. New York: Dell, 1969. 82–96. Printed by permission of Sentient Publications

Duffy, Melissa, "Inspiration," Printed by permission of Melissa Duffy.

hooks, bell, "writing autobiography," from *remembered rapture: the writer at work* by bell hooks. Copyright 1999 by Gloria Watkins. Reprinted by permission of Henry Holt and Company, LLC.

Vetter, Craig, "Against the Wind: Bonehead Writing," *Playboy* magazine (August 1985). Copyright © 1985 by Playboy. All Rights reserved.

Aronowitz, Stanley, "Writing is Not a Skill," From *The Knowledge Factory* by Stanley Aronowitz. Copyright © 2000 by Stanley Aronowitz. Reprinted by permission of Beacon Press, Boston.

Chapter 2

Boynton, Sandra, "The Five-Paragraph Theme," © Sandra Boynton. Used by permission.

Brandeis, Gayle, "Dyr Mom: Wy R You So Laveable." This article first appeared in Salon.com at *http://www.salon.com*. It and others like it can be found in Salon's archives. Reprinted with permission.

Wyche, Susan, "Time, Tools, and Talismans." Reprinted with permission from *The Subject Is Writing* by Wendy Bishop. Copyright © 2007 by Wendy Bishop. Published by Heinemann, Portsmouth NH. All rights reserved.

Stafford, William, "A Way of Writing." *Writing the Australian Crawl*, Ann Arbor, Univ of Michigan Press, 1978. 17–20. © University of Michigan Press. Used by permission.

Lamott, Anne, "Shitty First Drafts," from *Bird by Bird* by Anne Lamott, copyright © 1994 by Anne Lamott. Used by permission of Pantheone Books, a division of Random House, Inc.

Murray, Donald, "Internal Revision: A Process of Discovery." © Donald Murray. Used by permission.

Zinsser, William K., "Simplicity." *Writing Well*. Copyright ©1976,1980,1985,1988,1990, 1994,2001,2006 by William K. Zinsser. Reprinted by permission.

Chapter 3

Bryant, Lizbeth, "Disruptive 'Sexual' Voices in English 101." *Voice as Process* 2005. Reprinted with Permission from *Voice as Process* by Lizbeth Bryant. Copyright © 2005 by Heinemann, Portsmouth NH. All rights reserved.

Chapter 4

Chapter 5